MANAGING THE
EMPLOYEE BENEFITS PROGRAM

Managing the Employee Benefits Program

REVISED EDITION

Robert M. McCaffery

amacom
AMERICAN MANAGEMENT ASSOCIATIONS

Library of Congress Cataloging in Publication Data

McCaffery, Robert M.
 Managing the employee benefits program.

 Bibliography: p.
 Includes index.
 1. Employee fringe benefits—United States.
2. Compensation management—United States.   I. Title.
HD4928.N62U639   1983   658.3'25   82-73516
ISBN 0-8144-5760-6

First Printing

This book is dedicated to all my evening class students and seminar participants, who have taught me much of what I know about employee benefits.

CONTENTS

INTRODUCTION

The first edition of *Managing the Employee Benefits Program,* published by AMACOM in 1972, heralded the demise of the term "fringe benefits." In so doing, it traced the birth of the expression to 1943, when the War Labor Board ruled that benefits were merely a "fringe" on the border of wages. Pointing to the costs of benefits, which in 1972 averaged about 25 percent of payroll, the book declared that "fringe" was no longer an appropriate modifier of benefits and called for elimination of the misnomer from our business vocabulary.

In the past ten years, nothing has occurred to suggest that the earlier obituary for fringes was premature. On the contrary, employee benefits have achieved increased prominence in the U.S. economy and are now clearly recognized as a significant part of employee compensation. The Chamber of Commerce of the United States (CCUS) study *Employee Benefits 1981,* published in 1982, indicates that among 994 reporting companies benefits payments averaged 37.3 percent of payroll, $3.21 per payroll hour, and $6,627 per year per employee. Nationally, the CCUS estimated that employee benefits cost employers $485 billion in 1981.

As benefits progressed beyond the fringe during the 1970s, program managers universally attributed rising administrative costs and increasing plan complexity to the enactment of ERISA. The Employee Retirement Income Security Act of 1974 (or "Everything Ridiculous Invented Since Adam," according to some detractors) evolved from a presidential committee report issued in 1965. It was signed into federal law on Labor Day 1974, after nearly a decade of lobbying by a variety of interest groups and extensive congressional debate. ERISA specified reporting and disclosure provisions and fiduciary standards applicable to private pension and welfare plans; rules covering plan participation, vesting, funding, and plan termination insurance apply only to pension plans. ERISA also introduced the individual retirement account (IRA) for employees and liberalized Keogh plans for the self-employed.

Although many business leaders maligned ERISA, this landmark act spurred movement toward more professional management of employee benefits. Early evidence of this was the introduction in December 1976 of the Certified Employee Benefit Specialist (CEBS) program, a joint undertaking of the International Foundation of Employee Benefit Plans and The Wharton School of the University of Pennsylvania. As of mid-1982, 525 individuals had been certified through this program and almost 11,000 people had registered in one or more of the ten courses of study.

Employee awareness and understanding of benefits have been sharpened by ERISA; at the same time, major demographic shifts in the workforce have rendered most pre-1972 programs inadequate in meeting employee needs and wants. This is because most of the earlier benefits plans were designed for a prototypal male employee with a non-income-producing wife, two dependent children, and a heavily mortgaged home. As early as 1971, Peter Drucker signaled the folly of such assumptions:

> Underlying our entire approach to benefits—with management and union in complete agreement, for once—is the asinine notion that the workforce is homogeneous in its needs and wants. As a result we spend fabulous amounts of money on benefits which have little meaning for large groups of employees and leave unsatisfied the genuine needs of other, equally substantial groups.[1]

Drucker's observation has become increasingly pertinent as the composition of the workforce continues to change dramatically. Labor force participation of wives has risen from under 25 percent in 1950 to around 50 percent today. Marriage and birth rates are declining, and the divorce rate is rising. Mandatory retirement before age 70 for most employees is now illegal. As a result of affirmative action laws and employer efforts, there are more women, minorities, and handicapped people in the workforce.

The diverse needs and wants of a more heterogeneous workforce are now being served in a few progressive firms by "cafeteria" or flexible benefits plans. Such plans, adopted as early as 1974 by TRW, Inc., in Redondo Beach, California, and Educational Testing Service, Princeton, New Jersey, permit employees to allocate employer expenditures among several benefits plans and levels of coverage to obtain

---

[1] "What We Can Learn From Japanese Management," *Harvard Business Review* (March–April 1971).

Drawing by Dick Kramer; used with permission.

individually tailored programs. To date, only a handful of companies have installed similar programs because of the anticipated administrative and communications burden. But specific benefits plans are becoming progressively flexible, offering a variety of options to satisfy the varying needs and wants of employees.

The management of employee benefits has come a long way since 1972. This results from a combination of greater recognition of the costs at stake, legislative and regulatory requirements, professional education, and better informed and more demanding employees. Surely the Ebenezer Scrooge concept of benefits as guilt-expiating gratuities from the employer has practically vanished (see drawing). Still too many personnel administrators and operating managers continue to utter, and apparently believe, such shibboleths as:

Employment applicants are interested only in what the job pays, not in what benefits are available.

Unless our base pay is better than our competition in the job market, we can't expect to attract or hold good people—and don't tell me that benefits make a difference!

Benefits plans are all about the same from one company to another.

Only the "old-timers" here care about benefits; the young people couldn't care less.

You can't expect employees to contribute to the cost of benefits plans; they want the company to pay for everything.

A key goal for this book is to demonstrate that each of the above statements is invalid and that a fresh, more objective outlook is needed in the post-fringe era. Additionally, this edition is designed to provide a current overview of designs and alternatives for employee benefits plans and a summary of effective management practices.

CHAPTER 1

Beyond the Fringe

Since employee benefits have moved beyond the fringe, it now seems appropriate to define and describe them as they exist in the United States today. In doing so, it is important to recognize that benefits may be viewed as both an element of total compensation and a social obligation of the employer to employees that may or may not involve costs.

From a compensation viewpoint, employee benefits are a collection of nonwage payments and services that protect, conserve, and supplement base pay and are provided in whole or part by employer expenditures. This definition is consonant with the five standard categories of benefits that the CCUS uses in its widely referenced annual cost surveys. These categories are:

1. *Legally required payments* for such social insurance programs as:

Old-Age, Survivors, Disability, and Health Insurance (OASDHI)
Unemployment compensation
Workers' compensation
Nonoccupational, temporary disability income insurance

1

2. *Voluntary or agreed-upon payments* for basic benefits that protect or conserve base pay, including:

Retirement income (pension) plans
Group life insurance
Health care plans
Dental insurance
Long-term disability income protection
Discounts on goods and services

3. *Paid rest periods, coffee breaks, lunch periods, wash-up time.*
4. *Payments for time not worked* when away from the job, including pay to employees for:

Holidays
Vacations
Sick time
Absences for personal reasons

5. *Other items* that supplement or conserve employees' base income such as:

Profit sharing payments
Thrift (savings) plan contributions
Suggestion awards
Service awards
Educational benefits
Seasonal and other nonproduction bonuses

Perhaps the greatest contribution of the CCUS surveys to the field of compensation and benefits has been the standardization of content that has been maintained since the series began in 1947. By stabilizing the listing of included benefit categories, the U.S. chamber has minimized problems in ensuring comparability of data among reporting companies. Its studies also facilitate historical trend comparisons. For example, 175 companies submitted data in each of the chamber's surveys from 1961 to 1981. Exhibit 1 traces the growth of benefits costs during that period for this identical group of firms.

All the benefits mentioned so far normally require employer expenditures. But in fulfilling their social obligation to employees, companies provide other types of benefits for which they may incur no direct costs. For example, flextime (flexible work hours) is being offered

Exhibit 1. Comparison of the costs of employee benefits for 175 companies, 1961–1981.

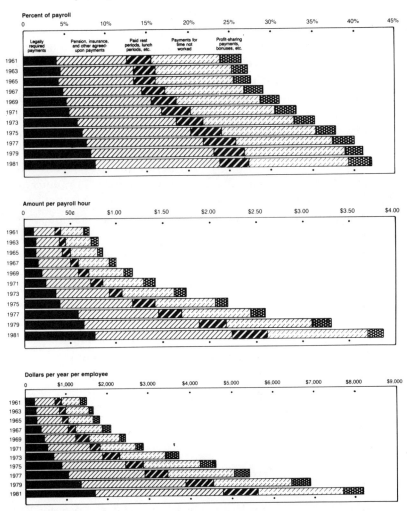

Source: Survey Research Center, Chamber of Commerce of the United States, *Employee Benefits 1981,* Washington, D.C., 1982.

by many firms as a response to the varying personal time pressures on today's more heterogeneous workforce. Flextime satisfies an important need of employees, yet it is not a cost item.

Company-operated or -facilitated van pools can benefit employees by offering them low-cost commuter transportation. But usually the fares paid by employees cover the employer's capital investment and operating costs, and the program runs on a break-even basis.

Another growing class of benefits that does not cost the employer anything out of pocket is known as voluntary or employee-pay-all. Through arrangements made by an employer with an insurance company, employees are able to obtain substantial discounts on such coverages as supplementary life and disability insurance, dependent life insurance, and automobile insurance. Insurers are able to offer reduced rates because their sales and administrative expenses are lower for group plans and premium collection problems are minimized by payroll deductions.

While doctrinaire compensation specialists may object to grouping no-cost items with benefits that account for significant employer expenditures, the belief that employees do not perceive any distinction between the two categories argues for taking the broader view in defining and classifying benefits. Ultimately, if employees refer to an employer consideration as a benefit, it *is* by definition a benefit! And, depending on individual needs and expectations, there may be no meaningful correlation between employer cost and employee satisfaction. In other words, for some people a no-cost flextime program might be far more desirable and useful than a pension plan costing 10 percent of payroll.

Historical Perspective

According to Washington Irving, one of the great surprises for Rip Van Winkle upon awakening from his 20-year slumber in the late eighteenth century was learning that instead of being a subject of His Majesty George III he was now a free citizen of the United States. While Rip was able to enjoy the fruits of political independence, chances are slim that he ever noticed any relief from tyrannies in employment. Employers were virtually unrestrained by government or unions. Workers were paid when they worked, but no provisions existed for paid time off or income protection during times of disability, unemployment, or retirement.

The Industrial Revolution had begun in England at about the same time that the American colonies started their revolt. However, during and after the Revolutionary War, Britain rendered illegal, at the penalty of fine and imprisonment, any attempt to provide the new nation with information on tools, machines, or processes. As a result of these restrictions, a significant industrial system did not develop in this country until after the Civil War. From that point forward, however, there has been a steady evolutionary growth of an industrial society that has incorporated a tradition of benefits, services, and considerations for the working class.

Exhibit 2 summarizes 44 milestones in the development of employee benefits in the United States. Reflected in this chronology are seven major influences that have propelled the average worker from a base of "no work, no pay" to a level of having an array of protections and extras that are now viewed as possessing sine qua non status.

Influences on Growth

INFLUENCE FROM WESTERN EUROPE

As indicated previously, the United States was a slow starter in the Industrial Revolution. Because of this, the countries of Western Europe not only gained an early competitive advantage but became world leaders in establishing statutory employee benefits programs. In Germany, the social reforms under Chancellor Otto von Bismarck in the 1880s included sickness and maternity coverages, pensions, and work injury benefits. France established a mandatory unemployment compensation program in 1907, and by 1911 Great Britain had a comprehensive system providing all the foregoing benefits.

The United States followed these leads, but slowly. An enduring state workers' compensation law was not passed until 1911, and it took another 24 years before old-age and unemployment income benefits were mandated with the passage of the Social Security Act. The influence of European programs has been evident in the design of the American counterparts in many ways, including the choice of

Exhibit 2. Historical milestones in the development of employee benefits in the United States.

1794 The first profit sharing plan set up by Albert Gallatin at his glass-works in New Geneva, Pennsylvania.

1818 Pensions established for war veterans.

1866 The Crane company introduced a medical department for employees.

1875 First private pension plan adopted; American Express Company provided benefits for employees 60 years of age or over who had 20 years with the company and were incapacitated for further performance of duty.

1880 First suggestion system installed by Yale & Towne.

1885 Procter & Gamble granted a Saturday afternoon half holiday for all workers with no reduction in pay.

1886 Westinghouse Corporation granted paid vacations.

1894 National Wallpaper Company and the Wallpaper Craftsmen negotiated a guaranteed annual wage.

1911 First state workmen's compensation laws enacted on an enduring basis in ten states.
       First group life insurance plan for employees inaugurated by the Pantasote Leather Company of Passaic, New Jersey.

1912 First major group insurance plan introduced at Montgomery Ward.

1916 Dennison Manufacturing Company of Framingham, Massachusetts, announced voluntary plan for payment of unemployment benefits.

1921 Edward Filene set up the Credit Union National Extension Bureau.

1926 Sun Oil Company established an employee savings plan with company contributions.
       Federal tax exemption extended to pension plans.

1927 George A. Hormel and Company introduced a plan guaranteeing workers 52 paychecks per year.

1929 Blue Cross concept of "service benefits" initiated at Baylor University Hospital in Texas.

1935 Social Security Act provided basis for a federal retirement system and state-administered unemployment insurance programs.

1937 Railroad Retirement Act federalized a private industry's pension program.

1938 Kaiser prepaid health plan (the basic model for HMOs) established for construction workers at Grand Coulee Dam in Washington State.

1940 National Labor Relations Board (NLRB) ruled that vacations, holidays, and bonuses were proper subjects for collective bargaining (Singer Manufacturing Company decision).

1942 Formation of War Labor Board led to wage freezes, an expansion of nonwage incentives, and the reference to benefits as "fringes."

1945 Caterpillar Tractor Company established first "broadbrush" employee assistance program (EAP), offering help to alcoholics and employees with other behavioral–medical problems.

1949 Supreme Court upheld NLRB ruling on Inland Steel and United Steelworkers negotiations that pensions are bargainable.

1952 Teachers Insurance Annuity Association (TIAA) established College Retirement Equities Fund (CREF) offering a pension option linking common stock performance with the lifetime annuity principle (variable annuity).

1955 Ford Motor Company and United Auto Workers negotiated supplemental unemployment benefits (SUB) plan.

1958 Welfare and Pension Plans Disclosure Act required employers and unions to disclose financial and other information about the operation of private employee benefits programs.

1962 United Steel Workers of America gained extended ("sabbatical") vacation plan in negotiations with American Can Company and Continental Can Company.
Self-Employed Retirement Act established tax-deferred pension plans for the self-employed (Keogh plans).

1965 President's Committee on Corporate Pension Funds and Other Private Retirement and Welfare Programs issued its report, *Public Policy and Private Pension Plans,* with recommendations that formed a foundation for ERISA.

1966 Medicare, developed to provide medical care for the aged under the Social Security program, became operative.

1971 Occupational Safety and Health Act (OSHA) strengthened employee safeguards and established a federal commission to study state workers' compensation laws (report issued in 1972).

1972 Equal Employment Opportunity Commission (EEOC) issued guidelines covering sex discrimination in employee benefits plans.

1973 Health Maintenance Organization (HMO) Act specified conditions under which employers must offer employees the alternative of having group medical benefits provided through a qualified health maintenance organization (HMO).
3M Company started the first employee van pool program.

1974 Employee Retirement Income Security Act (ERISA) established communications requirements and fiduciary standards for private pension and welfare plans, and set eligibility, vesting, and funding rules for pension plans.
TRW Systems Group (Redondo Beach, California) and Educational Testing Service (Princeton, N.J.) introduced cafeteria (flexible) benefits programs.

(continued on next page)

Exhibit 2.   Continued.

1975	Dental insurance became a significant employee benefit when Steelworkers of America gained coverage for 1.5 million individuals under contracts negotiated with ten major steel companies.
1978	Age Discrimination in Employment Act (ADEA) amended to prohibit mandatory retirement before age 70 in the private sector. (No age requirement to be used for federal employees.)
1979	Pregnancy Discrimination Act amending Title VII of the 1964 Civil Rights Act became fully effective. Employers required to treat disabilities caused by pregnancy the same as other disabilities under health, disability, and sick leave plans.
1981	President's Commission on Pension Policy issued its final report, *Coming of Age: Toward a National Retirement Policy,* with comprehensive recommendations covering the nation's retirement, survivor, and disability systems.
	Economic Recovery Tax Act (ERTA) liberalized rules on individual retirement accounts and Keogh plans; exempted tax-qualified benefits plans from constructive receipt doctrine.
1982	Tax Equity and Fiscal Responsibility Act (TEFRA) increased restrictions on employee benefits plans.
	Ford Motor Company and United Auto Workers agreed to *reduce* previously negotiated paid-time-off benefits.

age 65 as the normal retirement age under Social Security (patterned after the German system established in 1889).

One notable exception to our imitation of Western European social insurance benefits has been the failure to date of efforts to establish a universal health care system in the United States. The October 7, 1916, issue of *The Literary Digest* contained the following optimistic prediction for health insurance in the United States:

> Dr. Alexander Lambert, chairman of the American Medical Association's Social Insurance Committee, states that change will [soon] take place in the form of health insurance as is now compulsory under Government auspices in Great Britain. That this is inevitable for wage earners he positively asserts.

Seven decades later, Dr. Lambert's prophecy remains unfulfilled—although the introduction of Medicare in 1966 could be considered a giant step toward a national health care system.

A more recent example of Western Europe's influence on U.S. benefits is flextime. Started in West Germany in 1967, this concept of

flexible work hours began to receive acceptance in this country during the 1970s.

EMPLOYER INITIATIVE

From the introduction of a profit sharing plan by Albert Gallatin in
1794 to and beyond the adoption of a cafeteria-style benefits program
by TRW in 1974, private enterprise has continually played a leading
role in the invention and development of employee benefits. There
are many different motives for this—some economic and some hu-
manitarian. Both the early scientific managers and the employee
welfarists were concerned about worker fatigue, but for different reasons. They united in proposing break periods, holidays, vacations,
and shorter workweeks. The motivation for offering such incentives as
profit sharing or suggestion awards was frequently a quest for improved productivity. Henry Dennison's voluntary plan for payment
of unemployment benefits to his workers during seasonal slowdowns
was designed to stabilize employment and avoid the loss of skilled
craftspersons.

Certainly there have been many employer initiatives based on gen-
uine desire to minimize employee concern about loss of pay due to
poor health, layoff, or retirement. Using Frederick Herzberg's motivation model,[1] this would represent the removal of potential dissatisfiers.

Whatever the motives, employers have long recognized the needs
and value of employee benefits, and have frequently taken the leadership in designing and introducing benefits plans.

LABOR UNION EFFORTS

A widely accepted theory of management–labor relations is that,
when company leadership does not satisfy employee needs, the responsibility falls to union leadership by default. This seems just as
true in the field of employee benefits.

It has been estimated that during the depression of the early 1930s
up to half of the vacation plans existing in the 1920s were dropped by

---

[1] See Frederick Herzberg, *Work and the Nature of Man* (Cleveland: World Publishing, 1966).

employers. Also, the gap between vacations and holidays granted to hourly workers and to salaried employees widened, in favor of the latter. Bolstered by the National Labor Relations Act of 1935 and by subsequent National Labor Relations Board (NLRB) rulings, labor unions made rapid and substantial gains in securing contractual rights to paid vacations and holidays for hourly workers in the late 1930s.

Dental insurance, supplementary unemployment benefits, extended vacation plans, and guaranteed annual wage plans are examples of benefits given strong impetus through the gains of the United Auto Workers, the United Steelworkers, and other large unions in national bargaining. Overall, however, labor union influence seems to have been greater in securing and protecting benefits originated by employers than in introducing new programs.

In addition to gains achieved through collective bargaining, the major unions have had considerable influence on benefits legislation at both the federal and state levels. The labor viewpoint was certainly reflected in the text of ERISA, and in recent years, unions have lobbied aggressively for national health insurance and against reductions in Social Security benefits.

A point for employers to consider is that not all unions share the same philosophies and objectives about employee benefits. Such statements as "Unions do not like profit sharing plans" or "No union will negotiate a contributory health plan" are misleading and dangerous. Unions represent groups of workers whose needs and wants vary with age, education, marital status, seniority, job level, and the state of the economy. Organizing attempts and bargaining demands at any point in time will reflect these factors. The relative emphasis placed on wages and benefits, or on economic and noneconomic issues, has varied and will continue to vary with the needs of the moment.

WELFARE LEGISLATION

As labor unions have filled voids caused by individual company neglect, government legislation has provided or protected employee benefits—usually at employer expense—whenever industry at large has failed to offer adequate coverage.

Legislation concerning employee benefits has taken two basic forms. The first includes the federal Social Security program and the state unemployment, workers' compensation, and temporary disability insurance laws. These represent government-designed and -administered benefits programs. The second form of legislation is regulatory and covers private benefits plans. Included in this category are ERISA, the Health Maintenance Organization (HMO) Act, the Age Discrimination in Employment Act (ADEA), and state laws regulating group insurance provisions.

Although government has tended to play a progressively larger role in the field of employee benefits in the United States, there is still less government involvement here than in most developed countries throughout the world.

WAGE STABILIZATION

Because of the inflationary impact of rising wages and prices, the federal government enacted legislation during World War II, and again during the Korean conflict, to set price–wage controls. Faced with strict limits on the size and frequency of wage increases, employers and unions alike looked for other means of rewarding and retaining competent employees, who were in short supply because of military conscription.

The War Labor Board (and later the Wage Stabilization Board) tended to permit "reasonable" increases in employee benefits on the grounds that conditions of work should not be frozen. Also, from a political viewpoint, it seems probable that these government agencies were willing to make some concessions on fringes in order to gain labor–management cooperation on the wage freeze. This action prompted a shift in corporate compensation policies and, probably more than any other single event, triggered the dramatic expansion of employee benefits that occurred during the next 40 years. Interestingly, the Pay Board (1971–1974) and the Council on Wage and Price Stability (1978–1980) included employer contributions for fringe benefits in the definition of pay during subsequent control periods.

FAVORABLE TAX POLICIES

The stepped-up introduction of group medical and death benefits, pension plans, and educational assistance programs starting in the 1920s was largely attributable to the federal government's position on the tax treatment of these benefits. Subject to some limitations, employers have been permitted to take current-year tax deductions for their expenditures and employees have obtained the benefits on a tax-free or tax-deferred basis. In the case of pension plans, the employer-funded payments to employees following retirement are subject to tax, but typically at a lower rate than during active employment.

The tax-exempt or tax-deferred status of these major benefits plans has been secured by congressional action. In addition, the Internal Revenue Service (IRS) has tended to treat as nontaxable such special benefits as price discounts for employee purchases of company products; free travel for employees of airlines, railroads, and bus lines; free tuition for spouses and children of university faculty members and other employees; and free parking on employers' premises. About 1975 the IRS began to shift its position on this second category of benefits and immediately encountered strong congressional resistance. Unfortunately, the debate has created much confusion because of a failure to distinguish differences between executive perquisites (characterized by President Carter's 1978 attack on the "three-martini lunch) and benefits designed for the convenience of all employees and the employer (such as the company parking lot).

The future growth of employee benefits will depend a great deal on the continuing political battle between the IRS and Congress on the issue of taxing benefits.

INNOVATIONS BY INSURANCE AND FINANCIAL SECTORS

As employers and unions have sought professional assistance in satisfying identified employee needs, a new profession of benefits specialists in the insurance and financial sectors has arisen. These people are the architects and designers of long-term disability, comprehensive major medical, survivor income benefits, employee stock ownership, and savings plans, with an infinite variety of features developed to suit particular situations.

Many of the innovations from the insurance and financial specialists have helped to make benefits affordable in even the most profit-squeezed enterprises. By taking the maximum advantage of tax breaks, investment flexibilities, employee contributions, and coordination of benefits in the design of plans, a skilled benefits adviser/consultant can construct a program that will optimally meet objectives within defined cost limits.

Initially the primary sources for expertise in the development and design of employee benefits plans were resident in insurance companies and financial institutions. While those resources continue to be available to employers, a significant employee benefits consultant industry now exists, often in combination with actuarial services.

Current Views

Total compensation can be viewed as a partnership between direct cash payments (wages and salaries) and employee benefits (indirect compensation). The latter tends to be the junior member, but in "Elements of Sound Base Pay Administration," a 1981 joint publication of the American Compensation Association and the American Society for Personnel Administration (ACA/ ASPA), the following principle was advanced:

> Some organizations may emphasize direct cash payments, while others may minimize the relative importance of direct cash and place relatively more emphasis upon employee benefits. Organizations must have the freedom to make choices from the many alternatives available.

Beyond this, it is difficult to establish a universal set of principles for employee benefits management. However, during the past ten years, the following 12 statements have evolved from a steady flow of discussion with practitioners, educators, and students, along with extensive literature review. They are provided here as a foundation for closer inspection of particular program aspects in succeeding chapters, and as a basis for objective setting and self-audit by individual employers.

1. An employee's base pay income tends to create his or her standard of living; benefits protect it.

2. Because of current tax policies and group purchasing power, employers can obtain most employee benefits coverages more cheaply than can an individual employee.

3. Benefits programs that require or permit some employee contributions can offer broader coverage and tend to gain a higher level of employee awareness and understanding.

4. The overall responsibility for employee benefits management is best placed in the personnel or human resources function. Although a variety of supporting resources are needed (for example, tax, investment, insurance, actuarial, legal, accounting, and data processing), the logical focal point for centralized responsibility is the function most broadly concerned with employee needs and concerns.

5. To optimally manage the total compensation dollar, the functions of employee benefits and direct compensations should be closely coordinated, ideally on a peer level with a common supervisor.

6. Each organization should articulate its own set of objectives and priorities for employee benefits. These statements need to be consonant with other organizational and employee relations objectives; therefore they can be expected to vary from company to company.

7. The foundation for any firm's employee benefits program is the group of applicable federal and state mandatory benefits, such as Social Security, workers' compensation, and unemployment insurance. No private plan adoptions or revisions should be undertaken without a clear understanding of current requirements and projected changes in these public programs.

8. To be effective, benefits plans must be responsive to the analytically identified and/or the expressed needs of employees. This is ideally achieved through the cafeteria or flexible plan approach.

9. Benefits cost control is essential, but it must be performed openly and with employee understanding and involvement. Otherwise employee perceptions of the value of benefits plans may be overshadowed by suspicion and distrust.

10. Since many benefits are part of a hidden payroll, their value must be regularly and clearly communicated to employees through all available media to gain a desirable level of awareness.

11. Employees must have easy access to prompt and knowledgeable answers to individual questions about benefits. Meeting ERISA reporting and disclosure requirements is not enough. Provisions for effective two-way communication are essential.

12. At least annually, an organization should measure its performance against stated benefits objectives. This should include a review of the objectives themselves, results of short-term goals, individual plan performance, and some assessment of employee views.

CHAPTER 2

Employer Objectives and Employee Expectations

By definition, employee benefits are provided for employees. But employers, who now spend $5.01 on benefits for every dollar deducted from their employees' paychecks for this purpose,[1] should expect to gain some benefits—in terms of return on investment—too. Unfortunately, very few employers even know whether or not their return on employee benefits investment (ROEBI) is satisfactory. Most firms continue to manage benefits on a plan-by-plan basis. This approach may produce good performance in pension fund investments and health care cost controls, yet there is no assurance that total program results are in accord with broader company objectives and employee expectations.

Managing by objectives and collecting employee attitude and opinion information are two well-accepted management techniques that seem to have eluded executives with responsibility for directing employee benefits programs. Continued failure to use these techniques is bound to perpetuate the patchwork of overlapping, inadequate, and excessive forms of coverage that still characterizes many corporate benefits programs. To avoid or ovecome these barriers to

[1] *Employee Benefits 1981* (Washington, D.C.: Survey Research Center, Chamber of Commerce of the United States, 1982).

15

achieving optimum ROEBI, an employer needs to take five important steps:

1. Determine objectives and priorities.
2. Obtain and analyze employee views.
3. Publish and communicate a policy statement.
4. Establish responsibilities and accountability.
5. Provide for program performance measurement.

Determining Objectives

A University of Georgia study reported in the October 1978 issue of
Personnel Journal[2] confirmed that organizational objectives for benefits
programs tend to be fairly standard throughout U.S. industry. A
sample group of compensation managers was asked to rank in order
of importance to their organizations eight commonly cited objectives.

Although there was opportunity to insert other objectives, the 354
respondents made only two significant additions. The ten standard
objectives (in no particular order) were:

1. Improve employee morale.
2. Motivate employees.
3. Increase job satisfaction.
4. Attract good employees.
5. Reduce turnover.
6. Keep the union out.
7. Use compensation dollars better (by taking advantage of group
   funding and tax savings).
8. Enhance employee security.
9. Maintain a favorable competitive position.
10. Enhance the organization's image among employees.

All these objectives may be appropriate for any particular organization, but the assignment of priorities will vary depending on such
circumstances as company size, profitability, union status, employee
relations philosophy, workforce demographics, projected growth or
decline of the organization, and the influence of competitors' benefits

---

[2] Richard C. Huseman et al., "Getting Your Benefit Program Understood and
Appreciated."

in the community. Clearly, there is no right order of priorities, and the emphasis is likely to change from year to year.

The Employee Viewpoint

Concurrent with developing program objectives, an employer needs to be sure that the employee viewpoint on benefits is being accurately represented. Considering the increasing diversity of the workforce, it is no longer sufficient to rely on the personnel director or a group of employee relations specialists to "know what the people want" on the basis of daily walks through the factory or office. Such tours are undoubtedly useful for employee relations purposes, but they are hardly an efficient means for obtaining a balanced view of employee needs, wants, and expectations concerning benefits for themselves and their dependents.

The most formal and thorough method of obtaining employee views is the employee opinion survey. Often conducted by outside specialists, an opinion survey enables employees to express their ideas and feelings on company matters without fear of embarrassment or reprisal. Questionnaires are completed in privacy, and anonymity is assured by not requiring signatures. Questions on benefits may be included as part of a general attitude survey, or they may warrant a separate survey. Exhibit 3 is a sample from an employee benefits survey designed to measure three variables (understanding, importance, and satisfaction) related to existing coverages, and to elicit suggestions for program improvement. For reasons of cost, surveys of this type are usually limited in larger firms to a sample group of 20–25 percent of the employees.

A variation of the traditional survey approach was developed at General Electric's Behavioral Research Service, Crotonville, N.Y., in the mid-1960s. In the G.E. model, a representative sample of employees participates in an exercise involving choices for improvements in their pay and benefits within a defined limit. Choices are then matched with such demographic characteristics as age, stage of family cycle, work status of spouse, length of service, occupation, and income. From these data, general inferences can be ascribed to the total employee population for purposes of planning benefits.

Some firms have attempted to rely solely on demographics for rep-

Exhibit 3. Employee benefits survey.

I. Please indicate how well you understand each of the following benefits the Company provides. For each benefit listed below, would you say you understand "very well," "fairly well," "only partly," "not very well," or "not at all"?

PLEASE CHECK ONE ANSWER WHICH BEST APPLIES FOR EACH BENEFIT.

	Understand Benefit:				
	Very Well	Fairly Well	Only Partly	Not Very Well	Not at All
Life insurance	( )	( )	( )	( )	( )
Medical benefits	( )	( )	( )	( )	( )
Long-term disability insurance	( )	( )	( )	( )	( )
Dental insurance	( )	( )	( )	( )	( )
Vacation	( )	( )	( )	( )	( )
Retirement plan	( )	( )	( )	( )	( )
Savings plan	( )	( )	( )	( )	( )
Company holidays	( )	( )	( )	( )	( )
Sick pay	( )	( )	( )	( )	( )
Suggestion plan	( )	( )	( )	( )	( )
Educational assistance plan	( )	( )	( )	( )	( )

II. All individuals have different needs; thus, different employee benefits, provided by the Company, may be more or less important to each employee depending upon the individual's needs. Please tell us how important each of the following benefits is to you.

Circle *5* if the benefit is extremely important and circle *1* if the benefit is of no importance to you. Of course, you may circle any number between 5 and 1, depending upon how you feel.

PLEASE TRY TO SHOW DIFFERENCES BETWEEN THE BENEFITS.

	Extremely Important				Not at all Important
Life insurance	5	4	3	2	1
Medical benefits	5	4	3	2	1
Long-term disability insurance	5	4	3	2	1
Dental insurance	5	4	3	2	1
Vacation	5	4	3	2	1
Retirement plan	5	4	3	2	1
Savings plan	5	4	3	2	1

	Extremely Important				Not at all Important
Company holidays	5	4	3	2	1
Sick pay	5	4	3	2	1
Suggestion plan	5	4	3	2	1
Educational assistance plan	5	4	3	2	1

III. Again, depending upon your own situation, you may feel that some benefits satisfy your needs very well, while other benefits may be less satisfactory or not at all satisfactory. Please tell us how satisfied you are with each of the following benefits.

PLEASE CHECK ONE ANSWER WHICH BEST DESCRIBES HOW YOU FEEL ABOUT EACH BENEFIT.

	Satisfies Need:					Don't Know Enough to Rate It
	Very Well	Fairly Well	Only Partly	Not Very Well	Not at All	
Life insurance	( )	( )	( )	( )	( )	( )
Medical benefits	( )	( )	( )	( )	( )	( )
Long-term disability insurance	( )	( )	( )	( )	( )	( )
Dental insurance	( )	( )	( )	( )	( )	( )
Vacation	( )	( )	( )	( )	( )	( )
Retirement plan	( )	( )	( )	( )	( )	( )
Savings plan	( )	( )	( )	( )	( )	( )
Company holidays	( )	( )	( )	( )	( )	( )
Sick pay	( )	( )	( )	( )	( )	( )
Suggestion plan	( )	( )	( )	( )	( )	( )
Educational assistance plan	( )	( )	( )	( )	( )	( )

IV. Although you may generally understand the benefits provided to you, it is possible that you feel more information should be provided. If so, would you please describe below any specific information which you feel should be made available. (PLEASE BE AS SPECIFIC AS POSSIBLE)

_____

_____

(continued on next page)

Exhibit 3. Continued.

V. Please give us any additional comments you feel are important about the benefits listed on the prior pages.

_____

_____

_____

_____

_____

_____

_____

JUST FOR STATISTICAL PURPOSES, PLEASE INDICATE THE FOLLOWING:

Your Age:
( ) Under 30
( ) 31–49
( ) 50 or more

Payroll:
( ) Weekly
( ) Hourly
( ) Semimonthly

Marital Status:
( ) Single
( ) Married
( ) Legally separated
( ) Divorced
( ) Widowed

Company Service:
( ) Under 1 Year
( ) 1–5
( ) 6–10
( ) 11–15
( ) 16–20
( ) Over 20

resentation of employee needs and wants. Without the confirmation of expressed views, this can produce misleading assumptions. For example, an employer with a preponderance of unmarried employees in the 20–30 age range might infer from those data that there was a low level of employee interest in benefits compared with pay. However, a survey or a series of interviews could reveal a greater desire for educational assistance benefits, more time off with pay, group travel arrangements, and subsidized recreation than for fully taxable pay increases. The exhortation "Never assume!" may be overused, but it seems especially apt in this context. Statistical information about the workforce can be a useful tool in planning employee benefits, but it should never be used *in vacuo.*

Statement of Policy

A policy statement for the employee benefits program should be a natural product of blending employer objectives with information about employee needs and wants. It should be part of the organization manual that contains statements covering such subjects as equal employment opportunity, management development, health and safety, business conduct, and salary administration. The statement should convey a spirit of commitment to purposeful management of employee benefits and provide a set of standards against which program performance can be measured.

Exhibit 4 is an example of a policy statement incorporating both internal and external objectives for an organization that clearly emphasizes the importance of benefits as part of total compensation. A statement such as this need not be considered immutable, but neither should it require frequent substantial changes. A policy statement, custom developed for a given organization, should serve as a fundamental charter to which shorter term (for example, annual) goals can be appended. For instance, during a period of heavy recruiting requirements, an annual goal might be:

Review all benefits plan participation requirements and analyze feasibility of establishing earlier eligibility dates (temporarily or permanently) to enhance recruiting efforts.

If the company were faced with the reverse of this type of problem, and wanted to reduce its workforce as painlessly as possible, a short-term objective could be:

Develop a proposal (including cost estimates) with special benefits plan provisions designed to stimulate increased voluntary early retirements during the next 18 months.

Although statements of basic formal policy and of annual goals are essentially management documents, they should be given the widest practicable circulation within the organization. By treating them as top-secret material, some companies miss a golden opportunity to communicate relevant and realistic information to employees. At the same time, a failure to communicate openly is apt to be viewed by workers as a management cover-up.

Exhibit 4.   Prototype of company policy statement for employee benefits.

The management of the employee benefits program in this organization will be governed by the following internal and external objectives. The Vice President, Personnel, is responsible for implementation and accountable for results.

A. The following internal objectives deal with satisfying employee needs and expectations and meeting employer requirements.
   1. The company will provide sound and meaningful welfare and security benefits as part of compensation for competent and continuing service. These aids are intended to complement, not replace, the efforts of individual employees.
   2. Employee benefits shall be established and maintained on the basis of the employees' relative need for income protection, income supplementation, survivor benefits, retirement income, and paid leisure time.
   3. The company will review all benefits as part of an annual audit of total compensation. Costs of proposed new or improved benefits will be evaluated in relation to costs of projected increases.
   4. The total benefits program shall be evaluated on the basis of contributions to both morale and productivity. Criteria to be considered in this evaluation will include open positions, turnover, attendance, grievances, and responses to surveys of attitudes.
   5. To the greatest extent possible, basic benefits for employees will be provided through company contributions. Employees will be expected to pay at least part of the costs for *dependent* coverage.
   6. Since employees help create profits, they will in years when earnings permit be awarded a fair share of company profits before taxes on the basis of a published formula that takes into account years of service and annual earnings.
   7. All new and changed benefits will be discussed in detail with supervision before general communication to employees.
   8. Each employee will receive an annual statement itemizing the personal value of earned benefits, the related costs of company contributions, and any plan changes.
   9. Benefits for retired employees will be reviewed annually for adequacy and adjusted accordingly.

B. The following external objectives embrace labor market considerations, relationships with statutory benefits plans and requirements, union bargaining demands, and new developments and trends in the field of employee benefits.
   1. The employee benefits of the company will be compared each year as of July 1 with the programs of a standard group of 20 leading companies in our industry and geographic area. The overall value of benefits will be maintained at a level within the top 40% of this survey panel.

2. Through the industry association, management views on legislation and administration of legally required benefits and controls on private plans will be communicated to appropriate government officials.
3. All benefits plans will fully comply with applicable statutory and regulatory requirements.
4. All company benefits will be coordinated with related statutory plans that provide benefits to employees.
5. All trustees and carriers administering employee benefits plans will submit detailed annual reports to management for review, analysis, and communication to employees.
6. Benefits negotiated for unionized employees will be simultaneously extended to nonrepresented employees at the same location(s). These benefits usually will be identical, but if this approach is impractical, they may be extended in a different form representing the same level of company expenditures.
7. Personnel forecasts and reports of employment requirements will be reviewed annually to ascertain the need for changes in benefits to support recruitment.

Responsibilities and Accountability

The old bromide "You can't tell the players without a scorecard" described the status of employee benefits program management in most medium-size and large firms before 1970. If a telephone caller to one of these companies were to have asked to speak to the person in charge of employee benefits, the operator undoubtedly would have replied, "Which employee benefit(s) are you referring to?" From the caller's response, the operator then could refer to a "scorecard," which might have revealed:

Benefit plan	*Refer call to*
Group insurance	Insurance manager
Pension	Treasurer
Profit sharing	Compensation manager
Unemployment compensation	Payroll supervisor
Workers' compensation	Safety director
Service awards	Employee relations manager
Educational assistance	Training manager

The point here is that because most employee benefits programs are a collection of separate plans, rather than a planned unified system, their management historically has tended to be diffused. Inevitably though, organizations have found that this type of fractionated responsibility obscures purpose, creates confusion, and impedes control. As a result, there has been a significant trend toward more centralized management of benefits during the past ten years.

A 1980 survey of 72 companies conducted by Charles D. Spencer & Associates, Inc.,[3] revealed that while there was no "typical" benefits department, 56 departments reported to the personnel or human resources function; 7 were attached to a financial unit; and only 9 reported to more than one department.

Further confirmation of the movement toward centralized responsibility can be found in the scope of activities included in the standard position description for employee benefits manager used in the American Management Associations (AMA) compensation studies (see Exhibit 5). This position first appeared in AMA's *Middle Management Report* in 1962. Today it is a common title in most large organizations and many medium-size firms.

In small organizations, the plight of James Rast in the cartoon on page 26 is probably a more familiar occurrence than the problem of fractionated responsibility. Because of limited staff resources, one person is often expected to handle the complete benefits programs— and more!

To rescue all the Mr. Rasts in small companies, and to assist the full-time benefits managers in larger firms, many sources of technical information and professional consultation are available. First, and depending on company size, there are the in-house resources. To the extent available, tax, legal, financial, accounting, insurance, actuarial, data processing, real estate, and labor relations expertise within the organization should be accessed and utilized. Another internal resource that can be tremendously helpful, but surprisingly is usually ignored by benefits management, is the advertising and public relations area with its special skills in writing and graphics.

A second no-cost or low-cost source of help can be local industrial chambers of commerce and employers associations. Also, most large industries have national associations that conduct surveys and coordinate information sharing among member firms.

Finally, there are both profit-making and nonprofit external re-

---

[3] "Common Problems Found in Benefits Departments," *Employee Benefit Plan Review* (June 1980).

Exhibit 5.   Job description for employee benefits manager.

EMPLOYEE BENEFITS MANAGER

Position

The primary responsibility of this position is the administration of established company benefits programs. Develops and recommends new and improved policies and plans with regard to employee benefits. Assures compliance with ERISA requirements and regulations.

Specific Functions

1. Administers group life insurance, health and accident insurance, retirement programs, and savings plans.
2. Processes documents necessary for the implementation of various benefits programs and maintains such records as are necessary.
3. Recommends and approves procedures for maintenance of benefits programs and issues operating instructions.
4. Participates in the establishment of long-range objectives of company benefits programs.
5. Conducts surveys and analyzes and maintains an organized body of information on benefits programs of other companies.
6. Informs management of trends and developments in the field of company benefits.
7. Gives advice and counsel regarding current developments in benefits programs.
8. Acts as liaison between company and banks, insurance companies, and other agencies.
9. Conducts special studies as requested by management.

In addition, the employee benefits executive may be responsible for various employee services, such as recreation programs, advisory services, credit unions, and savings bond purchase programs.

---

sources. On a plan-by-plan basis, these include insurance companies, banks, Social Security field representatives, profit sharing and suggestion plan associations, service award suppliers, and employee relocation and recreation consultants and associations. On a broader scale, numerous private consulting firms are now equipped to offer comprehensive services related to the selection, design, administration, and communication of all aspects of the benefits program. A geographic listing of reputable consultants and advisers appears each month in *Employee Benefit Plan Review* (see Selected References).

The complexity of employee benefits management today mandates

Cartoon by Charles Saxon; used with permission.

the use of supporting resources by companies of all sizes. However, the person ultimately accountable for program performance—typically the top human resources executive—must ensure that these resources are used judiciously and that parochial interests and fascination with plan technology do not interfere with the pursuit of basic objectives. This is not a simple task. Managing to obtain assistance and advice from other areas within and outside the organization without losing control of the overall mission is a true test of executive ability. At IBM a contention system seems to be a helpful response to this challenge. An April 1980 *Pension World* article[4] contained the following quotation from R. N. Beck, an IBM benefits and personnel services executive:

> In a sense we are charged with developing appropriate personnel programs which have a price tag, and the financial people are charged with assessing the company's ability to fund the programs in the short and long term. We work closely together to come up with something which is best for the employee and best for the company. . . . In the end we may compromise on a design feature that will cost less to fund but will yield approximately the same in . . . delivery to the employee.

Specific responsibilities can be assigned or delegated, but accountability cannot. Whoever has ultimate accountability for employee benefits quickly learns that the buck can't be passed. Once this is clear, it is essential that this person provide for systematic measurement of program performance.

Measuring Program Performance

There appear to be four distinct levels for measuring the performance of employee benefits programs.

Individual plan performance. This is the easiest level of measurement from a quantification standpoint. A pension plan can be measured on fund investment performance; group health benefits can be assessed according to costs and processing time for claims; a suggestion plan can be judged on the basis of the use and value of adopted ideas; educational assistance plan expenses can be related to the impact on internal promotions and to projected savings in recruiting costs; and so on.

Certainly these kinds of measurements are important and useful, but it is critical to keep them in perspective. Analogous to "winning the battle, but losing the war" would be a record of achieving impressive savings in controlling health care costs while allowing turn-

---

[4] Ronald Derven, "IBM Computes Competitive Employee Benefits Plan."

over rates to rise, morale to decline, and a union organizing drive to succeed.

Program goals performance. Companies that use a management-by-objectives (MBO) process have a built-in mechanism for handling benefits program goals. In its simplest form, this management technique involves joint determination (for instance, between the vice president of personnel and the employee benefits manager) on certain major program aspects to receive special or intensified attention during a specified time period. As described previously, goals could involve adjustments to enhance recruitment or facilitate attrition, or they could be projects to improve benefits communication or reduce costs in certain areas. At this level, though, the focus begins to shift from individual plans to the overall program. Once goals are established and responsibilities assigned, milestones can be set for reporting, review, and, if necessary, revision.

Adherence to policy. As long as an organization has a statement of the type shown in Exhibit 4, it is easy to measure performance on the basis of adherence to policy. To assure objectivity, some companies utilize an internal audit staff to perform such checks. On a periodic basis, each of the objectives contained in the policy should be tested. Some, such as commitments to conduct competitive studies and attitude surveys, are quickly measureable; others, such as fundamental statements of philosophies, require more qualitative commentary.

Achievement of high-priority objectives. This can be considered the bottom-line evaluation of program effectiveness. As long as the organization was clear initially about what it wanted to achieve through its investment in employee benefits, this should be the ultimate standard of measuring performance of the person accountable for the program.

Assume that a company had determined that there were five key objectives for its benefits program. At the end of a year, the benefits manager might have highlighted performance in each category as follows:

Objective	*Performance Highlights*
Maintain union-free status.	Maintained status; no representation elections.
Reduce turnover.	Annual rate reduced from 10.8 to 6.3 percent.

Attract good employees.	Average number of qualified external applicants for each open position increased from three to seven.
Increase employee morale.	Company-wide attitude survey showed statistically significant improvement in favorable responses to 28 of 30 questions compared with previous survey.
Use compensation dollar more wisely.	Increase in total compensation per employee limited to 8.5 percent, compared with industry norm of 9.0 percent, because of changes in pay–benefits mix.

In this illustration, the key objectives were essentially fulfilled. It would be naive to give all the credit for high achievement to the benefits manager and staff. Surely many others, including the employment function, employee relations representatives, and line supervision, must have contributed a fair share to the achievement. But what counts is that the objectives were satisfied, and apparently in a cost-effective manner. The organization knew what it wanted, communicated the objectives, secured involvement of numerous people, and obtained an impressive ROEBI.

Of course, this kind of success can never be guaranteed; however, the total program planning approach described in this chapter will, at a minimum, provide employers with a compass and road map to help determine where they are and where they should be heading with their benefits investment. It is a proven method for successful business management, and employee benefits should not be excluded.

CHAPTER 3

Statutory Plans and Legal Requirements

Today's personnel executives recognize, without total acceptance, their partnership with government in the management of human resources. Labor laws, health and safety regulations, equal opportunity and affirmative action requirements, wage and hour rules, and employee rights legislation all consume great amounts of personnel administrative time and effort. Statutory plans and legal requirements applicable to employee benefits are no exception.

At both the federal and state level, government performs basically three major roles in relation to private benefits programs: plan designer and administrator, regulator, and facilitator.

Roles of Government

PLAN DESIGNER AND ADMINISTRATOR

At the federal level, the most visible government involvement is its nationwide operation of the Old-Age, Survivors, Disability, and Health Insurance (OASDHI) program, more familiarly known as Social Security. When this program got under way in 1937, benefits were limited to small pensions for workers at age 65 and above, coverage applied to slightly more than half of the total workforce, and the employer's maximum annual cost was $30 per employee. By 1983 the latter figure had increased to $2,391.90 per employee; with the exception of federal employment, almost all jobs in the United States were covered; and benefits had been extended to include disability income, survivor payments, health insurance, and early retirement pensions.

The unemployment compensation insurance (UCI) system in the United States operates as a federal–state partnership. The Social Security Act of 1935 laid the groundwork for a unique arrangement. Each state became subject to the Federal Unemployment Tax Act (FUTA) for employees engaged in industry and commerce. As soon as a state enacted its own unemployment compensation system, subject to minimal federal requirements, employers could offset FUTA taxes by up to 90 percent of the amount paid to the state program. Also, the state was eligible to receive federal grants for program administration. The states acted promptly, since they were allowed to decide what level of income replacement benefits they would pay, for how long, and under what conditions, and each state was responsible for meeting its resulting costs. Today, in spite of periodic legislative proposals for tighter federal standards, the states maintain primary control over administration of UCI benefits.

The entry of government into the business of operating employee benefits can be marked by the introduction of workers' compensation (WC) laws in ten states in 1911. By 1948 every state had its own program. Unlike the UCI programs, WC laws are strictly state creations. They evolved in response to employee, union, and public dissatisfaction with employer efforts to prevent occupational injuries and accidents and with their seemingly callous treatment of employee-victims. Also in contrast to the payment of unemployment benefits by public agencies, most states permit an employer to pay benefits to employees directly or through an insurance company. Each state specifies its own benefits levels and conditions. Benefits include temporary and permanent total disability pay, permanent partial disability awards, medical care benefits, rehabilitation, and survivor allowance. There are no absolute federal requirements, although many states have followed recommendations of the 1972 report by the National Commission on State Workmen's Compensation Laws. This commission proposed 19 essential improvements in the state programs or, alternatively, if these did not result promptly, federalization. Since the mid-1970s, numerous bills have been introduced in Congress to bring WC under federal control, but to date no such law has been enacted.

Closely related to WC benefits, which are applicable to work-connected injuries and illnesses, are state nonoccupational disability benefits programs. However, while every state has a workers' compensation program, only five states (California, Hawaii, New Jersey, New York, and Rhode Island) and the Commonwealth of Puerto Rico require temporary disability benefits (TDB) for off-the-job occurrences. Currently, only Hawaii does not operate its own public plan and only Rhode Island does not permit employers to substitute an insured or self-insured plan for a state-operated plan. Also, most TDB plans provide only short-term (typically 26 weeks) partial income replacement for an employee, in contrast with the broad array of employee–dependent–survivor benefits under WC laws.

REGULATOR OF PRIVATE PLANS

The principal controls that state governments have over private voluntary or negotiated benefits plans are the regulations and rulings issued by their insurance commissions. In addition to the basic regulation of carrier rates and service, these commissions review contract provisions (such as conversion and extended coverage), establish required coverages and minimum benefits levels, and monitor the way in which benefits are provided. Although there is a National Association of Insurance Commissioners, each state is autonomous in setting its rules and carrying out its program. As a result, there are significant variations among the states.

Somewhat related to the group insurance plan standards established by insurance commissioners are the health maintenance organization (HMO) standards established by some states.

Other areas in which state action tends to influence, if not regulate, decisions about employee benefits programs are the designation of holiday observances and requirements for providing employees with sufficient time off to vote.

Prior to the 1970s, the federal government exercised relatively little control over the management of private benefits programs. The Internal Revenue Service (IRS) had established certain limits on deductibility of benefits expenditures, and the Welfare and Pension Plans Disclosure Act of 1958 (amended 1962) gave the secretary of labor limited investigatory authority and the right to issue regulations covering benefits plans. Beyond that, except for some Securities and Exchange Commission (SEC) disclosure rules covering plans that offer benefits in shares of stock, the federal government practically ignored private plans.

The period 1972–1974 now appears to have been a time of a federal regulatory offensive, which started with the Equal Employment Opportunity Commission's (EEOC's) 1972 guidelines on sex discrimination in benefits plans. These were followed closely by the HMO Act of 1973. The final action in this three-year explosion was the passage of ERISA in 1974.

The question of sex discrimination in benefits plans has become increasingly complex and perplexing since guidelines were initially issued by the EEOC. The Pregnancy Discrimination Act of 1978 and subsequent revised EEOC guidelines (1979) have established the basic principle that pregnancy must be treated as any other disability in benefits plans. But, in spite of a 1978 Supreme Court decision[1] that ruled that women could not be charged a higher pension plan contribution rate than male counterparts, the federal government's specification of unisex mortality tables for determining annuities in defined-contribution pension plans was still being contested by several states in 1983. This has created a serious dilemma for private employers.

The HMO Act was intended to stimulate the growth of prepaid health care and, by stressing preventive medicine, to eventually reduce medical costs. The model for the government's initiative was the Kaiser-Permanente Medical Care Program, which had been widely accepted on the West Coast. By 1982 more than 11 million people were enrolled in approximately 270 HMOs throughout the country.[2] Employers who already offer health care benefits are required to offer the HMO option (referred to as "the dual-choice alternative") to employees only when formally approached by a federally qualified HMO. Also, the approach must satisfy certain criteria set forth in regulations issued by the Department of Health and Human Services. For employees who elect HMO participation, the employer must contribute no less than it does to other health benefits alternatives, but it is not required to contribute more.

ERISA has been called landmark legislation, and most benefits ad-

---

[1] *City of Los Angeles, Department of Water and Power* v. *Manhart.*
[2] *The Wall Street Journal*, December 14, 1982.

Table 1. Applicability of ERISA provisions to private benefits plans.

ERISA Provisions	Defined-Benefit Pension Plans	Defined-Contribution Pension Plans	Welfare Plans
1. Reporting and disclosure	Yes	Yes	Yes
2. Fiduciary standards	Yes	Yes	Yes
3. Plan participation rules	Yes	Yes	No
4. Vesting standards	Yes	Yes	No
5. Past service funding rules	Yes	No	No
6. Benefits accrual tests	Yes	No	No
7. Plan termination insurance	Yes	No	No

ministrators would consider that an understatement. Table 1 highlights the impact of ERISA on the design and administration of benefits plans. As of 1982, three federal agencies—the Department of Labor, the IRS, and the Pension Benefit Guaranty Corporation (PBGC)—were ensuring compliance with its various provisions.

As burdensome as ERISA may seem to some administrators, it does not go as far as some of the recommendations contained in the 1965 president's committee report that proved to be its genesis.[3] For example, that report supported the concept of the portability of pension benefits and the creation of a central private or public clearinghouse. So far, the proposal has been suppressed through intensive employer-interest lobbying.

In retrospect, ERISA no longer seems like the dragon that some antiregulation groups portrayed in 1974. In the first place, a law of this type was needed. That became clear when the president's committee report was published in January 1965. There were obvious weaknesses in the private pension and welfare plan system, and employee confidence in these plans was very low. Second, the legislation, signed into law on Labor Day 1974 by President Ford, was the product of much testimony, debate, and compromise by business leaders, labor union officials, human rights advocates, economists, and individual employees during a nine-year period. The impression that no one was *fully* satisfied with ERISA suggests that it reasonably bal-

---

[3] President's Committee on Corporate Pension Funds and Other Private Retirement and Welfare Programs, "Public Policy and Private Pension Programs" (Washington, D.C.: U.S. Government Printing Office).

anced many conflicting viewpoints. Finally, revisions and refinements since 1974 have simplified and clarified many of the seemingly insurmountable requirements in the original act.

After ERISA, the next major federal action in the area of employee benefits was the enactment of the Age Discrimination in Employment Act (ADEA) amendments of 1978. The original act (1967) had accepted predominant practice in the private sector by protecting employees only up to age 65. This effectively sanctioned mandatory retirement at that age. The 1978 amendments increased the protected age to 70 for most workers and prohibited any reduction in the benefits of older employees that could not be justified "by significant cost considerations."

When the law took effect on January 1, 1979, the Department of Labor was responsible for enforcement. On July 1, 1979, responsibility was shifted to the EEOC. As a result, considerable debate ensued about legislative intent versus administrative interpretation. Meanwhile, employers have had to modify plan participation requirements and benefit levels for older workers in ways that comply with their understanding of the regulations while attempting to avoid added costs.

In November 1978 President Carter established a Commission on Pension Policy to study the nation's retirement, survivor, and disability systems. This group issued its final report in February 1981. Among the key recommendations was a proposal for a mandatory minimum universal pension system (MUPS) to be funded by a 3 percent payroll tax on employers. In the face of President Reagan's objectives at that time of lowering taxes and eliminating excessive regulations, this proposal was quickly tabled by the administration. Other recommendations dealing with strengthening Social Security and encouraging individual efforts (for example, IRAs) were received more kindly and quickly led to a number of actions and revisions.

The Tax Equity and Fiscal Responsibility Act of 1982 (TEFRA) did not have as much impact as ERISA, but it did impose many restrictions on employee benefits plans. This federal act limited pension-plan contributions and benefits, set nondiscrimination rules for group life insurance plans, and prevented employers from substituting Medicare for company-provided medical plans as primary coverage for persons aged 65 to 69.

FACILITATOR OF PRIVATE PLANS

The greeting "I'm from the government, and I'm here to help you" generates about as much credibility among businesspeople as a sales pitch starting with "Buy this item before midnight, and receive a lifetime guarantee at no extra cost." In spite of skepticism about government involvement in private sector business, employee benefits continue to be aided in a variety of ways by federal government policies and actions. Some recent examples of this are:

HMO Act of 1973 authorized $375 million for a five-year period to stimulate development of the prepaid preventive health care concept as an alternative to existing fee-for-service group medical plans.

Tax Reform Act of 1976 provided that benefits employees derived from group legal services plans were not taxable income. It also increased maximum deductions for relocation allowances.

Revenue Act of 1978 liberalized rules on educational assistance plans by permitting employees to receive reimbursement for non-job-related courses on a tax-free basis (provision extends to December 31, 1983).

Miscellaneous Revenue Act of 1980 made it possible to have a three-way trade-off among cash, benefits, and deferred compensation in a flexible benefits plan without creating constructive receipt consequences for employees who choose other than cash.

Economic Recovery Tax Act of 1981 (ERTA) liberalized IRA and Keogh plan rules and maximum deductions; extended favorable tax treatment of group prepaid legal plans to the end of 1984; increased maximum deductions for recognition awards given to employees for length of service, productivity, or safety achievements; continued prohibition against IRS release of additional fringe benefits regulations, at least through 1983.

DYNAMIC NATURE OF GOVERNMENT POLICY
TOWARD PRIVATE PLANS

A system in which government simultaneously controls (restricts) and facilitates (favors) private sector benefits plans may at first appear incongruous. In reality, it is just another manifestation of our representational form of government operating under a series of checks and balances. At the federal level, members of Congress and executive branch leaders, including the president, must constantly listen to, evaluate, and act on expressed views from diverse constituencies. Similarly, the judiciary is guided to some extent by amicus curiae briefs. All three branches of government, not responsible to each other, must deal with a variety of interest groups and opposing viewpoints. In the ebb and flow of political tides, and depending on the relative effectiveness of competing lobbyists, employers can expect to win a few and lose a few in seeking government support for benefits plans, recognizing that there will always be another season.

A prime example of the dynamic nature of government policy affecting private benefits plans is the history of the law regarding pregnancy benefits that began with the Civil Rights Act of 1964. Included in Title VII of that law was a provision making it unlawful to discriminate with respect to "compensation, terms, conditions, or privileges of employment, because of . . . sex." Prior to this, most employers had reasoned that pregnancy was a condition uniquely applicable to women and therefore subject to special provisions in sick pay, disability, and medical benefits plans. Even states with temporary disability laws specified shorter durations of coverage for maternity disability compared with other disabling conditions. The 1964 Civil Rights Act seemed to rule that these special considerations were a form of sex discrimination, but in the absence of detailed regulations, many employers—and states—did nothing to change historical practice.

In 1972 the EEOC issued guidelines which stated, in part, that disabilities resulting from pregnancy "should be treated as under any health or temporary disability insurance or sick leave plan" that is available to employees. But these administrative agency guidelines, lacking the full force of law, were not universally adopted. Some employers protested that they exceeded congressional intent and that compliance would cause them great financial burden. Others proceeded to modify their plans to various degrees.

Then on December 7, 1976, the Supreme Court ruled[4] that exclusion of pregnancy in disability income protection plans was neither unconstitutional nor illegal under Title VII and the EEOC guidelines. While the major employer associations were celebrating the announcement of this decision, Karen DeCrow, president of the Na-

---

[4] *General Electric Company* v. *Martha V. Gilbert et al.*

tional Organization for Women (NOW), expressed "shock, anger, outrage, and amazement." She declared that NOW would "start drafting legislation immediately."[5]

Within a few months, bills to amend Title VII by specifically prohibiting sex discrimination on the basis of pregnancy had been introduced in both houses of Congress. On October 31, 1978, the Pregnancy Discrimination Act was signed into law. This law very clearly required that pregnancy, childbirth, and related conditions be treated in the same manner as any other illness or disability for all employment-related purposes.

Initiative then returned to the executive branch, and in April 1979, the EEOC issued amendments and an appendix to the 1972 guidelines. This document was undoubtedly more popular with NOW members than among leaders of the Business Roundtable; however, there was still an open issue. What about pregnancy benefits for wives of male employees? Some employers held that this coverage was not mandated by the Pregnancy Discrimination Act, and this led to litigation. Following conflicting decisions in the circuit appeals courts, the Supreme Court said in December 1982 that it will decide the issue.

Employer Influence on Legislation and Regulations

The preceding description of government roles in the field of employee benefits should reinforce the resolve of employers to exercise aggressively their rights to influence the course of government in this area. The stakes are high. Employers currently spend about $500 billion on employee benefits. Close to 30 percent of that goes into public programs.[6]

Obviously, employers cannot expect to shape the design of statutory plans or the controls on private plans with the same authority they have in managing their own plans. However, noninvolvement in the various processes of government means that opposing views may be accepted without challenge. That should never occur.

At both the federal and state level, there are clearly prescribed

[5] *The New York Times*, December 8, 1976.

[6] *Employee Benefits 1981* (Washington, D.C.: Survey Research Center, Chamber of Commerce of the United States, 1982).

ways to communicate ideas and opinions on issues that are dealt with by all three branches of government. Employers may choose to communicate views individually or through associations and political action groups. Such contacts include:

- Letters, telegrams, and personal visits to elected representatives.
- Letters, telegrams, and personal visits to members of key legislative committees (for example, House Ways and Means, Senate Finance).
- Testimony at legislative committee hearings.
- Participation in public hearings held by legislative committees and administrative agencies.
- Written comments to administrative agencies on proposed regulations.
- Filing of amicus curiae briefs in court cases.

Recognizing that labor unions, government administrators, and plaintiff-oriented groups participate actively in all these processes, it is essential that the employer voice not remain silent.

An excellent example of effective industry action was the response to New York Congressman Charles Rangel's proposed Pension Equity Tax Act of 1982. As a result of prompt and convincing lobbying efforts by industry, the Tax Equity and Fiscal Responsibility Act of 1982 (TEFRA) was enacted instead. This compromise act imposed much more moderate changes in restrictions on tax-qualified pension and capital accumulation plans than those contained in the original Rangel proposal.

Living with Government Involvement

Now that Social Security, workers' compensation, and unemployment compensation are firmly established in our economy, employers must learn to deal with them on four distinct levels. First, as already described, they should continue to lobby for cost-effective improvements in program features and requirements. Beyond that it becomes a matter of:

- Purposefully designing private plans in coordination with legally required benefits to avoid duplication of coverage and needless gaps.

- ○ Implementing operational programs and administrative cost-control measures to limit occurrences that cause unnecessary expense for the employer.
- ○ Developing and maintaining close liaison with government agencies to assist employees in obtaining appropriate benefits while guarding against abuses.

In more blunt terms, from an employer's view, this translates into "if you can't beat 'em, join 'em!"

Coordinated Plan Design

Elementary as it might seem, a checklist such as the one shown in Table 2 can be very useful in determining needs and opportunities for plan coordination and integration. A benefits analyst first must become familiar with key characteristics of the applicable mandatory coverages. These programs should be treated as the foundation for any current or prospective company plan.

The most obvious objective of this type of analysis is to avoid a duplication of benefits that could possibly exceed base pay. In some cases, the government makes specific provisions for this. For example, the Supreme Court ruled in 1981[7] that benefits from private pension plans may be reduced by workers' compensation payments. Conversely, state unemployment insurance benefits are offset by em-

Table 2. Benefits plan checklist for Excelsior Benefits, Inc.

Company Plans	Legally Required Plans			
	OASDHI	*UCI*	*TDB*	*WC*
1. Hospital, medical, surgical	X			X
2. Sick pay	X		X	X
3. Long-term disability payments	X		X	X
4. Survivor income benefits	X			X
5. Pension plan	X	X		X
6. Paid vacation allowance		X	X	
7. Severance pay		X		

X = Related; requires review.

[7] *Alessi* v. *Raybestos-Manhattan* and *Buczynski* v. *General Motors.*

ployer-funded pension payments to individuals who are retired involuntarily.

Also, government plans are coordinated with one another in a number of ways. State laws preclude duplication of payments by any of the three types of income protection plans (WC, UCI, and TDB). Under the OASDHI program, disability benefits are formally integrated with workers' compensation so that payments cannot exceed 80 percent of average earnings prior to the start of the disability.

Some of the considerations for designers of private plans are:

1. *Hospital, medical, and surgical benefits:* Offset coverage for retirees and dependents who become eligible for Medicare; nonduplication of benefits between basic group plan and workers' compensation insurance, especially when occupational relatedness is challenged.

2. *Sick pay:* Offsets for OASDHI, TDB, and WC payments; non-withholding of Federal Insurance Contributions Act (FICA) tax on certain payments.

3. *Long-term disability payments:* Length of elimination period (that is, when do benefits begin?); offsets for OASDHI, TDB, and WC payments; requirements to appeal denials of OASDHI benefits; no FICA tax.

4. *Survivor income benefits:* Offsets for OASDHI and WC survivor payments; awareness of all survivor benefits in mandatory coverages.

5. *Pension plan:* Integration by formula with OASDHI; offsets for workers' compensation payments.

6. *Paid vacation allowance:* Information given in response to UCI claims; status when TDB-qualifying illness or injury occurs during vacation.

7. *Severance pay:* Amount and conditions in relation to state UCI law; offsets for supplemental unemployment benefits (SUB) payments for UCI benefits.

Although it does not involve a program that is mandatory for employers, companies should also establish a policy on the relationship of veterans educational benefits to payments under tuition-refund programs.

It is important for employers to be open and candid in explaining to employees the purposes of coordination between benefits from government and company plans. Otherwise perceptions of reductions in basic entitlements may develop. A helpful analogy can be the coordination of benefits process in group health insurance. The primary provider will always pay the same amount to the claimant whether or not a secondary plan is available. When a secondary plan is involved (in this context, the company plan), additional benefits are usually provided. Also, employees will be more likely to accept coordination if the employer can demonstrate that savings derived from offsets are used to fund new and improved company benefits plans.

Operational and Administrative Cost Controls

Once coordination policy and design decisions have been made, employers should follow through to implement effective operational and administrative controls to contain the costs of mandatory benefits.

With respect to the costs of state unemployment compensation insurance, the prime objective is employment stability. Although state laws differ considerably, they are all rooted in the principle of experience rating. A company's UCI tax is based on its record of layoffs and other forms of involuntary separation that cause charges against its account. The less unemployment an employer causes, the lower its tax rate. From a preventive standpoint, this suggests care in hiring seasonal and other temporary employees who can quickly accumulate enough weeks of employment and earnings to be eligible for benefits. Alternatives to terminating regular employees, such as transfer, reduction in hours, suspension, job sharing, and leave of absence, are also worth exploring as a means of avoiding UCI charges. In many states, an employer may make a voluntary contribution to the unemployment fund in order to obtain a lower annual tax rate. Whenever a firm estimates that its taxable payroll will be the same or higher in the following year, a voluntary contribution may produce significant savings in UCI contributions.

Other actions that companies can take to control costs and abuses are:

1. *Good termination records.* Before an employee leaves the company, the basis of the separation should be clearly documented. If the termination is voluntary, a letter of resignation or a signed copy of the exit interview is desirable. When a discharge is involved, detailed statements of the cause and situations leading up to the action should be recorded. The employee must be given instructions for filing claims at the time of separation. Although it is illegal to try to deter an em-

ployee from filing a claim, a frank statement of the employer's position on a claim may avoid hard feelings and lengthy appeals at a later date.

2. *Prompt and accurate response to claims.* When a former employee files a claim, the state will contact the employer to request information about employment, pay, and the cause and conditions of the separation. Some states assess fines if their forms are not returned within five to ten days. A concise statement, such as "discharged for misconduct," "voluntarily quit without good cause attributable to his work," or "resigned, leaving the labor market," is usually adequate, but a supplementary statement explaining the circumstances is often helpful.

3. *Review and appeal of benefits determinations.* If an employee is ruled eligible for benefits, the employer should consider the possibility of an appeal if there is evidence of any false statement by the claimant or if the administrator's ruling seems questionable. In most states, employers are successful in overturning or modifying a majority of rulings they appeal. Even if there is no disposition to appeal the eligibility determination, it is important to check the amount and duration of benefits chargeable to the company's account, particularly if the company knows that the claimant had other employment during the base-year period.

4. *Claims-control card system.* Once a former employee begins to receive benefits, the state will notify the employer (usually weekly) of the amount being paid. At this point, it is very useful to begin recording the charges. A simple card-record system (see Exhibit 6) will enable the employer to review charges for accuracy each week. Errors can be corrected if reported promptly. Perhaps more importantly, a review of the cards for all claimants may suggest possibilities of recall or reemployment. Getting recipients of unemployment benefits back on the payroll is a worthwhile objective in many instances. Furthermore, if they refuse to apply for or to accept suitable work, benefits will usually be suspended.

Unquestionably the best control over workers' compensation costs is an effective accident-prevention program. Larger companies can usually justify a staff of safety and risk management specialists on the basis of preventing losses of life, time, property, and money caused by occupational injury and illness. Smaller firms usually must rely on supervisors and safety committees. Modern accident-prevention sys-

Exhibit 6. Sample card-record system for unemployment compensation claims.

UNEMPLOYMENT COMPENSATION COST CONTROL CARD

NAME		EMP. NO.	SOCIAL SECURITY NO.

POSITION	DATES OF EMPLOYMENT		EXPENSE CENTER
	FROM	TO	

REASON FOR SEPARATION

CHARGEABLE TO OUR ACCOUNT   DATE OF APPEAL

WEEKS @ $ PER WEEK

DECISION

U. C. BENEFIT

PERIOD COVERED	AMOUNT	PERIOD COVERED	AMOUNT	PERIOD COVERED	AMOUNT
	$		$		$
			TOTAL		$

44

tems include review of engineering plans, inspection of equipment, environmental studies, supervisory training, employee education, and provision of protective clothing and equipment. The value of safe practices at the work site was recognized in a slogan contained in a New York State workers' compensation brochure some years ago:

Practice Safety   *Avoid Injury*

Safety Pays Better Than Compensation

Another form of prophylaxis that employers should utilize is a preplacement physical examination. While remaining mindful of prohibitions against discrimination in employment of the handicapped, it is entirely proper and prudent for a company medical examiner to make a fair and relevant evaluation of an applicant's physical capabilities in terms of the particular position for which he or she is being considered. The same approach, of course, should apply in cases of periodic or return-to-work physical examinations. At all times, the health and safety of the employee should be the paramount consideration. The reduction of workers' compensation costs can be a welcome consequence.

From an administrative standpoint, employers can directly, or through their insurance carrier, monitor claims through home visitations, periodic medical examinations by company-appointed physicians, and challenges of charges submitted by claimants. However, a controls administrator who approaches every case with great expectations of uncovering dramatic opportunities for cost savings not only will be quickly disillusioned but, through his or her undue zeal, may do great harm to the firm's image of employee–management relationships.

Appealing compensation board rulings that appear to be inimical to company interests is another story. Whenever a company believes that a ruling is unjust, the right of appeal to a state court should be exercised. Some states permit a review of law and fact; others provide for a review of the law only.[8]

Controlling costs for state-required temporary disability benefits is

[8] For guidance in this regard, and on all matters relating to workers' compensation, the booklet *Analysis of Workers' Compensation Laws,* prepared and published annually by the Chamber of Commerce of the United States, is an excellent source.

intertwined with efforts to decrease any absence due to illness. Once again, safety professionals can contribute. Safety education programs covering vacation activities, driving precautions, hazards in the home, and other off-the-job causes of accidents can raise consciousness and help prevent time-loss disabilities.

Encouraging employees to maintain good health can have a salutory effect on reducing absences caused by illness. Such encouragement can be in the form of company-sponsored medical examinations, recreation and fitness programs, health bulletins, special diet foods in the cafeteria, and smoking cessation and employee assistance programs.

OASDHI does not offer the employer too many operational or administrative cost-savings opportunities. One area that should not be overlooked though is obtaining proof of age on all employees. This will help ensure timely coordination of group health benefits with Medicare and avoid inadvertent accrual of benefits beyond normal retirement age or extended employment past the mandatory retirement age. All these occurrences can create needless costs for an employer. Also, as noted earlier, FICA tax does not apply to certain payments under a formal sick pay plan. Administrative checks should be made to ensure that neither employee deductions nor employer tax payments are being applied to sick pay unnecessarily.

Liaison with Government Agencies

As a rule, district office managers of the Social Security Administration are receptive to company contacts requesting information for employees. Although they do not expect or want employers to explain the intricacies of OASDHI benefits, they welcome leads on employees about to retire or become eligible for disability benefits. These leads can facilitate processing and avoid or correct misunderstandings about Social Security benefits.

For the employer, good communication with local Social Security officials can produce many valuable services for employees. Small quantities of literature can be obtained without charge, and larger quantities purchased at minimal cost. In many cases, the explanatory booklets and brochures issued by the government are just as readable as, and more authoritative than, the more costly reading-rack material prepared by private publishers.

As an integral part of a preretirement planning program for employees, many companies have found it helpful to schedule presentations by Social Security officials. Lectures, question-and-answer sessions, and film showings can be arranged for large or small groups. Some organizations have avoided conflict with work schedules by permitting displays and booths attended by Social Security representatives to be set up in employee cafeterias during lunch periods. An inexpensive but effective gesture is to tell employees who are nearing retirement that they may take time off with pay about two months before retirement to visit their local Social Security office to initiate their claims.

When an employee has been disabled for more than three consecutive months and the outlook for a return to work within the next nine months is poor, the company should refer him or her to the Social Security office. This will help the employee obtain prompt payment of disability benefits if ruled eligible after the fifth month and enable the company to coordinate payments with other relevant coverages.

Companies can also aid employees by explaining the importance of periodically requesting a statement of credited earnings from the Social Security Administration. This is especially important to employees who work for more than one company in the course of a year. Unless errors are reported within approximately three years after the year in which wages were paid, correction of accounts may not be possible. Some district offices will furnish a supply of request cards (see Exhibit 7) to employers for distribution to employees.

Although company officials may be opposed to continual extension and liberalization of Social Security benefits, it seems sensible to enlist the assistance of the administrators of existing benefits in an overall program of communications to employees. Posters, news bulletins, and releases for reproduction in company house organs are additional forms of material that can be obtained from local offices to remind employees of entitlements that are financed by employer matching of their own contributions.

One of the requirements for receiving state UCI benefits is to register for work at a public employment office. One action that companies in a community can take to help one another is to list all their job openings with these employment offices. In addition to utilizing a no-fee recruiting source, and probably satisfying affirmative action objectives, placement of a person in one company may mean the end of a UCI benefits account charge for another.

Exhibit 7.   Social Security Administration's "Request for Statement of Earnings" card.

YOUR SOCIAL SECURITY EARNINGS RECORD

For a *free* statement of earnings credited to your social security record, complete other side of this card. Use card for only *one* person.

All covered wages and self-employment income are reported under your *name* and social security *number.* So show your name and number *exactly* as on your card. If you ever used another name or number, show this too.

Be sure to put a stamp on this card or it won't be delivered. You can mail the card in a stamped envelope if you wish.

If you have a separate question about social security, or want to discuss your statement when you get it, the people at any social security office will be glad to help you.

Form SSA-7004 PC (1-79)
(Prior Editions May Be Used Until Supply Is Exhausted)

POSTAGE
REQUIRED

SOCIAL SECURITY ADMINISTRATION
P. O. BOX 57
BALTIMORE, MARYLAND 21203

(Please read instructions on back before completing)
REQUEST FOR SOCIAL SECURITY
STATEMENT OF EARNINGS

Your social security number

Date of Birth

Month	Day	Year

Print Name and Address in ink or use typewriter

Please send a statement of my social security earnings to:

Name _____ __ _____

Number & Street ____ _____

City & State _____ Zip Code _____

Sign Your Name Here _____
                              (Do Not Print)

I am the individual to whom the record pertains. I understand that if I knowingly and willingly request or receive a record about an individual under false pretenses I would be guilty of a Federal crime and could be fined up to $5,000.

If you ever used a name (such as a maiden name) on a social security card different from the one above, please print name here:

_____

   Prompt, clear, and full responses to inquiries from state agencies concerning UCI claims is an excellent investment of time. In the first instance, the cost and annoyance of fines for late replies is eliminated. Beyond that, the quality of communication that employers develop with state administrators investigating UCI claims and with examiners conducting appeals hearings may indirectly affect eligibility rulings. State personnel are bound to form opinions of firms that create most of the traffic in their offices. The company that appeals every claim regardless of circumstances can expect to be dealt with in a less than friendly manner. The company that pays no attention to claims will create the impression that it does not care whether the former employee collects or not, and in questionable cases, the employee will get the benefit of the doubt. Companies that establish a reputation for being communicative with the state administration when they are asked for information, and for being reasonable and selective in their appeals, will earn the respect of agency personnel and can expect an objective review of all claims.

Finally, when a company decides it may want to reemploy an individual collecting unemployment benefits, it is important to formally communicate the job offer or opportunity to reapply. If the former employee ignores the contact or rejects a reasonable job offer, the employer should immediately notify the state unemployment administration. Some states supply forms for this purpose. A failure to apply for or to accept suitable work will usually result in a suspension of the claimant's benefits.

At the same time that employers complain about the many government agencies involved in administering ERISA, state workers' compensation administrators must decry all the company "cooks" who get involved in their business. Company medical directors, safety specialists, risk management staff, personnel directors, employee benefits managers, attorneys (in-house and outside), and insurance company representatives all seem to have roles in the WC area.

In addition to the obvious need for proper coordination within the company, there must be agreement on responsibility for liaison with the appropriate state agency. This is crucial in order to ensure:

1. Prompt and precise reports of injuries to state agencies.
2. Appeal of awards that seem excessive or inequitable.
3. Referrals to and reports from rehabilitation agencies.
4. Utilization of subsequent-injury funds (payments not chargeable to the employer).

CHAPTER 4

Basic Benefits: The Income Protectors

Employees in the 1980s tend to have rather definite expectations regarding employer-provided benefits. As a minimum, today's employees count on company programs that will protect their basic earnings during times of adversity. In *Profile of Employee Benefits*,[1] Mitchell Meyer and Harland Fox cite five common occurrences that fall in this category:

1. Hospital or doctors' bills that might bankrupt the family.
2. Loss of earnings because of sickness or accident.
3. Inability to work because of permanent disability or old age.
4. Untimely death of the breadwinner.
5. Layoff or loss of job.

In addition to plans that address needs resulting from these events, the basic, or core, benefits package typically includes rewards and recognition in the form of paid time off for leisure or civic duty and, fre-

[1] Report No. 645 (New York: The Conference Board, 1974).

quently, plans providing opportunities for capital accumulation. Of course, approaches, plan design, methods of funding, and benefits levels all vary from organization to organization. Factors causing the variations include:

- Industry and area practice.
- Company profitability.
- Philosophy regarding the mix of direct and indirect forms of employee compensation.
- Range and intensity of employee expectations and preferences.
- Unions.
- Cost-effectiveness of the design and management of the benefits plans.

Given an assignment to develop or upgrade a basic benefits program, managers have traditionally relied on the familiar compensation administration technique of conducting an industry or area survey of current practice. This is a useful, and probably necessary, step, but it usually reveals a myriad of plan design features. Although certain fundamental patterns may become evident, there are often more variations than similarities. The survey information can provide a good array of alternatives, but decisions must be based on a carefully balanced review of stated company objectives and employee expectations. Compensation managers can use survey data in a quasi-scientific way in revising a salary structure; the use of survey findings by benefits managers is more art than science.

This chapter is intended to offer assistance to managers who must operate within this "art form." It describes the most common plan features and alternatives for the five components in an employer's benefits program that are intended to protect employees' income. Where appropriate, prevailing practice in the early 1980s for major companies is cited.

Health Care

If a group of employees were assembled for a meeting on benefits and asked to make individual lists of the most important benefits, the odds are that health care would head most lists. This prediction is based on the results of dozens of similar exercises conducted in seminars and college courses over the past ten years. Explanations given for such a high rating include the near universality of health care coverage, frequency of utilization, applicability to the family, and intense concern about the rising costs of health care. Employers need to recognize the prominence of this benefit and take extra care in designing plans that will produce a high level of employee satisfaction.

ALTERNATIVE SOURCES

Health care benefits can be delivered to employees through four alternative sources:

Insurance companies.
Blue Cross/Blue Shield associations.
Health maintenance organizations (HMOs).
Self-funding arrangements.

Insurance Companies

Insurance companies are the most widely used alternative for group medical benefits, although in recent years employers have tended to adopt at least some degree of self-funding in combination with insurance contracts. Initially, insurance companies followed the practice of providing cash or indemnity benefits based on a schedule for hospital expenses. For instance, such a plan today might cover hospital daily room-and-board charge up to a limit of $150. In recent years, however, it has become more common for insured plans to specify coverage in terms of the hospital's standard rate for a semiprivate room. When this is the case, and when the employee elects to assign payments directly to the hospital, the delivery of benefits is virtually the same as in a Blue Cross arrangement. Proponents of insured health plans cite these advantages over other arrangements:

○ Insurance companies offer a broad and integrated package of coverages that can be tailored to a variety of needs (that is, not limited to health care).
○ The insurance company as a third party in the claims administration process can best reconcile problems between the patient and the purveyor of care—the physician or hospital.

○ Insurance companies provide coordination of benefits checks, claims analysis, and other administrative services to control excessive costs.

○ Insurance companies offer a variety of risk financing arrangements and rating techniques that allow employers flexibility in terms of risk management.

Blue Cross/Blue Shield Associations

Since the introduction of "service benefits" at Baylor University Hospital in Dallas, Texas, in 1929 for a group of schoolteachers, this approach has reached the level of covering more than 80 million Americans through state and local Blue Cross/Blue Shield associations. By meeting minimum standards set by the American Hospital Association, all these independent plans are permitted to use the Blue Cross identity, but their benefits and rates are primarily influenced by community standards.

Typically, a Blue Cross association has an arrangement with its member hospitals to reimburse the hospital for something less than 100 percent (perhaps 85–90 percent) of actual charges incurred by subscribers. As long as plan members are treated in participating hospitals, benefits are provided directly with minimal paperwork or noncovered expenses.

Blue Shield plans were developed by state and local medical societies whose members agreed to accept a fixed rate for medical and surgical services. For covered employees and dependents, this usually represents a full-service benefit. However, some plans operate on a schedule, and subscribers may be required to pay a portion of the physician's total fee.

Advantages of the Blue Cross/Blue Shield alternative include:

○ Employees are aware of the widespread use of these plans and know that most hospitals and doctors will readily accept them if they are covered by the "Blues."

○ The hospital discount is a competitive advantage for Blue Cross relative to insured plans.

○ In comparison with indemnity plans, the provision of service benefits simplifies the hospitalization process for the patient and plan administration for the employer.

○ Conversion opportunities for employees are relatively simple.

○ As nonprofit institutions, Blue Cross/Blue Shield associations have tax advantages over insurance companies.

Health Maintenance Organizations (HMOs)

The group practice prepayment method of providing health care dates back to the 1930s. By 1972 the Kaiser-Permanente Medical Care Program covered more than 2 million employees, mostly in northern California. That program served as a prototype in the development of the Health Maintenance Organization Act of 1973. Today, largely as a result of the federally mandated dual-choice alternative, there are approximately 11 million HMO participants in the United States.

By law, companies with more than 25 employees must offer HMO services as an alternative to conventional health insurance plans whenever a federally qualified prepaid plan makes timely and proper application for consideration. However, within any particular service area, an employer need offer that consideration to only one of each of the two basic types of HMO.

○ Group practice ("closed panel"). Physicians are employed by the plan or are under contract, and most medical services are provided at a central location.

○ Individual practice association (IPA) ("open panel"). Physicians continue to practice medicine individually but are paid by the IPA on a fee-for-service basis according to agreed-upon fee schedules. Services to members are provided from a variety of locations.

For employees who elect the HMO alternative over the conventional group health plan, the employer is required to make only the same level of payment as it is making to the conventional plan. If the HMO cost is higher, the added amount is normally paid by the employee. Although some employers have viewed HMOs as a government-imposed burden, many immediate and potential advantages are becoming apparent:

○ The emphasis on preventive medicine increases the likelihood of early diagnosis and treatment, thus reducing the incidence and costs of more serious illness.

○ There is a direct incentive for the HMO to keep members well, to eliminate unnecessary hospitalization, and to keep costs down.

○ Members receive comprehensive health care, often in an integrated facility.
○ The element of choice itself is consistent with the increasing desire among employees for flexible benefits plans.

Self-Funding Arrangements

Interest in self-funding has grown rapidly in recent years as employers have searched for ways to counter the rapidly rising costs of health care. Meanwhile, the insurance companies respond that their retention charges (risk and contingency charges, premium taxes, administration costs, and reserve requirements) are small (5–10 percent) in relation to paid claims, which they maintain can be better controlled with carrier involvement. Nonetheless, larger employers in particular have been persuaded to assume more of the health care risk in order to realize sayings, as typified in Table 3. As revealed in this example, the self-funding approach offers several advantages, including:

○ No state premium taxes.
○ Savings on administration and other carrier charges.
○ Improved cash flow.
○ Better investment earnings on reserves.

Companies that have elected a self-funding approach usually utilize insurance carriers in one or more ancillary ways. Frequently, an employer will sign an agreement for administrative services only (ASO) with an insurance company to handle claims management.

Table 3. Health care financing: insured vs. self-funded plans.

	Insured	*Self-Funded*
Beginning reserves	$ 800,000	$ 600,000
Income (premiums or deposits)	3,000,000	2,700,000
Paid claims	2,500,000	2,500,000
Operating costs		
Premium tax	60,000	—
Risk and contingency	30,000	—
Administration	200,000	150,000
Interest on reserves	(40,000)	(60,000)
Total	250,000	90,000
Addition to reserves	250,000	110,000
Total reserves	$1,050,000	$ 710,000

(Such agreements can also be made with third-party administrators.) Another common arrangement is stop-loss insurance, in which the employer buys coverage for claims that exceed a targeted level (for example, 120 percent of expected claims).

While technically within the traditional insurance framework, a minimum premium plan offers some of the advantages of self-funding. This is an arrangement in which the employer pays only a portion (for example, 10 percent) of its expected premium to the carrier, withholds the balance, and pays its claims directly up to an agreed-upon level (typically about 110 percent of expected claims). The carrier is responsible for paying claims above that level as well as for providing complete administrative services.

From a financial viewpoint, the use of a tax-exempt trust for a self-funded plan is an attractive alternative. Qualifying a trust under Section 501(c)(9) of the Internal Revenue Code permits the company to deduct its contributions as a business expense, and the trust's investment income is tax exempt.

COMPONENTS OF COVERAGE

In terms of delivery of benefits to employees and covered dependents, insured, self-funded, and Blue Cross/Blue Shield health plans cover essentially the same events and conditions. However, the scope and levels of coverage and claims arrangements tend to differ. HMOs typically offer a wider range of services with fewer restrictions and limitations. Whenever an employee has the opportunity to choose between an HMO and a conventional group health plan, the differences in coverage (and cost) come into sharp focus. Exhibit 8 is a chart an employer might provide that compares the benefits of each, neither recommending nor discouraging employees from electing HMO coverage. In this example, the HMO is meeting the conditions for federal qualification by providing basic services to enrollees without limit as to time, cost, or health status. The company plan is representative of those in effect for salaried employees of major U.S. employers in 1982.

Fundamentally, the model company plan used in Exhibit 8 provides basic hospital, surgical, and medical coverage subject to specified limits, supplemented by a major medical component with a coinsurance feature (80 percent paid by the plan; 20 percent by the covered person). This is still the most common configuration in group health care plan design. It results from major medical insurance hav-

Exhibit 8.   Chart comparing benefits for HMO versus conventional health plan.

Which health insurance plan is better for you?
Compare and decide.

Benefit	HMO	Current Group Plan
Inpatient hospital services	Umlimited days in a semiprivate room for each illness or injury	Up to 365 days in a semiprivate room for each illness or injury
Physician, consultations (office, hospital, and home)	Unlimited in HMO center, affiliated hospitals, and skilled nursing centers; in member's home (when medically required and with $7 copayment)	*In-hospital* 1st day—$15 2–7 days—$10 8–365 says—$5 Other visits under major medical*
Surgical procedures	Covered in full	Reasonable and customary charges**
Periodic health assessments	Covered in full	Not covered
Well-child care	Covered in full	Not covered
Outpatient diagnosis lab tests and X-ray	Covered in full	Up to $150 per year
Prescription drugs and medical equipment	Not covered	Covered under major medical*
Emergency health services	In HMO center or affiliated hospital at any time; when medically necessary at any approved hospital	Covered for treatment within 24 hours of accident or medical emergency at any location
Out-of-area coverage	Limited to emergency care	Covered on same basis as in area
Selection of physicians and hospitals	Limited to HMO staff and affiliated hospitals	Free choice of physicians and hospitals

(continued on next page)

Exhibit 8. Continued.

Benefit	HMO	Current Group Plan
Employee contribution		
Single coverage	$12.00	$7.00
One dependent	$17.00	$14.00
Two or more dependents	$25.00	$21.00

* Supplementary plan. After an annual deductible of $100 per person or $250 per family has been met, the plan pays 80% of covered expenses (hospital and surgical charges in excess of basic coverage, physician visits, and costs of prescription drugs). After the employee has paid total of $1,100, plan coverage becomes 100%. Maximum lifetime benefits of $1 million.

** Reasonable and customary is defined by the insurance carrier as any charge up to the 90th percentile of all surgeon's fees for a particular procedure performed in a postal ZIP code area.

ing been an add-on to existing basic hospital and surgical plans in most firms.

Many benefits authorities believe that a more logical and understandable design for health coverage is a comprehensive major medical plan. In this alternative, currently used by about 40 percent of U.S. employers, there is a single initial deductible, after which the plan begins to pay for a portion (usually 80 percent) of all covered hospital, surgical, and medical expenses. In both the supplementary and comprehensive forms of major medical coverage, most plans usually place a limit on the employee's coinsurance payments. For example, after the employee has paid $1,000 under the coinsurance provisions, many plans will pay 100 percent of covered expenses.

In contrast with HMOs, most conventional group health plans do not cover periodic health assessments. With growing awareness about the relationship between fitness and productivity, this omission will surely be reevaluated in the near future. In the meantime, some companies offer this benefit to a number of their employees through executive health plans and medical surveillance of employees subject to certain types of exposure.

Disability Income

Conditions causing employees to worry about loss of earnings due to disability can range from a sore throat to heart failure. In the first instance, the loss of one or two days' pay may create temporary financial presure; in the second case, the threat of a permanent reduction in income might aggravate the condition. A company's disability income benefits program must address the total range of concerns.

Government plans provide a floor of income protection, primarily for longer term disabilities, but there are major gaps in coverage for which employees expect benefits from their employers when the need occurs. The dilemma that most companies experience in dealing with this expectation is the conflict between normal compassion for sick and injured workers and a belief (suspicion?) that overly generous benefits breed malingering and create a disincentive to work. This section will cover the elements of a total approach to providing disability income benefits. The issue of cost control will be addressed more fully in Chapter 9.

PUBLIC PLANS

As stated previously, all state workers' compensation (WC) plans provide for both temporary and permanent disability income benefits. TDB laws covering nonoccupational disabilities exist in California, Hawaii, New Jersey, New York, Puerto Rico, and Rhode Island. Benefits begin on the eighth day of disability and are payable for up to 26 weeks (39 in California).

Social Security disability benefits begin after a 5-month waiting period if the condition prevents the person from doing any substantial gainful work and is expected to last for at least 12 months or result in death. Although these benefits can be paid in addition to WC, they are coordinated so as not to exceed 80 percent of earnings.

SICK PAY

Since none of the public plans specify full income replacement and in most cases provide no benefits for absences of one to five days,[2] most companies have adopted some type of sick pay plan to provide additional income protection. These plans, also called pay continuation plans, are designed to plug the hole in coverage for absences of less than a week. Also, they tend to reward seniority by granting progres-

[2] Most state WC and TDB laws have waiting periods of three to seven days for benefits. Typically, if the disability lasts for two to four weeks, benefits become retroactive to the first day.

Table 4. Provisions of a typical sick pay plan.

Years of Service	Maximum Pay (Days at Full Pay)	Continuation per Year* (Days at Half Pay)
3 mos–1 year	10	120
2–3	15	115
4–5	20	110
6–7	25	105
8–9	30	100
10–11	40	90
12–13	50	80
14–15	60	70
More than 15	75	55

* Offset by any WC or TDB payments.

sively longer periods of pay protection in relation to company service. A typical sick pay plan today might have the provisions shown in Table 4. Some plans eliminate coverage for the first one or two days of absence to control absences and costs. Another design alternative used for the same purpose is to permit carry-over or to pay a bonus for unused days.

LONG-TERM DISABILITY (LTD) PLANS

As sick pay plans supplement WC and TDB in the short run, LTD plans are designed to add to Social Security and WC disability income benefits in the event of more severe illnesses and injuries. Most LTD plans begin to pay benefits after six months of continuous disability and are integrated with public plans to avoid duplicative or excessive benefits. Three typical approaches are:

1. 50 percent of base pay, less primary Social Security benefits and any other public disability payments.
2. 70 percent of base pay, less maximum family Social Security benefits and any other public disability payments.
3. A dual-percentage formula, or "back door integration." In this approach, one percentage (for example, 50 percent) of pay applies if there are no offsets and a higher percentage (for example, 70 percent) is used to limit total payments under the plan and from public programs where offsets are applied.

Because the public disability programs replace a relatively high portion of base earnings for lower paid employees, LTD plans that offset these payments have been criticized by union leaders and some benefits experts as being phantom plans. In response to this charge, most employers provide a minimum monthly benefit in the range of $25–50. A small number of plans avoid the issue by providing a non-integrated disability payment of 15–20 percent of base pay.

Without question, LTD plans are most meaningful to higher salaried professional and managerial employees, who are least likely to receive workers' compensation payments and who receive a low percentage of income replacement from Social Security. With this in mind, many employers consider it important to periodically raise the maximum benefit level as salaries continue to rise. Ten years ago, a typical maximum in LTD plans was $1,500–2,000 per month; today, monthly limits are more frequently in the range of $3,000–5,000.

A common feature in most LTD plans is a two-stage definition of disability. Initially, the test involves the ability of the employee to perform his or her regular job. If the disability precludes this, benefits are usually paid for up to one or two years. At that point, the definition of disability changes to the inability to perform any occupation for which the person is qualified by education, experience, or training. This split definition, often called "his occ/any occ," is intended to encourage rehabilitation and, where appropriate, career redirection as well as to limit the employer's liability.

LTD plans frequently require employee contributions, and in some firms, they are offered on an employee-pay-all basis. Self-funding is not widely used by employers, since it is a relatively inexpensive benefit (particularly when employees share in the costs) and an insurance carrier can play a very useful role in monitoring long-term cases.

While LTD plans are clearly in the class of basic benefits for salaried employees in the United States today, a majority of firms have not extended this coverage to hourly workers. Some defend this on the basis of the adequacy of public program benefits; others cite the higher exposure to disabling injuries and the related impact on costs. From an employee relations viewpoint, the disparity in coverage seems to be at odds with the continuing trend toward equal treatment of employees regardless of payroll category.

PENSION PLAN BENEFITS

Before the widespread growth of LTD plans that began in the 1960s, it was common for pension plans to pay extended disability income benefits. Typically, a plan would pay actuarially reduced benefits to a vested participant who became permanently and totally disabled (the Social Security standard). Since vesting often required 15 or 20 years of service and the attainment of age 45 or 50, these provisions covered only a portion of a company's workforce. Now it is much more common to dovetail pension benefits with an LTD plan, as in this sample description for pension plan members:

> If you become totally and permanently disabled before age 62, you will receive LTD plan benefits and continue to accrue pension benefits until you recover, die, or reach age 65. If your disability continues to age 65, you will then be entitled to a pension based on the salary you were earning when the disability occurred. If your total and permanent disability begins after age 61, you will receive LTD plan benefits and continue to accrue pension benefits until you recover or die, or until the end of the period shown in the following table:[3]

Age when disability began	Period of payment (years)
62	3½
63	3
64	2½
65	2
66	1¾
67	1½
68	1¼
69	1

> At the end of the period shown in this schedule, pension payments will begin based on the salary you were earning when the disability began.

TAX IMPLICATIONS OF DISABILITY INCOME PAYMENTS

In designing a total program to meet employees' needs for income replacement during periods of disability, it is important to consider the tax treatment of payments from the various component plans. Since certain benefits are not subject to taxes, it is neither necessary nor advisable to replace 100 percent of base earnings during extended periods of disability. To do so could result in an employee receiving higher net income while disabled than while working—hardly an in-

---

[3] As specified by the Department of Labor in an interpretative bulletin of May 25, 1979, with respect to 1978 ADEA amendments.

Table 5. Tax treatment of various disability payments.

Type of Payment	Federal Income Tax	FICA
Workers' compensation	No	No
Social Security	No	N/A
Temporary disability benefits (TDB) (up to 26 weeks)	Yes*	Yes*
Sick pay salary continuation	Yes	Yes
Long-term disability plan (after 6 months of disability)	Yes*	No

* Except to the extent employee contributes.

centive to recover quickly. Under current laws, disability payments are subject to tax as shown in Table 5.

Survivor Payments and Benefits

No other category of basic benefits involves as many different plans, or functions so unevenly in meeting employee needs, as payments to and benefits for survivors. A collection of mutually exclusive plans has evolved in most firms largely because of a combination of inadequate communication between the personnel and insurance functions and effective marketing by the insurance industry. As a result, a typical array of company plans providing survivor income payments now includes:

Group term life insurance (basic and supplementary).
Accidental death coverage.
Business travel insurance.
Spouse's preretirement pension.
Survivor income benefits insurance (SIBI).

Furthermore, both the Social Security and workers' compensation programs pay survivor benefits. However, while these statutory programs relate payments to such need-related factors as marital status and parental responsibilities of survivors, most company plans do not. With the notable exception of SIBI plans, company survivor benefits tend to be influenced more by the cause of death and final pay level of the deceased. Because of an apparent overdependency on these fac-

Exhibit 9. Survivor benefit payments in a company without SIBI.

T.H.E. COMPANY SURVIVOR BENEFIT EXAMPLES

Leslie Johnson, who has worked with the company for 10 years, is 45 years old. She is married with four children (ages 12, 14, 16, 19). Her salary is $20,000 a year, and her husband earns the same amount. She develops a serious illness unrelated to her work and dies.

Martin Cummings, age 55, has been with the firm for 10 years. His annual salary is $40,000. His wife earns $20,000 a year. They have no children. While traveling on company business, he is killed in an airplane crash.

Company Plan	Benefits to Mr. Johnson	Benefits to Mrs. Cummings
1. Group term life insurance—two times salary	$40,000	$80,000
2. Accidental death—two times salary	N/A	80,000
3. Business travel accident insurance—three times salary	N/A	120,000
4. Spouse's pension—50% of accrued pension payable to spouse if death occurs after reaching age 55 and completing 10 years of service	N/A	4,000/year
TOTAL	$40,000	$280,000+ $4,000/year

---

tors, most employers' programs miss the mark in matching the level of benefits with the true needs of survivors.

Exhibit 9 dramatizes the unevenness of survivor benefits payments in a company without SIBI. Although both survivors in this illustration are employed and earning $20,000 a year, it seems reasonable to assume that Mr. Johnson's need for income replacement is greater than Mrs. Cummings's need. Three of his four dependent children are eligible to receive Social Security payments (limited by the maximum family benefit provision) until they reach age 19 (if they are still in primary or secondary school), but that amount will not come close to filling the income gap created by the death of his spouse. Mr. Johnson could invest his $40,000 life insurance proceeds and use the interest to supplement his income, or use an installment payment option for the same purpose. But neither of these alternatives seems to satisfactorily replace the loss of his cobreadwinner's income.

On the other hand, Mrs. Cummings's survivor income benefits are arguably more than adequate in terms of need. In addition to the $280,000 lump-sum payments and $4,000 per year spouse's pension, she would be entitled to a tax-free workers' compensation weekly benefit (for example, currently $215 in New York State) for life or until remarriage. With reasonable success in investments, her total income from survivor benefits sources could easily surpass her husband's earnings on an aftertax comparative basis.

Some employers believe that adverse public or employee reactions to a death that is work connected, especially when it results from a travel accident, can be mitigated by impressively high payments to survivors. This may be a fair judgment, but if such coverage is at the expense of needy survivors of employees who die from natural causes, the benefits structure seems illogical and inequitable.

SURVIVOR INCOME BENEFITS INSURANCE (SIBI)

A natural extension of the need-related basis of statutory survivor income programs is group survivor income benefits insurance (SIBI). SIBI plans seem to be ideally suited as a supplement to basic group term insurance. They provide a regular monthly benefit to a surviving spouse and dependent children, but unlike group term insurance coverage, payments usually are not made to any other class of beneficiary. A typical plan would specify a spouse's annual benefit at 25 percent of the insured employee's final pay, with an additional 5 percent for each dependent child (under age 19) and a maximum benefit of 40 percent. Some plans set the maximum benefit level at a higher percentage (for example, 70 percent) but apply offsets for Social Security and workers' compensation payments. In most plans, the spouse's benefit is payable until remarriage, death, or attainment of age 62, whichever occurs first.

If T.H.E. Company had adopted a typical SIBI plan as a substitute for its accidental death benefits and, at the same time, had lowered its business travel accident coverage to one times salary, the benefits for Mr. Johnson and Mrs. Cummings would have been as shown in the adjacent table. (Compare with Exhibit 9.) Under this alternative ar-

Company Plan	Benefits to Mr. Johnson	Benefits to Mrs. Cummings
1. Group term life insurance—two times salary	$40,000	$80,000
2. SIBI—25% of salary, plus an additional 5% for each dependent child (maximum 40%)	8,000/year	10,000/year
3. Business travel accident insurance—one times salary	N/A	40,000
4. Spouse's pension—50% of accrued pension payable to spouse if death occurs after reaching age 55 and completing 10 years of service	N/A	4,000/year
TOTAL	$40,000+ $8,000/year	$120,000+ 14,000/year

rangement, Mr. Johnson would have received an additional $8,000 per year of income replacement. Total benefits to Mrs. Cummings, while less than in Exhibit 9, would still seem reasonable.

In spite of the obvious logic of SIBI, its growth as an employee benefit has been surprisingly slow. One reason for this has been the relatively high cost of funding continuing payments to younger survivors. Because it is an expensive benefit, those companies that have installed plans tend to offer them on a contributory or employee-pay-all basis.

Although accidental death and business travel accident insurance are less expensive forms of coverage, it would seem worthwhile for employers to consider trade-offs between premiums for those special-purpose (and sometimes excessive) benefits and a more purposeful and equitable SIBI plan.

TAX CONSIDERATIONS AND EMPLOYEE CONTRIBUTIONS

In its familiar Jekyll–Hyde role of facilitator–regulator of employee benefits, the IRS has specified that the cost of employer-paid group term life coverage (and SIBI) is includable in an employee's taxable income, but only for any amount of insurance in excess of $50,000. To determine the cost value of insurance for tax purposes, the following schedule is specified under Section 79 of the Internal Revenue Code:

Age	Monthly cost per $1,000
Under 30	$ .08
30–34	.10
35–39	.14
40–44	.23
45–49	.40
50–54	.68
55–59	1.10
60 or more	1.63

For most hourly and nonexempt white-collar employees, the $50,000 rule means that there are no tax consequences from their company term life insurance plans, even if the insurance is fully company paid. Hourly employees often are covered by a flat amount of insurance that is unlikely to exceed $50,000. Nonexempt salaried employees are more likely to have basic insurance coverage that is equal to or two times base pay. Again, this is not apt to go above $50,000.

In recent years, the opportunity for employees to obtain supplementary term life insurance at group rates on either a contributory or an employee-pay-all basis has become increasingly popular. Not only are the rates favorable in comparison to rates for individual policies, but by paying for the insurance, employees can avoid or minimize the creation of additional taxable income. The following situations illustrate this effect.

Example A. Max Barnett, age 47, has $50,000 of company-paid term life insurance and $75,000 of supplementary coverage that is offered to employees on a contributory basis at a monthly rate of 40 cents per $1,000. His annual cost is $360 ($.40 × 12 × 75). The Section 79 tax calculation would reveal the following:

Total amount of group term life insurance	$125,000
Excludable from tax consideration	50,000
Balance	$ 75,000

Section 79 cost = $360 (.40 × 12 × 75)

Since Mr. Barnett's contribution is equal to the Section 79 cost, there is no imputed income subject to federal tax.

Example B. Shirley Novak, age 55, participates in a group term life insurance plan in which the employer pays for $40,000 of coverage, and she has elected an additional $40,000 on a contributory basis at a rate of 50 cents per month per $1,000. Her annual cost is $240. The Section 79 calculation would establish a cost of $396:

Total amount of group term life insurance	$80,000
Excludable from tax consideration	50,000
Balance	$30,000

Section 79 cost = $396 ($1.10 × 12 × 30)

Ms. Novak's imputed income from her employer's plan contributions in her behalf would be $156 ($396 − 240). If the additional coverage had been provided on an employee-pay-all basis (with a higher premium cost for employees), there would have been no tax consequence.

OTHER BENEFITS FOR SURVIVORS

In addition to income replacement requirements, there are several other needs of survivors that employers can satisfy, at least in part, when an employee dies. These needs and some typical company responses include:

Need	*Benefit*
1. Current funds for funeral and burial expenses.	Immediate lump-sum payment to the spouse (or designated beneficiary) of any salary and vacation entitlements plus salary for one additional pay period.
2. Health insurance.	Continuing coverage for surviving spouse and eligible dependents for one year at company expense, and then providing an additional 31 days to convert to an individual policy.
3. Employment.	For spouse and children, if requested, job or career counseling and consideration for employment. Priority consideration is given to children for summer employment during college years.

Retirement Income

The President's Commission on Pension Policy, which served from 1979 to 1981, essentially endorsed the "three-legged stool" approach to providing retirement income in the United States. This model, consisting of a public old-age benefits system, individual efforts, and private pension plans, was created with the signing of the Social Security Act by President Roosevelt in 1935. Since that event, coverage under the public program for private sector workers has become nearly universal, old age has been redefined to include people as young as age 62, and benefit amounts have risen steadily. In spite of recurring public concerns about the financial condition of the Social Security Trust Funds, retirement benefits from this source continue to represent a sturdy and dependable first leg.

Individual efforts to create retirement income have been hampered by inflation and taxation, but they were aided by the liberalized individual retirement account (IRA) provisions in the Economic Recovery Tax Act of 1981. As of January 1, 1982, virtually every working person in the United States became eligible to invest 100 percent of earnings up to $2,000 a year in a tax-deferred retirement account. Prior to that, IRA participation was restricted to employees who were not active participants in company pension plans, and individual contributions were limited to 15 percent of earnings, with a $1,500 yearly maximum.

Another factor tending to encourage individual effort in providing retirement income has been the accelerated rise in annual earnings allowed without any forfeiture of Social Security benefits. Between 1976 and 1982, this earnings limit increased from $2,760 to $6,000.

The significance to employees of private pensions as the third leg of a retirement income stool depends greatly on company size and length of service. Workers in companies employing 1,000 or more are almost certain to be covered by some type of pension plan. As long as they work for one company for at least ten years, they can expect some retirement income to be payable, probably anytime after reaching age 55. But for people working in small firms (fewer than 100 employees), or for anyone who changes employment more frequently than once every ten years, the odds on receiving retirement benefits from a company plan are poor.

It was because of this undependability of private pension plans as a third leg that the president's commission in its final report[4] recommended that a minimum universal pension system (MUPS) be established for all workers. Although this proposal has not been embraced by either the president or a significant number of congressional leaders, it advances a concept that employers cannot ignore—namely, mandatory private pensions. Unless voluntary efforts result in rapid progress toward providing pension plan coverage for the estimated 50 percent of the workforce not currently covered, support for MUPS will surely gain momentum.

INTEGRATING PENSION PLANS WITH SOCIAL SECURITY

By design, Social Security retirement benefits are intended to provide only a floor of income protection. However, because of the ceiling on wages that are counted in computing benefits, lower paid workers receive a higher percentage of income replacement than managers and other highly paid employees. For example, it has been estimated that a worker retiring in 1980 at age 65 with a gross preretirement salary of $10,000 would have received a Social Security benefit of $4,000 (40 percent) a year. A person earning $50,000 retiring at the same time and age would have received about $6,500 (13 percent).[5]

Recognizing this phenomenon, many employers integrate their pension plans with Social Security to provide proportionately greater benefits to higher paid employees through the private plan as a counterbalance. This they believe produces a more equitable overall income replacement ratio. At the same time, the cost of the pension plan can be reduced by approximately the cost of the employer's FICA payments. Of course, the Treasury Department has set guidelines that guard against any plans providing benefits that might unduly favor higher paid employees over lower paid employees. Currently, Revenue Ruling 71–446 specifies the integration limits for pension plans.

There are three basic approaches to integrating defined-benefit pension plans with Social Security. In order of utilization frequency these are:

[4] *Coming of Age: Toward a National Retirement Income Policy* (Washington, D.C.: Government Printing Office, 1981).

[5] Kenneth P. Shapiro, "An Ideal Pension System," *Personnel Journal* (April 1981).

1. *The offset approach.* This involves a reduction factor (offset) in the calculation of the pension plan benefit based on years of plan service and the primary insurance amount (PIA) payable to the employee under Social Security. For example:

$$\text{Offset} = 1.5\% \times 20 \text{ years} \times \$6,000 = \$1,800$$

The usual maximum offset is 50 percent of the PIA, although the Treasury Department allows up to 83⅓%.

2. *The step-rate approach.* In this approach, the benefits formula is split to reflect the greater influence of Social Security at lower pay levels. Typically, an integration level, or breakpoint, is set at or below the Social Security tax base level and raised periodically, not necessarily annually. An example of a step-rate benefits formula would be:

$$1\% \times \text{years of plan service} \times \text{earnings up to } \$12,000 \text{ } plus \text{ } 1.5\%$$
$$\times \text{years of plan service} \times \text{earnings in excess of } \$12,000$$

Under Treasury Department rulings, if the plan is based on actual yearly excess compensation, the maximum allowable rate differential is 1.4 percent; if an averaged annual excess compensation is used, the maximum differential is 1 percent.

3. *The excess-only approach.* A variation of the step-rate form of integration, this approach provides a private pension benefit only for earnings in excess of an integration level. For example:

$$1.2\% \times \text{years of service} \times \text{earnings in excess of } \$12,000.$$

This is an infrequently used approach that is sometimes offered on a contributory plan basis as a supplement to a noncontributory and nonintegrated fixed-dollar plan.

The president's commission 1981 report contained estimates of replacement ratios necessary to maintain the preretirement standard of living for retiring workers at various income levels. These ratios, or goals, were developed by reducing gross preretirement income by federal, state, and local taxes; work-related expenses; and savings and investments. For employees in major industrial, financial, and service companies who retire at age 65 with 30 years of employment, the combined benefits from Social Security and private pension plans come very close to meeting these goals (see Table 6).

Table 6. Meeting income replacement goals with Social Security and pension benefits (single worker).

Preretirement Salary ($)	Income Replacement Goal as Percentage of Salary	Percentage of Salary Replaced			Percentage of Goal Realized
		Social Security	Private Pension	Combined Benefits	
$10,000	73	40	28	68	93
20,000	61	29	28	57	93
30,000	58	21	32	53	91
50,000	51	13	37	50	98

Source: Kenneth P. Shapiro, "An Ideal Pension System," *Personnel Journal* (April 1981).

TYPES OF PLANS

Among large firms, most retirement income plans are of the defined-benefit type. In these plans the benefit, or method of determining the benefit, is specified. Contributions to a trust fund are determined actuarially on the basis of the benefits expected to become payable. Supported by plan insurance, as required by the Pension Benefit Guaranty Corporation (PBGC), these plans offer employees a high degree of financial security tantamount to a pension promise. For employers, defined-benefit plans are subject to the full array of ERISA requirements. They also lack cost-predictability because of the uncertainties of actuarial assumptions.

Since the arrival of ERISA, the majority of newly adopted pension plans have been of the defined-contribution type. These are individual account plans in which the rate of contributions is fixed by a formula. Benefits become whatever the amount accumulated and vested in the participant's account will buy. From an employee viewpoint, these plans tend to be easy to understand and they provide clear evidence of company contributions on a current and individual basis. On the down side, the employee bears the burden of poor investment performance and there are no guarantees or known levels of retirement income. Employers are attracted to defined-contribution pension plans because they are not subject to PBGC requirements or ERISA funding rules on past service liabilities.

Defined-contribution plans, such as the money purchase type, are widely used in retirement systems for public employees and by nonprofit organizations. This is mainly because of the difficulty plan sponsors face in projecting long-term costs for defined-benefit plans. For this same reason, both small and newly formed for-profit firms favor the defined-contribution approach. Larger and more mature companies often use a defined-contribution pension plan—typically a savings or thrift plan—to supplement a primary defined-benefit pension plan.

Although classified as pension plans under ERISA, savings and thrift, profit sharing, and employee stock ownership plans actually meet a variety of benefits needs, including capital accumulation, severance pay protection, and income supplementation during employment. They will be discussed in Chapter 6.

DEFINED-BENEFIT PLANS

In designing or reviewing a defined-benefit pension plan, the following elements require management decisions on issues that can have significant cost–benefit implications.

Eligibility

Under ERISA, employers may require employees to meet age and service requirements before they participate in a pension plan. The basic rule is that an employee must begin participation within six months of attaining age 25 and completing one year of service. An alternative rule permits three years of service requirement, but only if the plan provides full and immediate vesting. Also, an employer may exclude anyone hired within five years of the normal retirement age (usually 65) from participation in a defined-benefit plan. Most employers have adopted the basic ERISA rules. Firms that use more liberal eligibility rules reason that additional costs can be justified on the basis of satisfying recruitment and employee relations objectives.

Employee Contributions

Most plans today are noncontributory. This is understandable since employer contributions are tax deductible; employee contributions are not. However, employees can now make tax-deductible contributions to IRAs. Given that option, it seems unlikely that there will be much employee interest in contributing to defined-benefit plans, and employers probably won't count on that as a viable source of money for funding purposes.

Benefits Formulas

For salaried workers, the most prevalent type of formula is one in which benefits are related to "final" pay, usually an average of the highest five years of earnings. This is generally coupled with the offset approach to integration with Social Security. For example:

Pat Williams retires at age 65, after having participated in the Excelsior Benefit Corporation Pension Plan for 30 years. Final average pay (highest five years) is $25,000, and the PIA from Social Secuirty is $8,000. The benefits formula is 1.7% × years of plan service × final average pay less 1.5% × years of service × PIA

Calculation:

$$
\begin{array}{rl}
1.7\% \times 30 \times \$25,000 = & \$12,750 \\
\text{less } 1.5\% \times 30 \times \quad 8,000 = & \underline{3,600} \\
\text{Pension} \qquad\qquad = & \$\ \ 9,150
\end{array}
$$

This would be considered a fairly generous benefit by most standards in the early 1980s. However, a trend toward using the highest three rather than five years of earnings is becoming evident. Obviously, this increases plan costs, but many believe that it is more appropriate for meeting income replacement goals during times of rapid inflation.

Some plans still base benefits on career average earnings. These plans normally use step-rate integration with Social Security. To compensate for the steady rise in pay levels, and the effects of inflation, companies with career-average formulas will periodically upgrade accrued benefits.

Formulas in plans for hourly workers tend to be simpler, not integrated with Social Security, and not directly tied to pay. For example, the current pattern plan of the United Steelworkers of America specifies the following benefits: From August 1982 through July 1983—$17.50 per month for each of the first 15 years of service; $19.00 for each of the next 15 years of service; and $20.50 for each year thereafter. For a 30-year employee, this plan pays a monthly benefit of $547.50 ($6,570 a year). Combined with Social Security, this provides excellent income replacement for low-wage earners, but it seems marginally adequate for employees in higher pay grades. Because of their simplicity, relative certainty, and independence from Social Security, these so-called pattern or flat-amount formulas have been endorsed by most large unions, but it is questionable whether they are designed to best serve the needs of all union members.

Past-Service Benefits

When a company installs a defined-benefit pension plan, consideration should be given to crediting past service of current employees. Of course, costs would be extraordinary if a plan used the same formula that applied to future benefits. And if the past-service benefits had to be funded immediately, very few employers would be financially able to undertake such an obligation. To facilitate the granting of past-service credits, ERISA imposes no benefit standards and allows new plans to fund the accrued liabilities over a period of up to 30 years. With so much latitude, it is not too onerous for an employer to assume a past-service obligation that long-service employees will consider as being equitable, even though a somewhat less generous formula is normally used. For example, if Pat Williams (see above discussion of benefits formulas) had 10 years of past service and 20 years of current service, the benefits calculation might have been:

$$
\begin{array}{rl}
1\% \times 10 \times \$25{,}000 = & \$\ 2{,}500 \\
\text{plus } 1.7\% \times 20 \times 25{,}000\ \ = & \underline{\ \ 8{,}500} \\
& \$11{,}000 \\
\text{less } 1.5\% \times 30 \times \quad 8{,}000\ \ = & \underline{\ \ 3{,}600} \\
\text{Pension} & \$\ 7{,}400
\end{array}
$$

Although there are no legal requirements for granting a past-service benefit, the employee relations advantages of recognizing preplan service convince most firms to provide some benefit credits.

Funding

Funding is the process of setting aside assets in a trust account, or with an insurance company, to meet obligations to pay benefits in the future. Employer contributions, employee earnings, and appreciation of accumulated assets make up the fund from which benefits are paid. ERISA and IRS regulations specify funding standards and minimum and maximum tax-deductible contributions rules for employers. Generally, these rules require the plan sponsor (employer) to fund annually the full cost for current benefit accruals and amortize past-service credits over 30 years.

The funding process involves complex actuarial assumptions of mortality, employee turnover, rate of salary increases, and interest yield. These calculations, plus the company's financial position and funding philosophy, will determine the amount the company pays into the fund each year.

There are two general methods of funding a pension plan: through a pension trust and through an insurance company contract. Split funding is a combination of the two. Most early pension plans were of the insured type, but today trusteed plans are much more prevalent.

The yield on pension-fund investments is a factor that employers should watch carefully. Consultants estimate that if the yield on a mature plan's investments can be increased by 1 percent, the company's contributions can be decreased by as much as 20 percent, or benefits increased 25 percent. An employer can expect outside investment specialists to guide the management of a pension fund, but the sponsor can never abdicate the fiduciary responsibility to see that it is administered in the best interests of plan participants and beneficiaries.

Vesting

Vesting is a guarantee of accrued benefits to participants at retirement age, regardless of their employment status at that time. In the debate concerning minimum vesting standards that preceded ERISA, it became clear that, while some plans imposed ridiculously severe requirements (for example, attainment of age 65), a requirement of full and immediate vesting would be a disincentive for employers to establish or continue plans. The eventual compromise in ERISA was a choice of three standards:

Cliff vesting: full (100 percent) vesting after 10 years of service (with no vesting prior to completion of 10 years of service).

Graded vesting: 25 percent vesting after 5 years of service, plus 5 percent for each additional year of service up to 10 years (50 percent vesting after 10 years), plus an additional 10 percent for each year thereafter (100 percent vesting after 15 years).

Rule of 45: 50 percent vesting for an employee with at least 5 years of service when his or her age and service add up to 45, plus 10 percent for each year thereafter.

Under any of the options, an employee must be at least 50 percent vested after 10 years of service and 100 percent after 15 years, regardless of age.

Of course, a pension plan can adopt more liberal vesting standards, but so far, most employers have tended to use one of the ERISA prototypes. By far the most popular choice has been 10-year cliff vesting, probably because of its apparent cost-effectiveness and administrative simplicity. As a result, pressure for earlier vesting rules continues to be applied by unions and pension rights advocates who argue that a 10-year all-or-nothing standard causes too many workers to lose benefits. This is certainly understandable in light of the average worker job duration of 3.6 years reported by the Bureau of Labor Statistics.

Restrictive vesting rules may also undermine company performance. Eli Ginzberg, professor of economics at Columbia University's School of Business, has pointed out:

> It [vesting] often locks in workers who would do better work elsewhere if they could change jobs. The decision to move or not to move shouldn't be based on whether you're going to lose or keep pension rights.[6]

Sympathy for a 5-year cliff vesting standard is building, and at least one authority from the private sector (Donald Grubbs, Jr., of George B. Buck Consulting Actuaries) has estimated that this change would have a minimal effect on pension costs (for example, 7 percent).

Normal Deferred and Early Retirement Ages

The normal retirement age in a pension plan is the age when participants can retire with full benefits. Since unreduced Social Security benefits are available at 65, that continues to be the most common normal retirement age in private plans. The 1978 amendments to ADEA prohibit mandatory retirement prior to age 70 in the private sector, but there is still no requirement to credit service after normal retirement age for benefit accrual purposes, or provide an actuarial equivalent benefit to an employee who defers retirement until after the normal retirement date.

A majority of companies have taken advantage of this situation and elected to freeze benefits at the normal retirement age, suspending payment until actual retirement occurs. This clearly reduces plan costs and probably discourages extended employment (for example, from age 65 to age 70). From the standpoint of equity in compensation though, the practice must be questioned. At this time, each company needs to examine its own philosophy about benefits as compensation, as well as its position on encouraging or discouraging ex-

---

[6] Cited in Elliot Carlson, "Pension Portability," *Dynamic Years* (November–December 1981).

tended employment, before deciding on how to deal with this issue. However, it seems quite likely that government regulations will eventually require, at a minimum, actuarially increased benefits for employees who defer their retirement beyond the normal age.

Early retirement provisions allow eligible employees to retire before the normal retirement age (usually 65) and receive an immediate, reduced lifetime benefit. Virtually all private pension plans have such provisions, and most offer the option of deferring the pension and receiving an unreduced benefit at the normal retirement age.

The service requirement for early retirement is frequently equivalent to the requirement for vesting, but the most prevalent minimum age is 55. An implied superannuation before age 55 might be offensive to some employees, and a policy permitting retirement before that age could cause employees to leave while still in their peak productive years. Yet the military, as well as many public organizations, use years of service as the only retirement criterion, thereby allowing employees to retire after 25 or 30 years of service while still in their 40s, and sometimes with an unreduced benefit.

Since 1970 the labor contracts between General Motors Corporation and the United Auto Workers have contained special "30 and out" provisions. With progressively improved features, each successive contract has specified that employees with 30 years of service can retire with an unreduced pension and, if retirement occurs before age 62, receive a supplement until Social Security benefits are available.

Initially, most defined-benefit plans applied standard actuarial reductions to benefits commencing prior to age 65. This produced rather low benefit levels (for example, typically about 40 percent of accrued benefits at age 55; 61 percent at 60; 74 percent at 62) and tended to discourage early retirement. Today, it is more common for plans to have subsidized early retirement schedules. For example, many large company plans now pay unreduced accrued benefits at age 62 or 63. A more widespread practice is to use a uniform reduction schedule, usually 4 percent or 3 percent a year for each year prior to age 65, so that benefits at age 55 are 60 percent or 70 percent of accrued amounts.

Early retirement provisions, while frequently requiring employer consent, exist primarily for the welfare of employees. An employee who is not in good health, who has lost interest in a job, who wants to relocate, or who sees an opportunity for self-employment need not mark time until age 65. Since Social Security retirement benefits are available at age 62, that is a popular retirement age for many employees. Also, some company plans have a Social Security adjustment option that permits the employee to receive a larger-than-computed pension before the receipt of Social Security benefits, which is paid for by reducing plan benefits afterward.

Employers, too, need flexibility to encourage early retirement because of adverse business conditions, technological changes, or plant relocations. When companies have found it necessary to spur attrition through early retirement, it has been common practice to specify a combination of age and service, which employees usually call the magic number. This figure is frequently 70 or 80, but the precise number will depend on the depth of the necessary reduction in staff. Usually, no actuarial reduction factor is applied under programs of this type, and supplementary benefits are frequently provided at company expense until the employee qualifies for Social Security benefits. In recent years, most early retirement incentive programs have been offered for a limited period of time. (For example, the company offers a bonus to any one who retires within the next two months.) Such programs are called open-door policies or open-window policies. The major national union contracts guarantee special supplements to workers who are retired early at the company's option or under mutually satisfactory conditions.

Postretirement Increases

The image of inflation eroding the purchasing power of retirees attempting to live on fixed incomes is a familiar one. According to such organizations as the American Association of Retired Persons and the Gray Panthers, it accurately reflects the plight of almost all older Americans. However, employees who retire from companies with defined-benefit pensions should feel relieved from much of this anxiety. This is because most firms will periodically make ad hoc adjustments in their pension payments to compensate for the effects of inflation. A smaller number of companies (for example, Xerox Corporation, Equitable Life Assurance Co., Inco Ltd, and H. J. Heinz) have even indexed pension payments with the consumer price index (CPI) or some similar measure of the inflation rate. Ad hoc adjustments are now being made every two or three years in companies dedicated to this method of protecting retirees' real income. A typical formula relates adjustments to when the employee retired. For example:

Increase in pensions effective January 1, 1983, based on year of retirement:

Year	Increase
1981	3%
1980	6%
1979 or earlier	9%

Minimum increase = $20 per month

A 1981 study by the employee benefit consulting firm of Towers, Perrin, Forster & Crosby, which tracks the impact of postretirement increases by 95 major companies, indicates that retirees from these firms are generally doing no worse than active employees in battling inflation.

Employers also need to keep in mind that Social Security retirement benefits have been indexed to the CPI since 1975. Each June benefits increase if the index rises at least 3 percent. In 1980 the increase was 14.3 percent. Some authorities feel that these adjustments should be adequate for retirees and that expenditures for pension plan improvements should be concentrated on future benefits for active employees. Nonetheless, the practice of postretirement increases, at least in large firms, seems to be firmly established.

SIMPLIFIED EMPLOYEE PENSIONS (SEPs)

The Revenue Act of 1978 provided small organizations with an attractive alternative to the more complex qualified-type pension plans that are subject to myriad IRS and ERISA rules and regulations. This alternative is the simplified employee pension (SEP), which combines provisions for employer contributions with individual retirement accounts (IRAs) established by employees.

Under current rules, as modified in the Economic Recovery Tax Act of 1981, an employee may contribute up to $2,000 a year to SEP–IRA and deduct the amount contributed for income tax purposes. The employer may make deductible contributions to the plan of up to 15 percent of an employee's pay, provided the combined deductions do not exceed a maximum of $15,000.

Table 7. SEP–Social Security integration (example based on 1982 Social Security rate).

Annual salary	Employer target contribution (7.5% of salary)	Social Security Offset (6.7% up to $32,400)	Employer's SEP contribution
$10,000	$ 750	$ 670	$ 80
20,000	1,500	1,340	160
30,000	2,250	2,010	240
50,000	3,750	2,170	1,580
75,000	5,625	2,170	3,455

As long as the company has no other integrated plan, the full amount of the employer's Social Security taxes may be offset against plan contributions. This enables the employer to legally discriminate in favor of higher paid employees who receive a lower percentage of income replacement from Social Security (see Table 7).

The major limitation to establishing an SEP–IRA plan is that 100 percent of all eligible employees must set up an IRA or all other employees are prohibited from participating. Because of this requirement, the adoption of this type of plan has been restricted so far to small organizations with relatively few employees.

A UNIQUE RETIREMENT SYSTEM

Approximately 680,000 educators, researchers, administrators, and other staff members who work in colleges, private schools, and research institutions participate in a most innovative and flexible private pension system. It is the retirement program operated by the Teachers Insurance and Annuity Association–College Retirement Equities Fund (TIAA–CREF) headquartered in New York City. Although the total program, which includes tax-deferred annuities per Section 403(b) of the Internal Revenue Code, may not be appropriate for all other industries, at least two of its elements, portability and variable annuities, warrant inspection and consideration.

Portability is an arrangement under which the contributions of several employers who are parties to a pension plan are pooled in a central fund, where they are credited to individual employee accounts. If an employee changes jobs within the group of participating employers, there is no loss of pension credits and contributions to the account continue. In the TIAA–CREF retirement system, the group consists of approximately 3,500 institutions. This includes about 80 percent of four-year colleges and universities, public and private combined. For the career educator or researcher, this permits a high degree of mobility without loss or interruption of pension accruals.

Portability tends to conflict with the values of many business persons who believe that stability should be rewarded and turnover deterred. However, the TIAA–CREF retirement system offers a challenge to industry. In that organization's 1969 annual report, Chairman William C. Greenough referred to its program as "people-oriented pensions." He further stated:

> Most government and industrial pension plans tend to overemphasize the employer's needs at the expense of the individual participants. It is frequently heard that the main purpose of such pension plans is "to make possible the retirement of older employees whose efficiency has declined," or "to tie our employees to us during their working years." The employee's rights to benefits are contingent—part or all of his benefits will be lost if he dies before retirement age, changes jobs at the wrong time, or retires ahead of schedule.

> But through the use of individually owned annuity contracts, with provisions that are uniform throughout the TIAA–CREF system, employers orient their retirement plans toward the participants themselves. Whether you work for one or several of these institutions, die before retirement, retire early or late, their contributions to your annuities can be counted as part of your total compensation.

A *variable annuity* plan is one in which accruals and payments are expressed in terms of units of benefit rather than a fixed amount of money. The units are revalued periodically against an index. CREF accumulation and annuity units are revalued monthly to reflect changes in the market prices and dividends of common stocks owned by the fund. In the TIAA–CREF program, the participant may allocate up to 100 percent of contributions to the purchase of accumulation units in CREF; the balance (if any) goes toward a fixed-dollar annuity in TIAA. The number of units accumulated in CREF depends on monthly evaluations of unit value. Rising market prices for CREF's securities make the accumulation unit value rise; falling prices make the unit value fall. Conversely, for a level rate of contribution, more units are accumulated when the unit value is lower, fewer units when the unit value is higher. This relationship is comparable to that of the mutual-fund concept of investing.

At the time of retirement, the participant's stock of accumulation units is converted into annuity units in accordance with actuarial standards. Thereafter, payments from CREF are based on this fixed number of units whose value is adjusted annually on the basis of investment experience and actuarial factors. In addition to the CREF annuity, which will vary, the participant will receive a fixed-dollar payment from any TIAA accumulations as a hedge against any sharp drop in value of the CREF unit.

Proponents of variable annuity plans cite their inherent ability to protect retirees against the long-term upward trend in the cost of living. The initial value of the CREF *accumulation* unit in 1952 was $10.43; at the end of 1981 it was $48.33. However, the *annuity* unit, which was valued at $35.74 in 1972–1973, had dropped to $26.27 in 1980–1981.

The unpredictability of the stock market in recent years has slowed the growth of variable annuity plans, yet TIAA–CREF remains committed to the concept. Perhaps significantly, the most popular choice of allocations of contributions between the two funds among participants continues to be 50 percent/50 percent, and as of December 31, 1979, 63 percent of the participants were directing at least half of their premiums to CREF. In spite of some Cassandra-like prophecies, it appears that the idea of variable annuities is not going to die.

Pay for Unemployment

It has been estimated that, at the depths of the Great Depression of 1929–1933, 25 percent of the U.S. workforce was unemployed. Of the 48 states existing at that time, only Wisconsin and Ohio had any type of public income replacement system, so most of the unemployed had to rely on family support, savings, and charity.

Today, with federal support, every state administers an unemployment compensation system that offers some protection to virtually every worker against the economic hazards of involuntary unemployment. But the statutory plans replace only a portion of wages. For example, in New Jersey, as of 1982, a displaced worker with average base-year weekly earnings of $210 received a UCI benefit of $140 (two-thirds of the earnings amount). Yet a person earning $225 (or more) was limited to the maximum benefit of $145 (one-half of the statewide average wage rate on September 1, 1981).

To supplement state UCI benefits, particularly for higher paid employees, most companies provide some form of severance pay or pay continuation to involuntarily separated employees.

Some employees and most unions regard severance pay as an earned right and a form of deferred compensation. They consider it to be not simply a plug for the gap between UCI benefits and regular pay but also a fund to be used in covering the extra expenses incurred in searching for work and replacing company-paid benefits coverages. In response to these viewpoints, many companies establish a severance allowance schedule specifying lump-sum payments based on company service. A typical plan for nonexempt employees in 1983 might have these features:

Years of service	Severance payment (in weeks of salary)
0–1	1
2–3	2
4–5	4
6–7	6
8–9	8
10–12	11
13–15	14
16–19	17
20 or more	20

The payments would not be made in instances of discharge for cause, mandatory retirement, or voluntary quits. It should be noted that a severance pay plan set out in an employer's personnel policy manual is considered an employee welfare benefit plan covered by ERISA.

In the mid-1950s, the United Auto Workers and the United Steelworkers of America succeeded in negotiating supplemental unemployment benefits (SUB) plans for hourly workers with the major auto and steel companies. These plans, integrated with state UCI benefits, are now used to provide income replacement of up to 95 percent of aftertax base wages for six months and longer (SUB durations of four years have occurred in the rubber industry). Because of high costs and a growing belief that it is more sensible to avoid layoffs than to pay SUB benefits, the once expected expansion of these plans all but ended after 1960. It is now estimated that less than 15 percent of large manufacturers have SUB plans.

Exhibit 10. Benefits of outplacement services: responses to two survey questions.

Please rank the benefits of outplacement services to your organization:

(1 = greatest benefit, 6 = least benefit)

Rank		Average Rank
1	Helped the individual	1.28
2	Continued good morale	2.54
3	Reduced anxiety of person doing termination	2.74
4	Maintained good public relations	2.84
5	Made decision to terminate sooner	2.92
6	Reduced length of severance pay	3.49

Please rank the benefits of outplacement services to the individual:

(1 = greatest benefit, 5 = least benefit)

Rank		Average Rank
1	Rebuilt confidence	1.97
2	Assessment of self and/or career direction	2.12
3	Helped individual accept the loss	2.23
4	Developed effective employment search techniques	2.38
5	Faster relocation	2.78

Source: "Termination Policies and Practices: Survey Results and Analysis," Drake Beam Morin, Inc., New York, February 1981.

For managerial and professional employees subject to involuntary separation, it is now more common to provide a period of salary continuation than a lump-sum severance payment. The concept of an income bridge for terminating employees is one that combines dignified and compassionate treatment of workers with a potential bar to costly UCI claims against the employer. Once the termination decision is made (the reasons can range from cutbacks and shutdowns to unsatisfactory performace, but not disciplinary matters), a maximum period of pay continuation is set. The duration is usually a function of length of service, job level, salary, performance, and (sometimes) age. During the specified period, the person receives full pay and benefits coverage and may utilize company facilities and services, but is relieved of all job responsibilities. Proponents of salary continuation as an alternative to severance payments believe it facilitates a person's job search efforts and may negate the need to file for UCI benefits if a new position can be found within the prescribed time.

A relatively recent technique utilized by companies to ease the pain of termination and to expedite the process of finding a new job is outplacement. A 1981 survey report[7] with responses from 449 companies revealed that 75 percent of the companies had used external outplacement consultants. These firms, which charge employers fees ranging from a flat $2,000–2,500 to 15 percent of the employee's pay (group rates are lower), offer numerous advantages to both the organization and the employee, as indicated by the responses to two questions in the survey (see Exhibit 10).

[7] "Termination Policies and Practices: Survey Results and Analysis," Drake Beam Morin, Inc., New York, February 1981.

CHAPTER 5

Time Off with Pay: The Hidden Payroll

The first American Labor Day parade in September 1882 displayed the slogan:

8 HOURS OF WORK
8 HOURS OF REST
8 HOURS FOR WHAT WE WILL

At that time, a work schedule of 11 hours a day, six days a week in manufacturing was common. Vacations and holidays, with or without pay, were rarely granted, and hourly workers put their jobs in jeopardy if they missed a day or requested time off for personal reasons. Time off without loss or pay was a major battle cry of the emerging trade unions.

As manufacturing became more scientific and as employers became somewhat more humanistic, awareness developed about the effect of time off on productivity. Long work periods with little time for rest or leisure were found to be a major cause of industrial accidents. An employee's efficiency dropped when fatigue became evident. This awareness led to two developments that increased paid leisure time— shortening of the workweek and time off with pay.

The Shorter Workweek

As a result of worker demands and employer beliefs about productivity, the standard workday and workweek have declined steadily. Today the pattern in manufacturing firms is eight hours a day, five days a week. In nonmanufacturing industries, the standard workday is typically seven or seven and a half hours. A reduction in the scheduled hours of work is almost always accompanied by a rise in the rate of pay. This means that employee income remains the same. It also has the effect of providing pay for time no longer worked, but employees rarely perceive the change in that context.

Since the publication of *4 Days, 40 Hours: Reporting a Revolution in Work and Leisure,*[1] there has been much publicity about—and scattered examples of change to—a shorter workweek that permits a three-day weekend. On the surface, this rearrangement of work hours into four 10-hour days does not seem to have any direct implications with respect to employee benefits. There is no change in pay for time worked in weeks when the 40-hour work schedule is observed. But when employees are granted time off for illness or for personal reasons, the costs for a 10-hour day, or 25 percent of the workweek, are obviously greater than the expense of an 8-hour day, which is 20 percent of the workweek. Also, demands for a third rest period during the workday are bound to arise. There is even greater concern among many employers that the "4-40" schedule is merely a prelude to union demands and lobbying for a "4-32" pattern for industry. If, or when, the latter schedule is implemented without any reduction in base pay, industry's costs for time off with pay would increase markedly.

Paid Time Off

Most business forecasters believe that continued expansion of paid leisure time is more likely to occur from an increase in the number of paid holidays and extended vacations rather than from a drastic shortening of the workweek. A milestone in a long-term trend toward

---

[1] Riva Poor, Ed. (Cambridge, Mass: Bursk and Poor Publishing Company, 1970).

more paid time off in industry was the labor contract signed by Ford Motor Company and the United Auto Workers (UAW) in 1976 following a month-long strike. This agreement, which became a pattern for the auto industry, provided each Ford worker with 12 additional days off, besides regularly scheduled holidays, over the life of the three-year contract.

Calling this a "toe in the door" to the year-round four-day work-week with five days' pay, Arvid Jouppi, an independent industry analyst, estimated that it would shorten auto industry working time by about 2 percent.[2] By 1981 a factory worker at Ford with 20 years or more of service could count on a total of 46 paid holidays, personal days, and vacation days per year. At that point, U.S. auto industry executives were citing "pay for not working" as a key factor in their firms' productivity decline and inability to remain competitive with Japan's auto manufacturers. This led to unilateral reductions in time-off allowances for salaried workers and some negotiated concessions on take backs with the UAW in 1982.

In cost calculations, pay for time not worked is an inside payroll item. In other words, it is included in the employee's basic pay as quoted by the employer. For that reason, these benefits become hidden and taken for granted by the employee, who expects to receive the same amount of pay each week or month regardless of actual work time. To the employer, a paid absence of an employee is a separate item of expense for which there is no direct counterpart in output. Furthermore, it may require extra expense in the form of replacement workers or overtime payments.

In the U.S. Chamber of Commerce survey for 1981, pay for time not worked, away from the job or from the work site, averaged 13.2 percent of payroll in manufacturing firms and 13.5 percent in non-manufacturing companies.

Vacations

Traditionally, there have been two basic reasons for granting paid vacations. One is the need for rest and relaxation away from the physical demands and mental stresses of work. The other is the belief that

[2] *The New York Times,* October 7, 1976.

Table 8. Summary of vacation practices in average and leading edge companies.

	Years of Service to Qualify	
Weeks of Vacation	*Average Company*	*Leading Edge Company*
3	7	5
4	15	10
5	25	20
6	(not provided)	30

Source: Mitchell Meyer, *Profile of Employee Benefits: 1981 Edition* (New York: The Conference Board, 1981).

employees are entitled to a reward in the form of vacation pay for faithful service. In recent years, a third reason has evolved. The sabbaticals or extended vacation programs first negotiated by the United Steelworkers in 1962–1963 were designed to create additional jobs. In fact, in the container industry, these benefits are called expanded employment programs.

SERVICE REQUIREMENTS

Service requirements for vacation eligibility tend to vary by industry, locale, and company size. Although the gap between salaried and hourly employees has closed substantially, the latter still have longer waiting periods for earning one- and two-week vacations in many companies. According to *Profile of Employee Benefits: 1981 Edition*,[3] which summarizes benefits practices in 1,368 companies, requirements for longer vacations in "average" and "leading edge" companies are currently as shown in Table 8.

Obviously, a company has to weigh its obligations to senior employees against the recruiting incentive of early eligibility whenever it considers changing service requirements for vacations. In a time when salaries are being compressed, a clear advantage in vacation entitlement is almost essential to the preservation of good morale among long-service employees. At the same time, an employer is disadvantaged in trying to hire experienced workers if they are going to lose paid vacation time by changing jobs. For this reason, some companies use an age factor or credit years of prior experience in determining vacation eligibility.

[3] Mitchell Meyer (New York: The Conference Board, 1981).

Another feature that has gained more popularity among banks and insurance companies than in manufacturing firms is the service anniversary bonus vacation. After an employee reaches the basic maximum on vacation allowance, say four weeks, he or she receives an extra week or two in major anniversary years, such as the twenty-fifth, thirtieth, and so on. This can help give the anniversary more meaning, but it has a built-in disadvantage—the employee may feel deprived in the following year.

SCHEDULING CONSIDERATIONS

Except for manufacturing companies that schedule plant shutdowns, the limited vacation season is no longer an important consideration in industry. At one time, it was common practice to specify that vacations be taken somewhere between June 1 and September 30. This was based on assumptions that employees preferred vacations in the warmer months, that business would be slow anyway, that it was better to limit the work interruptions to a short period, and that student replacements were available if needed.

These assumptions may have been valid when most employees were limited to one or two weeks of vacation and there was only one breadwinner in a family. Now that three or four weeks' allowances and dual-income marriages are common, many employees prefer split vacations. Companies could not operate if all the earned vacation time had to be taken in a three- or four-month period. In most companies, it is mutually satisfactory to have vacations spread over the full year. Unfortunately, many companies fail to communicate and promote this fact. As a result of either habit or lack of knowledge, employees continue to request their time off in the months of July and August. To counteract this tendency, these companies not only should communicate information about their policies but also should consider publicizing the lower travel costs and other attractions of off-season vacations.

For some manufacturing companies, a shutdown of plant operations is a necessity; some consider it an advantage in terms of vacation scheduling. Shutdowns are required when equipment cannot be overhauled during normal operations. Production managers may specify that all machinery must be checked and parts replaced by the maintenance workers once a year. In such cases, the machines must be out of operation; there is no work for the production operators, and it becomes logical to send them on vacation so that they do not lose pay.

Those who see extrinsic values in vacation shutdowns claim that:

- The Christmas–New Year's period (a popular vacation time) may be used as the shutdown.
- They eliminate the need to employ replacement workers.
- Administration is simplified for the company.
- Employees can plan activities better when there is a fixed time for everyone's vacation.

Some of the disadvantages of shutdowns are:

- Employees have no choice. This is particularly troublesome when spouses work in other firms and there is no flexibility for matching the vacations.
- Employees without full eligibility lose pay unless special assignments are available. If not, they may collect unemployment compensation after a brief waiting period.
- There is a general lag in production involved in closing down and starting up operations.
- Customer service may require costly special orders and call-in pay.

When most employees have vacation eligibility in excess of the shutdown period, dissatisfaction diminishes, and the company does not have to be concerned with providing work or being charged for unemployment claims. If an employee is entitled to four weeks and has some freedom in selecting the time for two of these weeks, he or she can usually tolerate having the other two weeks scheduled by the employer. An important factor, though, is early notification. Companies should try to schedule shutdowns during the same time each year, or at least announce the timing six or more months in advance.

Three other aspects of scheduling that employers should explain in their policies are qualifying dates, split weeks, and carry-overs. A qualifying date establishes when current-year vacations are earned. This date governs when vacations with pay may be taken and sets a cutoff date for vacation pay at termination. Unless employees have eligibility of less than a week, split-week or single-day vacations are usually discouraged. They are cumbersome to record and control, and the employee misses the restorative pluses of a lengthier vacation.

Requests to carry over or accumulate vacation time from one year
to the next were once rather common when employees needed longer
time periods for travel. Now that three- and four-week vacations are
common, the need for carry-over has lessened. From the company
viewpoint, pyramiding of vacation time can be harmful to operations,
and it is normally restricted to unusual circumstances or emergencies.
For control purposes, if carry-over is granted, it is helpful to require
the employee to specify when the time will be taken and to limit this
to the first three to six months of the following year.

PAY CONSIDERATIONS

When vacations were considered primarily a rest from work, pay administration was simple. Today the view that vacation is an earned
right is more dominant, and questions of entitlement and calculation
can be extremely complex. A pattern that was established in the steel
industry in 1969, and that employers can expect to see grow, is the
vacation bonus. This is an extra amount of pay, which the employee
receives on top of base pay, to help cover the added expenses associated with travel and recreational vacations. For example, Chem-
Trend Inc. of Howell, Michigan, pays time and a half to its vacation-
ing employees, so that an individual earning $300 a week is paid $900
for two weeks' vacation.

As a form of employee compensation, vacation pay needs to be
checked against a variety of policies covering related items. Employers should review their vacation policies to make sure that they provide adequate, clear, and consistent answers to question about pay.
Exhibit 11 is a checklist of typical employee questions for employers
to use in reviewing their existing vacation policies.

Answers to these questions will vary among companies, of course,
because philosophies differ and the terms of other coverages will influence vacation pay policies. Within any given company, however,
supervisors should be able to give employees timely, accurate, and
thorough replies to all questions of this nature.

SABBATICALS

The word *sabbatical* had its origin in biblical times, when it meant a
rest from agricultural work every seventh year. In more recent years,

Exhibit 11. Checklist of typical employee questions about vacation pay policy.

VACATION PAY POLICY CHECKLIST

1. If I am ill when my vacation is scheduled to begin, can it be postponed?
2. Do I receive sick pay in addition to vacation pay if I become ill while on vacation?
3. Can I be paid in lieu of vacation under any circumstances?
4. Do I receive pay for unused vacation if I leave the company (a) voluntarily? (b) involuntarily?
5. If I die before taking vacation, will my beneficiary receive the equivalent pay?
6. Will I receive additional time off, or pay, if a holiday occurs during my vacation?
7. What happens to my vacation allowance and pay if during my vacation (a) a member of my immediate family dies? (b) I am called to jury duty? (c) I am placed on active military duty?
8. How is my vacation pay computed if (a) I am on layoff status for part of the year? (b) I work a part-time schedule for a portion of the year?
9. Does my vacation pay take into consideration (a) shift premiums? (b) overtime pay? (c) incentive earnings?
10. Can I take my vacation before the annual qualifying date and receive the pay at that time?
11. Can I suspend voluntary deductions (credit union, savings bonds, thrift plan) from my vacation pay?
12. What will my pay rate be if I am required to come in to work during my vacation?

---

it has been used in universities to denote a 12-month vacation for professors, also every seventh year.

Most of the employee sabbaticals that the United Steelworkers of America (USWA) have negotiated with the major companies in the can, steel, and aluminum industries provide a 13-week vacation every five years to long-service hourly employees. The emphasis in these plans is on creating more jobs, and this is patent in the statement of purpose from an American Can–USWA contract:

> The purpose of this Expanded Employment Program is to further employment opportunities in the Company and to permit certain long-service employees to take periodic leaves.

In the early 1960s, sabbaticals seemed to be on their way to becoming a standard benefit in industry, but this has not materialized. Some of the reasons for this are:

○ The union's objective of creating more jobs has not been achieved. Through automation and reassignment of work, companies have kept additional hiring to a minimum.
○ Some workers have experienced problems of maintaining skills and the required physical condition during the extended leaves.
○ Salaried employees usually cannot be spared and are offered alternative benefits, such as added thrift plan payments or pension credits. This tends to create discriminatory feelings between the salaried and hourly groups.

VACATION BANKS

At one time, most vacation policies stated or implied that if allowances were not taken in the year earned they became forfeited. The message to employees in other words was "Use it or lose it." The opportunity to carry over vacation time to the next year on a limited basis has existed in plans for many years, but recently a number of companies have gone one step further and provided for permanent vacation deferral.

As indicated above, companies that grant sabbaticals to hourly workers have found this to be impractical for salaried employees. American Can Company and Bethlehem Steel Company are representative of a number of firms that adopted deferred vacation plans as an alternative benefit to sabbaticals for their salaried employees. IBM, Bristol-Myers, Kimberly-Clark and Schering-Plough are some of the major employers that introduced vacation banking as a broad-based vacation option for all classes of employees.

Philosophically, the option to defer, or bank, vacation time is a departure from the traditional company view that an annual vacation is necessary for employee physical and mental well-being. However, defenders of the banking option point out that most plans permit only a portion of the annual allowance to be deferred. For example, one large firm allows banking of each year's vacation allowance in excess of three weeks. Another employer permits employees with six weeks of eligibility to defer just one week. With such limitations, the plans maintain the fundamental rest and relaxation values while offering greater flexibility to the employee. Furthermore, the employer effectively regains employee availability during productive working years in exchange for paid time off at the time of retirement or other final separation from the company.

Other typical features of vacation banks are:

○ Irrevocable election to defer the time until separation. (This practice may be modified as a result of changes in the definition of constructive receipt for tax purposes in the Economic Recovery Tax Act of 1981.)

○ A limit on the total number of weeks to be accumulated in the bank (for example, 26 or 30).

○ Provisions to pay for the time either at the current rate when actually taken, or at a computed rate reflecting CPI changes or investment performance during the years since the time was banked.

Holidays

In 1939 only 12 percent of 2,200 manufacturers surveyed by the National Industrial Conference Board provided holidays with pay to hourly workers. Today hourly workers (along with salaried coworkers) in the United States can generally expect to be paid for at least 9 holidays from work; 11 holidays are common in the Northeast and Middle Atlantic regions, and 12 or more holidays are guaranteed in 18 percent of firms included in a 1981 Conference Board study.

In addition to granting holidays with pay, companies now pay premium rates to hourly employees who have to work on company holidays. Typically, this is time-and-a-half or double-time pay, plus holiday pay. Salaried employees frequently receive compensable time off when they are required to work on a designated holiday, or this may be offered as an alternative to premium pay.

The type of business tends to influence both the number and observance of holidays. For example, banks are controlled by state laws that specify certain closing days and frequently prohibit closings on two consecutive weekdays. The retail trade is historically a trailer in granting holidays, and most store owners would consider closing on such traditional sale days as Washington's Birthday, Columbus Day, or the Friday after Thanksgiving to be a form of economic suicide. However, for manufacturers, these three days are very attractive choices for observance, since they do not create the inefficiencies of a midweek shutdown and start-up. Hospitals must provide continuous patient and emergency service, which makes it impossible to release all employees from work on any designated holiday. This creates a need to establish complex schedules to permit an equitable allocation of traditional holidays and substitute days to employees.

There are also geographic variations in terms of both numbers of holidays and particular observances. The West Coast has tended to lag behind the East in the number of days granted, but this gap has been closing, probably as a result of the establishment by national employers of uniform benefit levels. In the southern states, Jefferson Davis's and Robert E. Lee's birthdays are often observed. In Massachusetts and Maine, Patriot's Day is a standard holiday, and in Alaska, Seward's Day is widely recognized.

In setting the number of holidays in a company, the employer must be sensitive to area and industry patterns. In selecting the particular days for observance, the employer has much more flexibility and should carefully evaluate both operational needs and employees' preferences. Many national firms permit some local option in setting annual holiday schedules.

THE SOLID SIX

Regardless of industry or area, six holidays are observed and paid for by virtually all employers in the United States:

New Year's Day
Memorial Day
Independence Day
Labor Day
Thanksgiving Day
Christmas Day

Three of these (Memorial Day, Labor Day, and Thanksgiving Day) always fall on the same day of the week. The others vary each year. None of the six occurs in the same month, although three (Thanksgiving, Christmas, and New Year's) fall within a six-week period, and two (Memorial Day and Independence Day) have about the same span. These facts are quite significant in terms of company planning.

For example, recognizing that Thanksgiving is a Thursday holiday has led many manufacturing companies to establish the Friday after Thanksgiving as a standing holiday. This gives most employees a four-day weekend and avoids a costly shutdown and start-up process for the employer.

Realizing that three of these basic holidays can fall on any day of the week, companies have adopted policies covering holidays that occur on a Saturday or Sunday and have used the concept of floating holidays. Generally, when a holiday falls on a Saturday it is observed on Friday, and Sunday holidays are observed on Monday. Hourly workers see this as five days' pay for four days of work. In some cases, manufacturing requirements or union pressure will cause an employer to remain open on the Friday or Monday before or after a holiday. This is usually handled by providing an extra day's pay ("six for five" in the worker's parlance), but some unions have argued for holiday premium pay when this situation arises. The floating holiday permits employers to designate the Friday after a Thursday holiday, or the Monday before a Tuesday holiday, for company observance. This has the same universal appeal as Thanksgiving Friday.

Taking into account employee needs for periodic rest and relaxation, companies in moving beyond the basic six holidays have tended to select days that occur in other months. As a result, Washington's Birthday (February), Good Friday (March or April), and Columbus Day (October) have become familiar holidays in industry. An employee who can observe these three holidays plus the basic six has at least one day off in all but three months of the year—and June and August are months in which some vacation time is usually taken.

THE MONDAY HOLIDAYS LAWS

With rare concurrent support from the U.S. Chamber of Commerce and the AFL–CIO, a Monday Holidays Law was enacted in 1968 to be effective in 1971 for federal government employees. Subsequently, nearly every state acted to shift observance of four holidays to particular Mondays in order to create long weekends. Although the change from November 11 to the fourth Monday in October for observing Veterans Day was soon rescinded because of adverse public reaction, the following designations are now almost universally recognized:

Washington's Birthday—third Monday in February.
Memorial Day—last Monday in May.
Columbus Day—second Monday in October.

Although the laws do not compel private industry to grant these holidays, they tend to control the observance dates. The Monday holidays have achieved great popularity with employers who abhor the stop–start interruptions of midweek holidays and employees who enjoy the advantages of a minivacation. Happiest of all, though, is the travel industry, which hailed the passage of the federal law in 1968 as "the greatest thing since the invention of the automobile."

RELIGIOUS AND OTHER HOLIDAYS

Employers in New York City and other metropolitan centers, where there are large numbers of Jewish employees, have found it desirable to recognize certain major Jewish holidays as regular company holidays. The two most prevalent observances are Rosh Hashanah, the Jewish New Year, and Yom Kippur, or Day of Atonement. They fall about a week apart and occur in September or October. Some companies with predominately black workforces have observed January 15, Dr. Martin Luther King's birthday, as a company holiday.

When such dates are not personally significant to the majority of employees, it is not feasible to observe them generally, and in some companies, this creates difficulties for management. The granting of time off usually is no problem, but the question of pay is. If a minority of employees are given pay for these days, the majority may expect compensatory allowances. If no pay is granted, employees who are docked may feel that they have been unfairly penalized for following fundamental beliefs.

One alternative to resolving these problems is to permit employees to use a floating holiday or vacation day on the date of religious or special observance. In one New York City firm with an equal number of Christian and Jewish workers, either Good Friday or Yom Kippur may be chosen by employees as a holiday. Another approach that is gaining in usage involves the application of a limited number of unspecified days each year (usually one to three) that employees can use for any personal reason without loss of pay.

The employee's birthday is now granted as a holiday by about one out of seven companies, the cost being considered relatively inexpensive. Observances are spread over the full year, so there is no need to suspend operations. Unlike absences due to illness or personal reasons, birthdays are known in advance and work schedules can be adjusted accordingly.

PAY FOR HOLIDAY WORK

In addition to providing extra pay for time worked on a holiday (which is considered to be a form of overtime premium, not a benefit), companies find it necessary to specify a number of rules governing the granting of holiday pay. From management's viewpoint, one of the more important factors is some qualification on work in the holiday week. A familiar statement in union contracts and employee handbooks is: "In order to be eligible for holiday pay, an employee must perform work on the day before and the day after the holiday."

Such clauses are intended to deter absenteeism, particularly on days surrounding a midweek holiday. Usually absences for illness and specified personal reasons will waive compliance with these rules.

Although most companies consider all employees immediately eligible for holiday pay, it is not unusual to withhold this benefit from probationary and temporary employees, including summer employees.

Paid holidays, like paid vacations, are now viewed by most employees more as an earned right than as a rest from work. The questions posed in Exhibit 12 can be used to make a comprehensive check on company holiday pay policy to avoid inconsistent applications.

Personal Absences

One of the conditions for being exempt from the overtime pay requirements of the Fair Labor Standards Act is that the "employee must be paid on a salary basis" at a minimum rate that is set and revised periodically by the federal government. A "salary basis" has been held to mean that the employee regularly receives for each pay period of a week or longer a predetermined amount that is normally not subject to reduction in a week in which he or she performs any work. Some employers have interpreted this to mean that an exempt employee must be paid in full for all personal absences. This is not

Exhibit 12. Checklist of typical employee questions about holiday pay policy.

HOLIDAY PAY POLICY CHECKLIST

1. Do summer or other temporary employees receive pay for company holidays?
2. Do new employees receive pay for holidays that occur during their probationary period?
3. Do employees who are absent for the following reasons receive either holiday pay or additional time off?
   a. Short-term illness
   b. Long-term disability
   c. Vacation
   d. Personal leave of absence
   e. Jury duty
   f. Honeymoon leave
   g. Short-term military service
4. If holidays occurring during vacation time can be carried over, does the employee have any choice in selecting the time for observance?
5. a. If an employee is absent on the last working day prior to a holiday, does he or she receive holiday pay?
   b. What if he or she is absent on the day following a holiday?
6. Are shift premiums included in holiday pay?
7. Is overtime pay considered in calculating holiday pay?
8. Are extra incentive payments included in holiday pay calculations?
9. If an employee is required to work on a holiday, what rate of pay applies?

---

true. Although custom and competitive factors may suggest that it is wise to treat an exempt employee's pay as irreducible, it is not a legal requirement. The following guidelines may help clarify the law regarding payments on a salary basis to exempt employees:

1. Deductions from salary may be made when the employee is absent for a day or more for personal reasons.

2. No deductions may be made for absences occasioned by the employer or by the operating requirements of the business, or for absences of less than a day for personal reasons.

3. If an employee loses time from work during part of the week because of jury duty, attendance as a witness, or temporary military leave, the employer may offset any amount received by the employee as fees or military pay against the salary due for that week. If the em-

ployee receives no jury or witness fees or no military pay, no deductions from salary can be made.

4. Deductions may not be made for disciplinary reasons, except for infractions of safety rules of major significance.

5. Full salary need not be paid for the initial or terminal week of an individual's employment if, as a result of employment beginning or terminating after the start of the week, the employee does not work the full week; pro rata payment will suffice.

Pay for personal absences is one of the RHIP ("rank has its privileges") benefits that companies extend to exempt employees to help assure their compensation edge over subordinates who receive overtime pay. However, when special overtime pay is extended to certain levels of exempt employees for this same reason, unlimited payment for personal absences may be superfluous. In any event, employers should check both legal requirements and cost experience in evaluating their pay policies for personal absences of exempt employees.

With the exception of paid time off to vote, as required in some states, nonexempt employees need not, according to law, be paid for any personal absences. In spite of this, most companies specify several categories of absences for which pay is allowed to the nonexempt as well as exempt employees.

TIME OFF TO VOTE

About half of the states require that employees be given time off to vote, but not all of those states specify that it must be time off with pay. The normal maximum for time off is two hours. Employers should familiarize themselves with applicable state laws and voting hours.

In states where the maximum time off is three or four hours, many companies have found it preferable to schedule a full holiday on election days. Banks controlled by state banking laws generally treat election days as a standard holiday.

JURY DUTY

Jury duty is a civic responsibility that employees at all levels of the organization may be called on to fulfill periodically. Normally, an assignment as a petit juror will last two weeks, and a person should not be summoned more frequently than every two years. Jurors receive a small daily allowance to cover transportation and parking, and this may be deducted from salary. Banks, insurance companies, and public utility firms usually do not deduct jury fees; employers in manufacturing and the retail trade industry usually do. Those who deduct claim that an employee should not make extra money while excused from his job. Since any citizen can volunteer for jury duty, the opportunity to earn more while away from work might become too attractive for some employees. Companies that let employees retain the fees cite the administrative problems for the payroll department and reason that the allowances are given because the employees incur extra expenses.

Employers should become aware of court procedures and make sure that employees understand their responsibilities. Since many judges do not like to commence trials on a Friday, jurors are often excused on that day. Employees should be reminded that jury service is not the same as a vacation and that the company expects them to report to work whenever they are excused for a major portion of a workday.

SHORT-TERM MILITARY LEAVE

Short-term military leave typically takes the form of a two-week summer encampment for military reservists and members of the National Guard. The law requires employers to grant time off without prejudice to the person's employment status, including the vacation allowance, but there is no statutory requirement to pay for this time off. Nonetheless, common practice in all industries is to provide some form of salary continuation. Most employers pay the difference between normal wages or salary and the base military service pay. A small percentage of companies also include clothing, quarters, and sustenance allowances as part of military pay for offset purposes. To the extent that these allowances are intended to cover extraordinary expenses for the employee, it would seem that they should be ignored in computing the offset.

Members of the military reserve and National Guard are also subject to call-ups for emergency duty. Most employers apply the same pay principles to these instances as they use for summer training assignments. However, since emergency recalls can extend into several months or longer, policies should be specific with regard to time limits for salary continuation and should be carefully integrated with other policies covering regular military leave.

MARRIAGE AND HONEYMOON

Marriage and the attendant honeymoon may put an employee in a state of bliss that is quite incompatible with good performance. This is one argument in favor of paid honeymoon leaves, but except for banks and insurance companies, it is not a widespread benefit. Of course, with adequate planning, vacation time can be used for the honeymoon.

In response to those detractors who shout that benefits are for the old only, time off for marriage is one benefit with special appeal to the young. Companies that hire large numbers of young people directly from high schools and colleges may find that a reference to honeymoon leave in their recruiting literature is a helpful plus.

Time off for marriage and honeymoon is frequently only one day, but a growing number of companies now allow three or five days. The waiting period for this benefit may be longer than for other time-off categories, and if a week or more is granted, it is not unusual to make the pay contingent on the employee's continuing employment after the honeymoon. Other issues that should be covered by policy are the number of honeymoon leaves that any employee is entitled to during employment with the company and the definition of marriage for benefit purposes.

DEATH IN THE FAMILY

Most employers understand that a death in the family requires a certain amount of time off for mourning and making arrangements for survivors. The most typical allowance is three days with pay for death of a member of the immediate family (see Exhibit 13 for definition). Although some leading edge companies are now allowing five days for situations requiring overnight travel, some companies stipulate that the employee must attend the funeral to be eligible for this pay.

When policies indicate an allowance of up to three days, it is usually expected that when a death occurs on a Saturday the employee should return to work on Tuesday or Wednesday following the normal time for the funeral. Because this is a very difficult rule to administer, many companies today consider the three days' pay to be inviolate. In some cases, vacations are specifically extended when an employee's close relative dies during that time period. It is worthwhile to establish pay policy covering time off at the time of death of other relatives and coworkers.

MISCELLANEOUS REQUESTS FOR TIME OFF

Miscellaneous requests for time off can range from illness in the family and dental appointments to graduation ceremonies and court appearances. Exhibit 13 represents one approach to handling the variety of occasions for which employees need or desire time off. Eleven separate reasons have been specified and maximum allowances established. No exceptions are permitted for nonexempt employees. This approach offers the advantages of consistency, simplified administration, and clear understanding of which situations will qualify for pay.

However, no list, no matter how lengthy, can cover every legitimate employee request. Moreover, employees often consider the maximum allowance to be a full entitlement. In one company, an employee was told that the maximum allowance for a required National Guard physical examination was one day. His examination was completed at 11 A.M., and he returned to work. His supervisor was about to congratulate him for devotion to the job when the man asked: "Will it be all right if I take the remaining five hours next Friday?"

During the course of a year, an employee might not require time off for any of the reasons listed but could be prevented from coming to work because of water in the basement, snow in the driveway, or a fire in the garage. To avoid prejudging which causes should be listed, many companies establish a pool of personal days for each employee to cover emergencies and the uncontrollable causes of personal absence. An employee may be allowed two to five days' paid personal absence for any reason whatsoever each year. In this way, the employee is the judge of whether a particular occurrence is important enough to be charged against the allowance. Once the pool is depleted, any further absences in the year are unpaid.

Exhibit 13.   Statement of payment policy for personal absences.

Purpose

To ensure consistent payment for certain types of personal absences.

Scope

Applies to all domestic employees of XYZ Company and subsidiaries.

Authorization

Managers authorized to sign employee payroll records will control the allowed hours and approve payment for personal absences. Completion of at least three months' employment is required for all personal absences listed below except jury duty.

Reason for Personal Absence	Maximum Allowance (Days)
Jury duty	15
Military reserve or National Guard (per year; base pay less military income)	10
Physical examination required by military, National Guard, or Veterans Administration	1
Workers' compensation hearing	1
Mandatory court appearance when not directly involved in litigation	2
Election board duty (base pay less allowance)	1
Social Security office visit (within three months of retirement)	½
U.S. citizenship	
1. Application process	½
2. Administration of oath	½
Honeymoon following a marriage recognized under laws of the state of permanent residence (Employee must have completed two years of employment and continue employment after the honeymoon)	5
Death in family	
1. Mother, father, wife, husband, son, daughter, brother, sister, in-law, or blood relative living in the same household	3
2. Other relative—funeral attendance	1
Death of employee in same department (funeral attendance; department manager must approve number of representatives)	½

Paid Rest Periods

The U.S. Chamber of Commerce's employee benefits surveys contain a separate category for paid rest periods—lunch, coffee breaks, wash-up time, travel time, clothes-change time, or get-ready time. In the 1981 study, their average cost as a percentage of payroll was 3.4 percent. In some cases, these allowances are essential to operations. In others, they are thought of as beneficial to the health and attitudes of employees. Some paid rest periods do not apply outside of manufacturing, but the coffee break is universal.

It is very useful to separate benefits that involve nonworking time during the workday from benefits that involve time away from the work site, such as vacations, holidays, and personal leave. The latter are relatively free from abuses, and their costs can be closely estimated and controlled. The former are always subject to stated time limits, but the observance of those limits depends on a combination of employee respect and supervisory surveillance.

The costs of extended coffee breaks and rest periods are not included in benefits surveys, and employees are not inclined to recognize such costs as meaningful. However, the costs can be considerable either in terms of work not completed or in terms of extra personnel required to absorb the loss of productive time. The following case illustrates this point.

The Ajax Insurance Company employs 60 secretaries and clerks. They are scheduled to work a seven-hour day, which includes two coffee breaks of 10 minutes each. The average pay is $210 a week ($6 per hour). Although the work load is currently sufficient to utilize every employee for the full day without a need for overtime assignments, a backlog is developing. It appears to the office manager that either overtime or extra help is needed. When she checks with the supervisors, she finds that the coffee breaks are being extended by an average of 20 minutes per day. To impress her supervisors with the costs of this laxity, the office manager makes the following analysis, which she expects the supervisors to use as background in gaining employee cooperation.

Time Lost by Extending Breaks
   60 employees × ⅓ hour × 5 days = 100 hours/week
Cost of Extended Breaks
   100 hours @ $6.00 = $600/week
Overtime Cost of Completing Work
   100 hours @ $9.00 = $900/week

Additional Staff to Perform Work
  3 employees @ $210 = $630/week

When employees are confronted with this type of analysis in a logical and nonthreatening manner, the reasonableness of placing limits on breaks should be apparent. The extra costs imposed on the company because of squandered time could easily reduce its ability to improve wages and benefits. They could also hurt the firm's competitive position, which could lead ultimately to the loss of jobs. Faced with such gloomy alternatives, any rational employee would readily agree to get back to work after a 10-minute coffee break.

Employers can use certain techniques to help control abuses and legitimate losses of time associated with the various breaks during the day. Bringing carts to a station near the work area will reduce the time needed to go to a cafeteria or out of the plant or office for coffee. Staggered meal schedules will cut down the time used in standing in line for lunch. In plants, adequate lockers and washroom facilities will help to keep nonproductive preparatory and wash time within the stated limits.

The allowances for time off during the workday are significant and costly. But as long as employers continue to exercise their right to manage by controlling the excesses, the following pessimistic portent will never materialize.

Notice to Employees

Somewhere between starting and quitting time and without infringing too much on the lunch period, coffee breaks, rest periods, story telling, ticket selling, and vacation planning, it is requested that each employee find some time that can be set aside to be known as the "work break."

The Management

CHAPTER 6

Income Supplements and Capital Accumulation Plans

Frederick Herzberg, the prominent behavioral scientist widely known for his motivation-hygiene theory, tends to relegate employee benefits to the status of "dissatisfiers," claiming their importance is felt only in their absence.[1] He believes that people are dissatisfied if benefits are missing or inadequate, but their existence has little effect in motivating people to improve their work.

This view of employee benefits seems accurate if the definition of benefits is limited to those basic entitlements that employees expect and receive from most companies today. It is doubtful if employees work harder because they are protected by group health plans, participate in pension plans, enjoy vacations and holidays, and receive pay when they are absent because of illness. The absence of any of these benefits, however, is almost certain to create serious dissatisfaction among today's employees.

Stock options, management incentive bonuses, and deferred-income and phantom-stock plans are widely used for top management employees, but their application is a subject for executive compensation planning and not an issue for discussion in an analysis of benefits for all employees.

---

[1] Cited in Harold M. Rush, *Behavioral Science: Concepts and Management Application* (New York: The Conference Board, 1969).

Annual Christmas bonuses and length-of-service bonuses are considered direct compensation by some authorities and benefits by others. In either case, they have declined in use during the past decade or so. This decline can be attributed in part to their tax treatment as current income and in part to employer recognition that employees easily take these benefits for granted. They have little motivational value, do not provide a distinctive way of rewarding loyalty, and lead employees to believe that the amounts paid are merely a form of discount from their basic pay.

There is, however, one category of employee benefits that offers definite, but underexploited, potential for employee motivation. That is the category of plans that offer employees the opportunity to receive extra income and, in most cases, accumulate capital without requiring additional hours of work. This category includes suggestion award plans, productivity gain-sharing plans, supplemental profit sharing plans, savings (thrift) plans, and stock bonus plans. Although each of these types of plans functions quite differently, they all have the following common characteristics or potentials:

- ○ They are usually available to all or a large segment of employees in the company.
- ○ Rewards can be related to individual and/or group contribution to profitability and operational improvements.
- ○ In contrast with the basic employee benefits, these plans can create additional income or capital for employees.
- ○ Unlike overtime premium payments, there is no requirement to work extra hours to receive extra compensation.
- ○ Except for suggestion award and productivity gain-sharing plans, these plans offer employees distinct tax advantages over cash bonus payments.

Among major companies, it is now probable that employees will find at least one of these four types of plans in the total benefits package. But this is less likely to be so in smaller firms. Employer payments for these plans averaged less than 2 percent of payroll among the 994 companies reporting in *Employee Benefits 1981* (a study done by the Survey Research Center of the Chamber of Commerce of the United States), suggesting that many firms contribute little or nothing. Clearly these are exceptional benefits, and perhaps that special status contributes to their motivational value in those companies that do offer them to employees.

Suggestion Award Plans

Without doubt, no phase of personnel administration has suffered from more lampooning than the employee suggestion plan. Jokes and cartoons about suggestions that tell the boss "what he can do" or "where he can go" are legion. Following a boom during World War II, suggestion plans declined in popularity for a while, perhaps because many employees expressed cynicism about them. Yet this attitude was often a product of employer neglect and insensitivity. An employee who has to wait a year to receive an answer to a suggestion can lose respect for the plan. When the answer is a form response that says, in effect, "This is not a new idea, we thought of it first," or "This is a good idea, but it will never work here," the employee can be completely discouraged from further submission of ideas.

Companies that jumped on the suggestion plan bandwagon without setting up adequate administrative systems have learned that the very existence of a suggestion plan can dissatisfy employees. However, a recent report from the National Association of Suggestion Systems (NASS) indicates that most systems today are carefully structured and there is a renewed growth in plan adoptions.

According to NASS, there are four reasons for this renaissance: (1) the need to cut costs as inflation erodes profit; (2) the rising level of customer complaints; (3) the desire of companies to devise methods for dealing with service problems; and (4) the relatively new problems of environmental pollution. Although the moving force for adopting a plan might be any combination of the above, a successful program can make at least five important contributions to the employee-management relationship:

1. Employees are encouraged to use their creative powers to help solve problems and improve conditions.
2. Employees can gain recognition as well as tangible awards through the plan.
3. Management can identify the more inventive and resourceful employees in the organization by reviewing participants in the plan.
4. The plan serves as a means of two-way communication between management and employees. This is especially valuable in very large organizations, where informal personal communications are more difficult than in small firms.

5. Positive attitudes can develop when employees are encouraged to think in terms of company objectives.

All these seem to qualify as satisfiers, or motivators, in Herzberg's theory of work motivation.

PLAN ADMINISTRATION

A hallmark of the early suggestion plans was protection of suggester anonymity. In the mode of secret ballot elections, suggesters dropped a form in a suggestion box and retained a stub for purposes of numerical identification. Receipt of the suggestion would be acknowledged by a coordinator, who was the only person aware of the suggester's identity while the idea was being investigated, reviewed, and acted upon.

At one time, this behind-the-curtain approach seemed appropriate to both employers and employees. Presumably it was designed to produce objective evaluations with less emphasis on who made the suggestion and more on idea value. During the 1960s, some firms, notably the Maytag Company, began to recognize that this type of plan could interfere with the natural flow of communication between worker and supervisor. This led to a widespread shift to the "fully identified" suggestion system, which, according to a 1981 NASS report, is now the dominant type of plan in the United States. Exhibit 14 shows the steps involved in handling suggestions in a typical fully identified suggestion system. Unlike in traditional systems, there is no suggestion box, the employee is encouraged to discuss the idea with the supervisor, and a committee serves only to set and monitor policy, not to evaluate suggestions.

AWARDS

In determining awards for suggestions, it is necessary to distinguish between "tangible" and "intangible" ideas. The former relate to improvements where an actual reduction in costs or an increase in sales can be calculated. The latter do not produce measurable improvements but contribute toward improved operations or conditions. Usually ideas affecting safety, housekeeping, and public relations are of the intangible type.

Exhibit 14.   Process chart for a fully identified suggestion plan.

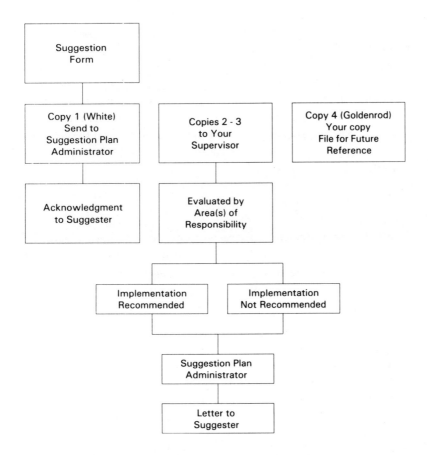

Tangible ideas lead to the largest awards, which are usually based on a percentage (for example, 10–25 percent) of the first year's net savings. In 1981 the highest award payment reported in the annual NASS survey was $84,529. Awards of this size have a profoundly stimulating effect on plan participation, and they provide favorable public relations for the company. Realistically, though, the bread-and-butter inputs of successful suggestion plans are those ideas, tangible and intangible, that produce awards of $25–100. Most plans specify a minimum payment for acceptable ideas. Today this is most likely to be $25–35, but the amount should be reviewed every year to be sure that inflation has not rendered it meaningless.

PLAN PROMOTION

Although awards, and their attendant publicity, are probably the best type of promotion for stimulating suggestions, additional forms of communication are needed to sustain a successful program. Thought-inspiring posters, films, and sound-slide presentations are available from NASS and a number of service organizations. The formation of Thinkers Clubs for winners of five or more awards, payroll inserts, desk ornaments and jewelry symbolizing awards, campaigns directed at specific areas of problem solving, and sweepstakes are some of the more popular techniques developed by companies to sell their plans to employees.

EVALUATING PLAN EFFECTIVENESS

The following statistical data, taken from the 1981 *Annual Statistical Report* of the National Association of Suggestion Systems, indicates some norms for measuring plan performance. These averages are based on information submitted by 236 companies and government agencies in 1981.

Number of suggestions per 100 eligible employees—14
Number of employees submitting per 100 eligible—11
Average processing time—139 days
Adoption rate of suggestions processed—27 percent
Average award payment—$182.49
Average net savings per adoption—$1,827
Net savings per 100 eligible employees—$11,437

Productivity Gain-Sharing Plans

According to James Day Hodgson, former U.S. ambassador to Japan and former secretary of labor, this nation's No. 1 industrial problem today is poor productivity.[2] This generally accepted condition has led companies to a variety of programs in their quest for a quick remedy. Quality circles, performance development reviews, worker participa-

[2] "An Impertinent Suggestion for Personnel Practitioners," *Personnel Administrator* (August 1981).

tion plans, quality of work life programs, and "cracker-barrel" sessions with top executives are some familiar employer efforts to improve employee productivity. While much emphasis is being placed on stimulating worker involvement and a spirit of cooperation at the work place, many productivity authorities believe that there needs to be some element of gain sharing for these management efforts to succeed. This view has created renewed interest in the Scanlon and Rucker type of productivity gain-sharing plans that have been available for nearly half a century.

Joseph Scanlon, a representative of the United Steelworkers of America, conceived a system in 1937 in which employees, supervisors, and management participate in the development of suggestions to improve productivity and also share in the gains. In a Scanlon plan, bonus payments are based on a ratio of labor costs to the sales value of production. If that ratio is reduced, a portion of the computed savings is distributed to employees monthly. The plan is not a form of profit sharing, since employees benefit from reduced labor costs regardless of a firm's profit. Proponents of Scanlon plans claim this is a more equitable system, since profits are influenced by many factors outside the worker's control.

Some firms that have reported considerable success with Scanlon plans, in terms of both improving productivity and providing meaningful pay supplements (for example, up to 20 percent per year), are Donnelly Mirrors, Inc. (Holland, Michigan), Parker Pen Company (Janesville, Wisconsin), Atwood Vacuum Machine Co. (Rockford, Illinois), and the Pfaudler Co., division of Sybron Corp. (Rochester, New York).

The Rucker plan of group incentives and team productivity, offered as a professional service by the Eddy–Rucker–Nickels Company of Cambridge, Massachusetts, is similar to the Scanlon plan in philosophy but involves more complex analysis. The long-range sharing plan adopted by the Kaiser Steel Corporation and the United Steelworkers of America in 1963 is another example of a plan in which employees are offered a share in cost reductions in order to make their interest in the business, and their desire for its success, as strong as management's.

Productivity gain-sharing plans have not become a cure-all for lagging productivity in industry, but in firms with successful programs, the following advantages are evident:

- Employees are willing to provide large numbers of useful cost-savings ideas.
- The usual negative reaction to technological change is less than normal.
- There is better teamwork and cooperation between workers and supervisors in complex problem solving.
- Employees share ideas with fellow workers and create their own forms of sanctions against loafers.
- Conscious restriction of output disappears.
- Employees feel comfortable and natural in working with management rather than against it.
- Competition between employees and controversy over ownership of ideas and eligibility for awards that can occur in individual suggestion award plans are avoided.

Profit Sharing Plans

The Profit Sharing Research Foundation (PSRF) reported net growth of 25,556 deferred profit sharing plans during 1978. This one-year gain was greater than the total number of plans in existence in 1959. Other PSRF statistics reveal that from 1950 to 1974 the number of plans doubled every five years.

The enactment of ERISA (1974) caused many firms to adopt a profit sharing plan as an alternative to a defined-benefit pension plan because of the additional funding and insurance requirements placed on the latter. Small companies in particular tend to use profit sharing as a substitute for a standard pension plan because their income and reserves may not be adequate to make any commitments for fixed contributions or benefits payments. In this chapter, however, profit sharing will be discussed as a supplemental benefit.

The traditional definition of profit sharing, formulated at the International Cooperative Congress in Paris in 1889, is "an agreement freely entered into by which the employees receive a share, fixed in advance, of the profits." The Profit Sharing Council of America (PSCA), a nonprofit association of approximately 1,400 profit sharing employers, has refined this definition to include "any procedure under which an employer pays or makes available to regular employees subject to reasonable eligibility rules, in addition to prevailing rates of pay, special current or deferred sums based on the profits of the business." Profit sharing is therefore clearly distinguished from productivity sharing, conventional pension plans, and most thrift or savings plans governed by factors other than profits.

PLAN OBJECTIVES

Although ERISA and the IRS specify numerous rules and standards, the employer still retains considerable latitude in plan design. For that reason, it is important to be clear on plan objectives and priorities. At a minimum, these five basic objectives should be considered:

1. Provide a retirement income supplement.
2. Create flexibility and additional benefits through loans and withdrawals for various needs. (The Economic Recovery Tax Act of 1981 [ERTA] eased restrictions on in-service withdrawals from profit sharing plans.)
3. Encourage individual savings by permitting employees to make voluntary contributions to the plan. (ERTA introduced the possibility of permitting employees to make tax-deductible contributions to a profit sharing plan subject to IRA withdrawal rules.)
4. Offer inflation protection through several investment fund choices (for example, fixed income, diversified common stock, company stock, money market).
5. Stimulate productivity by encouraging employees to participate in the success of the business and its profits.

There is considerable controversy about the incentive value of profit sharing plans. Advocates maintain that employee awareness of the possibility of gaining almost an extra eight weeks' pay a year is a sufficient incentive to encourage cost consciousness, regular attendance, attention to the job, and constructive criticism of operations. They hasten to add that to achieve these goals the plan must be supported by an active program of communications and be part of a well-founded and credible employee relations program. Skeptics assert that profits depend on a large number of factors, many of which employees cannot influence. They point out that the most intelligent and intensive effort of employees may not increase profits if customer preferences change, if competitors introduce better products, or if government tax policies are altered. Conversely, employees generally may have little to do with increased profits that occur as a result of revised pricing policies, changes in currency exchange rates, new stylings, or company acquisitions.

Regardless of their intrinsic incentive values, profit sharing plans, particularly deferred plans, continue to be adopted at an ever increasing rate. Undoubtedly, the tax attractions to both employer and employee, plus the fact that the employer is not committed to making payments when there is no profit, are major factors in this growth. But another important reason has been cited by Bert L. Metzger:

> Because of its versatility, profit sharing programs can be developed in a variety of ways to solve a variety of industrial problems. A careful analysis of particular problems to be solved and goals to be reached can lead to the selection of provisions for the profit sharing plan calculated to do the designated job.[3]

The following tabulation lists some of the specific problems or needs employers have faced and the particular facets of profit sharing plan design that have helped to resolve or ameliorate the difficulty.

Problem or Need	*Plan Feature*
1. Anticipated major reduction in staff within five years.	Deferred accumulation to serve as severance pay.
2. High turnover among employees with one to three years' seniority.	Participation in a deferred plan after one year on a 50 percent basis, with full participation and partial vesting after two years, and full vesting after five years.
3. Need to update pension benefits, but inadequate funds to cover past service.	Allocation of profit sharing weighted heavily for past service.
4. Compression between wages of skilled hourly group and first-line supervisors.	Allocation of cash profit sharing to supervisors at a ratio of 1½ to 1.

[3] *Profit Sharing in Perspective* (Evanston, Ill.: Profit Sharing Research Foundation, 1966).

5. Excessive absenteeism.   Allocation of cash profit sharing weighted to reward good attendance and to penalize absenteeism.

TYPES OF PLANS

There are three basic types of profit sharing plans: cash, deferred, and combination.

Cash plans provide full and direct payment of profit shares to participants shortly after profits have been determined. This may be monthly, quarterly, semiannually, or annually.

Most of the early profit sharing plans were of the cash type. They offer the advantages of frequent and clearly evident rewards, freedom of choice to the employee in using the money and to the employer in making allocations, simplified administration, and a close relationship between performance and results. Disadvantages of cash plans include employees' tendency to become discouraged quickly whenever payments drop, their tendency to spend the payments rather than use them for security needs, and the lack of built-in tax or investment advantages.

Small companies with fewer than 50 employees favor cash plans as a contingent bonus with flexibility and incentive features. Some have graduated into deferred plans as profits became stabilized and the company grew.

Deferred plans specify that a share of profits is to be placed periodically in a trust fund for future distribution to employees. According to a formula related to earnings and years of service, employees receive a distribution, at retirement or termination, based on contributions to the fund, fund earnings, and appreciation. The deferred approach to profit sharing gained preeminence in the 1940s because of favorable tax rulings and wartime constraints on increases in current income. Today 80 percent of PSCA members have deferred plans.

Deferred plans have the attractions of long-term growth and security. Employees are less affected by short-term fluctuations in profit, and they are able to build a tax-deferred nest egg for retirement or emergencies without altering their current living patterns. The large accumulations possible through deferred funds provide impressive case reports, such as that of a Signode Corporation employee:

At Signode Corporation, a participant with thirty-five years of profit sharing participation who retired at a final average pay of $14,466 received $127,752 in profit sharing. This was an annuity equivalent of $15,300 per year rather than the $6,582 that he would have received as the typical pension benefit from a standard pension plan using his final average pay/service.[4]

In this company, the profit sharing plan and a defined-benefit pension plan are coordinated, and employees are guaranteed a minimum retirement income. This is a safeguard against any decline in the value of individual profit sharing accounts, which is an inherent risk in deferred plans. Employees can become quite disenchanted with the company as well as the plan when account balances drop. This was evidenced by a profit sharing plan participant at Marriott Corporation who brought suit against the plan sponsor because the value of her account fell from $17,764 in 1972 to $8,638 in 1975 when she retired after 15 years of service.

Younger workers may become impatient with the extended requirements for realizing benefits under a deferred plan, and all participants may resent the limited access to money and/or stock that is shown in their account statements.

Combination plans combine the features of both the current and deferred distribution methods. A part of the share is paid currently and the remainder at a later time. A combination option or elective plan allows participants to choose distribution from among several cash and deferred options, as in this sample annual election notice:

Election. You may elect to have your 1982 share of profits distributed in any of these ways:

A. 100 percent in the cash account. After three consecutive years of allocating money to this account, you will receive a cash payment amounting to approximately this year's contribution.
B. 100 percent held in trust in your individual account(s), with payment deferred until retirement or other termination. Money will be invested according to your directions below.
C. 50 percent into the cash account as in A, and 50 percent deferred as in B.

Investments. Money placed in the cash account will be invested in short-term securities. If you elect to defer 50 percent or 100 percent of your

---

[4] Bert L. Metzger, *Profit Sharing in 38 Large Companies* (Evanston, Ill.: Profit Sharing Research Foundation, 1978).

share of profits, you must direct the trustee to invest that amount in one or more of the following funds (minimum investment in any one fund = 5 percent):

1. Diversified common stock fund.
2. Fixed-income securities fund.
3. Money market type fund.

Only 16 percent of PSCA members have combination or elective plans, but it seems reasonable to expect that use of this type of plan will grow as the trend toward more flexible benefits plans that surfaced in the 1970s continues in the current decade.

PLAN DESIGN AND ADMINISTRATION

As already indicated, current profit-sharing plans are relatively simple to design and administer. There are no special tax considerations or investment policies to be evaluated. But deferred, combination, and elective plans require knowledge of law, finance, and taxes as well as of employee and organizational needs. There are many rules, but there are even more choices.

For employers considering a profit sharing plan, a checklist developed by PSRF is an excellent guide. PSRF was organized in 1951 to meet the needs of objective fact finding in the profit sharing field. Located in Evanston, Illinois, this nonprofit educational foundation conducts objective research studies to guide organizations formulating or administering profit sharing plans.

Some of the points included in the PSRF checklist are:

Type of plan (for example, deferred or combination).
Definition of employees.
Waiting period.
Definition of continuous employment.
Definition of profits.
Definition of compensation.
Allocation of company contributions.
Allocation of forfeitures, trust earnings, and appreciation or depreciation of fund assets.
Full and partial vesting.
Form and timing of distribution.
Duties of administrative committee and trustee.

Payment of administrative expense (company or trust fund).
Contributory or noncontributory.
Internal Revenue Code requirements.

Another useful resource for prospective profit sharing sponsors is a prototype profit sharing plan adopted by PSCA. This prototype plan, which has IRS approval, consists of three documents:

1. A basic plan containing provisions applicable to all companies, with elections for coverage, contributions, and vesting.
2. An adoption agreement that can be executed, indicating the company's choice of elective features.
3. A trust agreement to be signed by the employer company and its selected trustee concerning the handling of the trust, investment policy, and the fiduciary responsibility involved.

To be able to use PSCA's prototype plan, a company must join the council, since the plan and all the services offered with it are for use by members only.

TAX CONSIDERATIONS

For the employer, one of the major attractions of deferred profit sharing is the IRS approval to deduct as a business expense up to 15 percent of annual compensation of participants. There are also provisions for carry-over that permit deducting up to 25 percent of a participant's compensation in a year under certain circumstances. In order to qualify for this consideration, the plan must:

- Be primarily a deferred compensation plan.
- Be a permanent arrangement and not a temporary expedient.
- Be in writing and communicated to the employees.
- Be for the exclusive benefit of employees.
- Cover either a specified percentage of employees or a nondiscriminatory class of employees.
- Provide nondiscriminatory benefits and contributions to the employees covered.
- Contain a predetermined formula for allocating the profits among participants, as well as for distributing accumulated funds.

During active service, a deferred or combination profit sharing plan offers employees an attractive tax shelter. Employer contributions and all investment gains on funds in the trust accumulate without any current tax consequences for individual participants. Also, if the employer agrees to make the necessary arrangements, each employee may make voluntary tax-deductible contributions of up to $2,000 a year to the plan.

When the employee is separated from the company, there are a number of possibilities for handling profit sharing distributions resulting from employer contributions. Under current federal income tax rules, these several options are basically treated as follows:

1. *Lump-sum distribution.* The portion of the distribution attributable to plan service before January 1, 1974, is subject to capital gains tax; the balance is treated as ordinary income. However, the recipient may elect to treat the entire amount as ordinary income in order to use a special ten-year averaging procedure.
2. *Annuities and installment distributions* are taxed as ordinary income in the year in which they are received.
3. *Rollover to an IRA or another qualified profit sharing or pension plan.* As long as this is accomplished within 60 days of receipt, all tax consequences are deferred.

UNIONS AND PROFIT SHARING

Historically, most unions have viewed profit sharing plans as a means of detracting them from their goal of higher wages and as a management technique to speed up production. The "progress sharing" contract negotiated in 1961 between the UAW and American Motors Corporation did not ignite a trend of plan adoption through collective bargaining, but it did demonstrate the feasibility of such agreements.

Profit sharing has been a key element in contracts between the American Velvet Company in Stonington, Connecticut, and the Textile Workers Union of America since 1940. While the textile industry in New England has suffered a long-term decline, American Velvet has enjoyed considerable growth and prosperity. As quoted in the July 1975 issue of the *Journal of the Connecticut Business and Industry Association,* the local union president, Charles Gencarella, credited profit sharing and its underlying philosophy for much of the success:

The management has made it clear over a long period that its interests and those of employees are tied closely together. The profit sharing is extremely important but the attitudes of management in its relations with the union are equally important. I would say that progress both on the side of ownership and on the side of employees is due very much to our excellent relations with the company as well as to profit sharing.

For the nonunion employer, there is some evidence that profit sharing may be a deterrent to union organizing efforts. A research project conducted at the University of Iowa's Center for Labor and Management, covering the period 1961–1966, showed that unions were significantly less successful in organizing plants that had profit sharing plans. More recently, in his book *Personnel Policies in Nonunion Companies,*[5] Fred K. Foulkes noted the prevalence of profit sharing plans among the 26 companies studied. Eleven of these major firms had supplemental plans, and five used profit sharing as the primary retirement benefit. (Eight of the remaining ten companies had a savings or thrift plan in addition to a defined-benefit pension plan.)

These two studies may not conclusively prove a causal relationship, but it does appear that the spirit and benefits of profit sharing can be very compatible with a positive-minded union avoidance philosophy.

COMMUNICATION

Effective communication has been called the lifeblood of profit sharing. Through a variety of oral, written, and visual media, management must provide a balanced communications effort that informs, satisfies, and motivates employees. Informational material is particularly important in elective plans where employees have to make decisions involving distribution and investment options. A basic plan booklet is essential, and annual statements reviewing plan highlights can help guide the employee in making choices.

For a plan to be successful, employees must be aware that it exists. That statement may seem truistic, but it is not difficult for a profit sharing plan to fade into the background and lose its value as an employee satisfier. Without active promotion, the plan can be forgotten and taken for granted, or it can become suspect. If the company is not open in sharing information with employees about profit calculations and investment peformance, a credibility gap will quickly develop. Detailed individual reports to employees, supported by the type of

[5] Englewood Cliffs, N.J.: Prentice-Hall, 1980.

general financial information given to stockholders, is needed to ensure employee satisfaction with a plan.

If employers believe there is an incentive value in profit sharing, they must nourish it with motivating communications. A formal suggestion plan in tandem with profit sharing can help stimulate workers to seek ways of improving profits. Posters, payroll stuffers, articles in the company newspaper, and contests are some of the media that have proved successful in engendering employee concern about improving operations.

Obviously, each organization must develop an approach that fits its character, but the Profit Sharing Council of America offers a variety of materials and services that can serve as the foundation for a comprehensive communications program.

SIGNIFICANT TRENDS

Annual surveys of PSCA members by Hewitt Associates indicate that the average employer contributions to profit sharing plans consistently range between 9 and 10 percent of payroll. Plan eligibility is most frequently based on one year of company service, with relatively few companies using the ERISA age 25 standard.

Vesting in profit sharing plans tends to be faster than in defined-benefit pension plans. Graded vesting is most common, and full vesting typically occurs within six to ten years.

An increasing number of plans now (undoubtedly influenced by ERTA provisions) permit voluntary employee contributions; very few have mandatory contributions.

Employee Savings Plans

Employee savings, or thrift (the terms are interchangeable), plans have much in common with deferred profit sharing plans. They both:

- Represent an opportunity for employees to receive pay supplements.
- Offer capital accumulation opportunities.
- Qualify for tax advantages under the Internal Revenue Code.
- Typically offer employees a choice of investment media.

○ Utilize employee contributions (all savings plans; some profit sharing plans).

○ Tend to be multipurposed in terms of benefits utility.

But there are two very definite differences between the two types of plans. First, in terms of cost to the employer, a savings plan is much less expensive—about 1–2 percent of total payroll. As indicated earlier, profit sharing payments can be as high as 15 percent of a participant's salary, and they usually average around 9–10 percent. Second, profit sharing benefits are a direct function of company profits. Even if a plan accepts voluntary employee contributions, this doesn't affect the amount of profit sharing allocated to an employee. In a savings plan, an employee must agree to save in order to qualify for any company contribution. In a small number of savings plans, the company's contribution rate may vary according to profits, but employee contributions remain as the primary factor; profits are secondary.

Once associated primarily with the petroleum industry, employee savings plans experienced dramatic growth during the 1970s, as indicated by these comparisons from two Conference Board studies covering all industries:[6]

	Percentage of Companies with Savings Plans	
Category	*1973*	*1980*
Office employees	18	35
Nonoffice employees	12	22

HOW THE PLANS WORK

The waiting period for participation in most savings plans is one year. (Under ERISA, it cannot be longer.) Some firms allow earlier participation, but because of the administrative costs of opening and closing accounts, it is customary to require at least completion of the probation period for plan eligibility.

The employee may elect to contribute a percentage of pay, usually between 2 and 10 percent. The most frequently specified maximum

[6] Mitchell Meyer and Harland Fox, *Profile of Employee Benefits*, Report No. 645 (New York: The Conference Board, 1974) and Mitchell Meyer, *Profile of Employee Benefits: 1981 Edition* (New York: The Conference Board, 1981).

employee contribution that will be matched by the employer is 6 percent. Typically, about seven out of ten eligible employees join a savings plan, and most save as much as is allowed.

As just mentioned, a few companies vary their contribution according to profit experience, but in the most common type of plan, the company puts up 50 cents for each dollar contributed by employees. Some firms also use a length-of-service criterion in which the percentage of company matching increases progressively with years of employment or plan participation.

All contributions are placed in a trust fund, where the employee gains the advantage of tax-sheltered investment earnings and appreciation. Typically, the employee has three or four choices for investment, including various combinations of company common stock, U.S. government bonds, a guaranteed-income fund, and diversified securities.

While by definition savings plans are intended to encourage thrift and long-term accumulation of capital, employees are generally allowed to make withdrawals of funds during active employment. The Economic Recovery Tax Act of 1981 took away the constructive receipt issue as a limiting factor on withdrawals, but most employers still impose penalties to help maintain plan objectives and administrative controls. For example, a typical plan might permit withdrawal of employee contributions and fully vested company contributions in cases of hardship. But in the absence of such evidence, only partial withdrawals are allowed, and an employee who makes such a withdrawal is suspended from the plan for six months or a year.

Vesting of company contributions is usually based on either a graded standard, with full vesting occurring after five to ten years, or a class-year system. In class-year vesting, each year's contributions from the company become 100 percent vested after a specified amount of time elapses. Under ERISA, the elapsed time cannot be greater than five years; most plans specify two or three years. For example, if 100 percent vesting takes two years after participation in the plan begins, and if the waiting period for participation is one year, then an employee hired in 1979 would first participate in the plan in 1980; and such an employee would be entitled to the company's 1980 contributions at the end of 1982, to its 1981 contributions at the end of 1983, and so on. Under this plan, unless a separate provision states otherwise, the employee never "catches up" with the full amount of the company's contributions to date. After working for 20 years, the employee is entitled to 17 years' worth of employer contributions.

SPECIAL ATTRACTIONS OF SAVINGS PLANS

Although they are not tied directly to productivity or profit improvement, employee savings plans serve many of the same purposes as plans that are. Some of their most familiar goals are to encourage employee thrift, to encourage employees to become stockholders in the company, to stabilize employment, and to improve general attitudes.

As the trend continues toward employer payment of the full cost of such basic benefits as health insurance, pensions, and income-protection coverage, it would seem that savings plans and contributory profit sharing plans will become increasingly more popular with both employees and employers. Many behavioral scientists continue to maintain that employees resent paternalistic benefits that, intentionally or not, create a relationship of dependence on the employer. At the same time, it is evident that employees want different kinds of benefits at different stages of their careers, according to numerous factors.

Savings plans offer employees the opportunity of participating in a program in order to produce a superior level of benefits for themselves. Also, the options in most plans permit the use of plan funds for any number of purposes, thereby giving employees considerable flexibility. From the vantage point of the employer, as long as employees are paying most of the costs, there is bound to be a greater willingness to tailor the plan to employee desires.

In contrast with the great majority of profit sharing plans, savings plans require an employee commitment to put aside some of his or her own money in order to gain from company contributions. Although savings plans rarely produce as much extra employee income as profit sharing, and may not be as strong an incentive for productivity, they may prove to be a more practical alternative as a supplemental benefit.

RELATIONSHIP TO CASH-OR-DEFERRED PLANS

In November 1981 the Internal Revenue Service published proposed regulations covering Section 401(k) of the tax code, which had been adopted in 1978 to cover cash-or-deferred options in profit sharing plans. The 1981 proposed regulations, not finalized as of late 1982, opened the door for some firms to introduce salary reduction plans that channel part of pay into long-term savings accounts for employees, thus lowering their current tax obligations. The pay conversion plan introduced by Honeywell in 1982 (see the end of Chapter 8) was one of the first of these plans.

Companies with established savings or thrift plans quickly recognized the attractions of combining cash-or-deferred features with these plans. For example, it is now possible to offer employees an option of designating part or all of their "mandatory" contributions (that is, contributions that the employer matches by some percentage) to a savings plan as tax deductible. If these contributions are withdrawn from the employee's account prior to age 59½, they are subject to regular and penalty taxes unless there is evidence of disability or severe financial hardship. Also, the IRS has specified nondiscrimination rules that limit the amount of tax-deductible contributions by the higher-paid one-third of eligible employees in relation to contributions by employees in the lower-paid two-thirds of the group.

In spite of the restrictions on liquidity, and the amount that may qualify as a tax-deductible employee contribution, the current IRS position on cash-or-deferred arrangements is expected to result in the modification of most existing savings plans as well as a wave of new plan adoptions.

Stock Bonus Plans (ESOPs, TRASOPs, and PAYSOPs)

From an employee benefits standpoint, a stock bonus plan is similar to a deferred profit sharing plan, except that employer contributions do not necessarily depend on profits and distributions are in the form of employer stock. Until the mid-1970s this type of plan was associated with executive compensation, but several factors since that time have caused employers to adopt broad-based plans:

1. The so-called people's capitalism theories of Louis Kelso, a San Francisco attorney and economic theorist, gained acceptance as concerns rose over falling productivity. Generally credited with developing the leveraged-type employee stock ownership plan (ESOP), Kelso has ascribed nearly supernatural powers to this approach:

By turning every worker into a capital owner we can enhance worker productivity, raise the capital needed to accelerate economic growth, reduce unemployment, and defuse the conflict between management and labor that underlies the wage–price spiral.[7]

2. ERISA exempted ESOPs from the diversification of investment requirements that apply to other funded plans and singled them out as the only type of plan that could be used as vehicles for corporate borrowing.

3. The Tax Reduction Act of 1975 and the Tax Reform Act of 1976 provided employers with a 1 percent tax credit for business investment if they made an equivalent contribution to an ESOP (plus an additional ½ percent credit if voluntary employee contributions were permitted and matched). These plans became known as Tax Reduction Act stock ownership plans (TRASOPs).

4. TRASOPs were exempt from the federal pay guidelines that were applied in 1979–1980.

5. The Economic Recovery Tax Act of 1981 (ERTA) extended tax credits for ESOPs through 1987.

Up to now, TRASOPS have become most popular in electric and gas utilities and among capital-intensive manufacturers. This is because the tax credits were related to capital investment. But starting in 1983, the tax credits are based on covered payroll. This should make such plans (now called PAYSOPs) more attractive to a broader cross section of employers.

LEVERAGED ESOPS

Many employers are attracted to ESOPs as a financing tool as well as an employee benefit, since it offers a way to raise additional capital through corporate borrowing with repayment of the loan through tax-deductible dollars (see Exhibit 15). The cost of raising capital in this way is approximately half that paid in conventional financing arrangements, assuming the corporation is in a combined 50 percent federal–state tax bracket. That is because company contributions to the employee stock ownership trust, which in turn are used to repay both principal and interest on the loan, are tax deductible. In a con-

[7] Cited in "Employee Stock Plans Begin to Catch Fire," *Business Week* (March 1, 1976).

Exhibit 15.   Mechanics of an employee stock ownership plan.

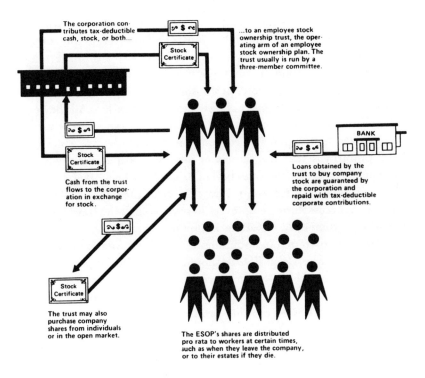

The corporation con-
tributes tax-deductible
cash, stock, or both...

...to an employee stock
ownership trust, the operating arm of an employee
stock ownership plan. The
trust usually is run by a
three-member committee.

Stock
Certificate

BANK

Cash from the trust
flows to the corpor-
ation in exchange
for stock.

Stock
Certificate

Loans obtained by the
trust to buy company
stock are guaranteed by
the corporation and
repaid with tax-deductible
corporate contributions.

Stock
Certificate

The trust may also
purchase company
shares from individuals
or in the open market.

The ESOP's shares are distributed
pro rata to workers at certain times,
such as when they leave the company,
or to their estates if they die.

Source: John H. Crichton and Robert A. Manley, "How to Motivate Your Employees and Raise Capital, Too." Copyright October 1976 by *Nation's Business,* Chamber of Commerce of the United States.

ventional loan arrangement, only the interest payment would be tax deductible.

LIMITATIONS OF STOCK BONUS PLANS

As a sole source of capital accumulation for employees, PAYSOPs— with a tax credit limit of ½ percent of covered payroll in 1983–1984 (increasing to three-quarters of 1 percent for 1985–1987)—do not appear to offer great promise. Besides, these plans do not enjoy the degree of permanency under our tax laws that other qualified plans have had. They should probably be viewed as simply a form of frosting on the cake. However, they can help satisfy the nondiscrimination test in a Section 401(k) plan by increasing the amount credited to the lower paid two-thirds of a covered group.

Leveraged ESOPs will probably continue to grow in favor with employers because of their financial advantages. However, in spite of the messianic prophecies of some advocates, these plans do have some fundamental limitations as employee benefits. A major disadvantage in comparison with deferred profit sharing and employee savings plans is the lack of investment choice and diversification. All the benefits eggs are in one basket in an ESOP. This can serve as a motivator, but it places participants' accumulations at considerable risk. The basic problem is that the success of an ESOP depends heavily on company success and the valuation of its stock in the market, but employees do not have full control over either of these factors. Despite numerous success stories, employees in some companies have come to regard the promises of ESOPs as more fable than fact.

Employers interested in obtaining technical information and communications materials on ESOPs should contact the Employee Stock Ownership Council of America (see list of special resources in the back of this book). This is a nonprofit trade association of companies who have either ESOPs or some variation thereof.[8]

---

[8] For more information on PAYSOPs, see Howard A. Sontag and Gary G. Quintierl, "PAYSOPs: ERTA's Revised TRASOPs," in *Compensation Review* (Second Quarter 1982).

CHAPTER 7

Those All-Important "Other Benefits"

Personalized benefits statements (described in more detail in Chapter 10) are now distributed to employees regularly by most large companies. These reports provide employees with a useful summary of their accrued and projected pension benefits; medical, disability, and survivor protections; and, where appropriate, capital accumulation plan balances. Many statements also itemize the employee's vacation, holiday, and paid personal time allowances. Invariably, there will be some reference to "other benefits." A review of the other benefits section in a sampling of company statements for 1980–1982 shows that the most frequently mentioned items are:

Tuition-aid plans.
Children's scholarships.
Matching gifts.
Relocation allowances.
Product and service discounts.
Credit union.
Subsidized food service.
Commutation assistance.
Group social and recreation programs.
Health services.

Employee assistance programs (EAPs).
Service awards.

Several of these items (for example, relocation allowances and children's scholarships) might be classified as special-purpose benefits, since they can be utilized by only a small portion of the workforce. All other items are available to most employees, and many are broadly utilized.

Collectively, these other benefits represent a significant employer response to the expressed needs of employees. In some instances (for example, tuition aid and subsidized food services), they account for substantial expenditures; in other cases (for example, commutation assistance), they are virtually no-cost items. Whatever the cost, they are important benefits that deserve more recognition than the brief mention they usually receive in personalized benefits statements and benefits brochures.

Tuition-Aid Plans

A tuition-aid plan is one of the best methods of keeping employees up to date on advances in their fields and helping them to get ahead in their company. Such a plan can augment the company's efforts to train employees for present and future job assignments and can help enrich employees' lives.

Tuition-aid plans embody the contributory principle more fully than most benefits plans today. While the employer covers the direct costs of tuition and required fees, the employee is usually required to pay for books and materials, is responsible for costs of meals and transportation, and attends classes and studies after work hours. In some cases, an employee may even have to forgo overtime assignments. For the individual who sees opportunity ahead, these sacrifices can lead to recognition, advancement, and new career directions that can return much more than the investment.

The principal considerations for an employer in setting up a tuition-aid plan are:

Employee eligibility rules.
Definition of acceptable courses and schools.
Definition of covered expenses.

Time-off policy.
Extent, conditions, and time of payment.
Tax treatment.
Employee records.
Communication.

EMPLOYEE ELIGIBILITY

Most firms extend eligibility to every full-time employee after about six months on the payroll. A small and declining number of companies restrict participation to salaried or managerial employees. Such restrictions seem particularly inappropriate today, when so much attention is focused on the need for assisting disadvantaged and underutilized workers to upgrade their skills. The exclusion of part-time employees seems reasonable, since many of these people are moonlighters who have coverage from their principal employer or full-time students who have no career ambitions with the part-time employer.

DEFINITION OF ACCEPTABLE COURSES AND SCHOOLS

Any course directly related to an employee's present job with the company should qualify for tuition aid. Beyond this obvious goal, it is necessary to provide some guidelines to govern eligibility of other courses. Each company must evaluate the advantages against the costs of covering courses that have little relation to employees' present jobs but may help them prepare for advancement.

A relationship between a course and some phase of company operations is a useful guideline, but exceptions should be considered for courses required in a degree program. If, for instance, a bachelor's degree in English is a job requirement for a company librarian and if an employee needs to complete courses in philosophy and history to achieve the degree, these courses probably should be covered. However, some limits on elective courses should be imposed. An employee in the chemicals industry who is working for a degree in business administration and must take a course in either chemistry or astronomy to satisfy a science requirement should be advised which course to take to receive company reimbursement.

Acceptable schools are usually defined as accredited secondary schools, colleges, and universities, plus technical institutes, specialty programs, and correspondence schools. The latter may be included only if clear evidence exists that classroom instruction is unavailable or inaccessible. The growing interest in speed reading, public speaking, business writing, and memory courses has led some companies to design their own after-hours programs as a less expensive alternative to subsidizing individual attendance at outside courses.

DEFINITION OF COVERED EXPENSES

Although the term "tuition aid" is still used widely to describe these plans, it is becoming a misnomer. Since most plans cover registration and laboratory fees, and some subsidize books and supplies, "educational expense allowance" and "continuing education allowance" seem to be more descriptive terms.

Other expenses that are paid for in a minority of plans today include entrance examinations, thesis costs, graduation fees, health fees, professional certification, and activity fees. Employees receiving educational allowances under the G.I. Bill are usually expected to apply the government aid before requesting company support.

TIME-OFF POLICY

Many educators believe that as management becomes more aware of, and concerned about, the knowledge explosion in progress today, the classic separation of education and work will disappear. However, most companies still draw a line between in-plant training programs that are considered essential and outside educational programs that have been termed "desirable." This results in employees having to take courses on an after-hours basis in most situations. But some companies will permit employees to adjust their work schedules to permit class attendance as long as this does not interfere with operations, and flextime can accommodate many employee time requirements.

EXTENT, CONDITIONS, AND TIME OF PAYMENT

The customary allowance for an approved course of study was originally 50 percent of the cost of tuition in most industrial plans, but today 75 or 100 percent of tuition costs and related fees is the norm. For an employee to qualify for reimbursement, most companies require a passing grade or specify "successful completion" of courses where no grade is given. Some companies vary the allowance with grades. For instance, 100 percent of the costs might be reimbursed for an A, 75 percent for a B, and 50 percent for a C. Other companies reject this approach on the basis that grades are subjective evaluations that vary from school to school and that too much pressure on grade attainment could adversely affect an employee's job performance.

Most employers impose limits on allowances, in the form of either a maximum number of dollars or a number of credit hours per semester or academic year for which payment will be made. Firms that set dollar maximums have found it necessary to adjust the limit frequently as tuition costs continue to rise at a rapid rate. Limiting the credit hours or courses allowed guards against employees overextending themselves in the pursuit of knowledge to the detriment of their health and work effort.

By definition, most tuition-aid plans are refund or reimbursement arrangements. An employee obtains advance approval from the employer, enrolls in a course or program, pays the institution, and, if he or she successfully completes the educational requirements, submits a request to the company for reimbursement. Recently, to aid employees who may be deterred from enrollment because they lack available cash, some companies have arranged for advance payments or loans. Where an employee credit union is operative, educational loans can usually be obtained conveniently, and the employer may agree to pay the loan interest.

TAX TREATMENT

Prior to 1979, there was a great deal of confusion about the tax status of payments to employees from a tuition-aid plan. The 1978 Revenue Act clarified the situation until at least the end of 1983. Currently, educational assistance plan payments are not included in taxable income if the following conditions are satisfied:

1. The plan does not discriminate in favor of officers, owners, or highly paid employees.

2. Not more than 5 percent of total benefits are paid to shareholders or owners.
3. No choice is offered between educational assistance and other compensation includable in income.
4. Payments are not for education involving sports, games, or hobbies.

EMPLOYEE RECORDS

Small companies should have no problem maintaining records of employee course enrollment, participation, and completion in a central file. Summary reports can be prepared periodically and circulated to key managers so that individual attainment can be recognized and possibly rewarded through advancement. If a clerk or mechanic receives a degree in business administration, this fact is quickly known and he or she can be sure of at least consideration when a job in purchasing, inventory control, or office services becomes open.

In large organizations with a number of divisions and locations, the link between educational assistance and employee development and advancement is often tenuous. Both company and employee can suffer a serious loss if employment specialists and line supervisors do not have access to up-to-the-minute information about employees' educational attainments when transfer and promotion decisions are made. An employee may appreciate tuition refund as a benefit, but its value is limited if educational accomplishments are overlooked when promotions are made. Administratively, it seems preferable to have the employee benefits or personnel staff handle the processing of enrollments and reimbursements. However, information about course completion should go into the employee's basic file, and the corporate unit responsible for employee placement and development should be apprised of all major attainments. This is an area where computerized systems can be of great value.

COMMUNICATION

The most frequently mentioned objectives for employee tuition-aid plans are to:

Enable employees to get ahead in the company.
Make employees more productive.

Enrich employees' lives.

Create a reserve of promotable employees.

Attract promising new employees.

Any company that subscribes to these beliefs should be sure that all applicants and employees are aware of its educational assistance program. Unfortunately, too many firms limit their publicity of these plans to a page in the employee handbook and a brief mention in the annual benefits statement. If a program is to be worthwhile, and if management expects it to fulfill such lofty objectives, it must be promoted more aggressively.

Certainly recruitment literature should emphasize the highlights and advantages of educational assistance. Special notices on bulletin boards and displays in cafeterias and employee lounges, particularly a few weeks prior to school registration periods, are excellent reminders for employees. Articles in employee publications can dramatize the relationship between educational accomplishment and job progression. Special memorandums or letters to the home are effective vehicles for transmitting information about plan improvements. Supervisors should be reminded to mention the plan to employees whenever overall job performance and individual development needs are being discussed as part of a merit rating or appraisal program. An effective way to use the personalized benefits statement to promote educational assistance is to quantify the benefit for both participants and nonparticipants by using alternative messages. For example:

Participant

> During [1982], you received [$450] in educational assistance plan benefits. Since your employment in [1973], you have received a total of [$3,225] in plan benefits.

Nonparticipant

> You are eligible to participate in the educational assistance plan. During 1982, 737 employees received a total of $224,500 in benefits from this plan.

Children's Scholarships

Although tuition aid is the most prevalent form of educational benefit offered by employers, only 3–5 percent, on average, of employees utilize the benefit. In a company where utilization is even lower, a college scholarship program for employees' children may serve as a more attractive benefit.

A 1981 Conference Board Information Bulletin[1] indicates that approximately three out of ten firms now provide this benefit, typically through an arrangement with the National Merit Scholarship Corporation (NMSC) of Evanston, Illinois. In this type of arrangement, the sponsoring company determines how many scholarships it will fund—either a fixed number, all finalists or semifinalists in the testing competition, or some combination of each approach. Other than communicating rules and procedues to employees and publicizing the winners, the sponsor has no involvement in program administration. NMSC processes the results of the eligible students' Preliminary Scholastic Aptitude Test and advises the employer of the number of award qualifiers. NMSC also calculates the amount of the four-year scholarship—typically ranging from $1,000 to $2,500 per year—on the basis of financial need.

A unique combination of employee tuition-aid and family educational benefits was introduced by Kimberly-Clark in 1974.[2] A three-part educational opportunities plan was established:

Employee self-development ("KimEd"). Each employee receives an annual allotment in a personal bank account to be used for self-development. The allotment is based on several factors, including company earnings and the employee's performance rating. In certain circumstances, up to two weeks' time off the job can be granted.

Family education savings ("FamEd"). Each year an amount equal to 25 percent of the employee's KimEd allotment is credited to a FamEd account that may be used for educational expenses of the employee, spouse, and children. The employee may also contribute up to $200 a year to this account. The company matches 20 percent of employee savings.

Extended education leaves. Each year the company may grant paid education leaves of two weeks to one year.

During the first three years of operation, the participation rates for KimEd and FamEd were 30 percent and 12 percent, respectively.

---

[1] *Personal Practices III: Employee Services, Work Rules.*
[2] "Tuition-Aid Concepts at Kimberly-Clark Show Dramatic Results," *Training and Development Journal* (December 1977).

Matching Gifts

Employees are now accustomed to receiving solicitation letters from colleges, hospitals, museums, public TV and radio stations, and other tax-exempt institutions that exhort them to "check with your employer regarding a matching gift." From the fund-raising standpoint, this is tantamount to the salesperson's credo, "Always ask for the order."

For the employer, a matching gifts plan can be viewed as a contributory benefit plan that effectively shares the gift-giving obligation with employees. The operation of a plan is relatively simple. The employer defines eligible donees, sets gift limitations (for example, minimum gift—$25; maximum annual matching—$5,000), and communicates and administers the plan. Employees determine to whom they wish to make donations, how much and how often. Although the advantage is not publicized, it is quite likely that some individuals reduce the amount of their personal donations because of the amount being added by the company in a matching gifts plan.

Relocation Allowances

In the early years of this century, company-sponsored housing facilities were quite common in the mining and textile industries. To many workers, they represented the best available housing in their communities, but in some cases, the company town and the company store became a trap that restricted the mobility of labor. What was once a symbol of benevolent management became a target of labor union ridicule in the 1950s, when Kohler, Wisconsin, a company town, suffered labor strife for most of that decade. In 1970 Cannon Mills' domination of Kannapolis, North Carolina, was Ralph Nader's target in a television special sponsored by the Ford Foundation and shown on the public television network. In this report, Nader criticized the shortcomings of corporate paternalism and the oppressive environment of a company town.

Today the thrust of company benefits in the area of housing is toward facilitating rather than restricting mobility. National and multinational employers want to be able to move key employees throughout their systems. Companies that decide to relocate from urban centers to suburbia or exurbia want to retain as many employees as possible. Firms that move out of state usually attempt to bring at least a cadre of salaried workers with them. Local shortages of qualified managers, scientists, and business specialists cause employers to explore job markets far removed from their places of business.

RELOCATING NEW EMPLOYEES

Very few businesses today can rely on the local labor market to satisfy all their employment needs. Certainly any company that must recruit recent college graduates knows that they must seek students from distant locations. A company in Virginia might want to hire someone who is graduating from a university in Massachusetts but lives in Wyoming. Fortunately, most young people are willing to relocate for a superior job opportunity, and in many cases, their relocation expenses are limited to transportation costs.

If their needs are critical enough, some companies now extend many of the same allowances to new employees that they provide for transferring employees. Generally, though, the new employee is offered coverage for only travel expenses and the costs of moving possessions. If required, temporary living expenses may be covered, and the company might agree to pay for storage of furniture for a limited time. Except for key executives, new employees usually do not receive allowances related to the costs of selling and buying a house. These costs, normally covered under policies for transferred employees, can be considerable, and most companies are unwilling to assume such a heavy liability for a person whose value to them may not become clearly evident for a year or more.

Those companies that do provide more comprehensive allowances to newly hired employees believe that it is a cost-effective recruitment policy. To quote one company executive:

> With soaring relocation expenses, two-income families more common than ever before, high costs, and complicated procedures involved in home sale and purchase, a relocation policy offering complete, comprehensive, and realistic coverage can play a major role in determining acceptance or rejection of job offers.[3]

---

[3] Howard G. MacMillan, Jr., "Your Relocation Policy as a Recruiting Tool," *Mobility* (November–December 1980).

Exhibit 16 is an example of a 1980–1981 relocation policy that, while still somewhat more liberal for a transferee, covers most areas of concern for a new hire quite well. Advocates of this approach believe that it facilitates the recruitment process and relieves pressure on starting salaries.

ALLOWANCES FOR TRANSFERRED EMPLOYEES

In addition to the basic or bare bones allowances given to new employees, most companies provide a variety of allowances and services for transferees. These usually include:

Cost allowances for selling a house.
Search expenses for finding a new residence.
Temporary living expenses.
Allowances and loans for purchasing a house.
Assistance in finding employment for a spouse.
Practical assistance.

House-selling costs. During the 1970s, there was a dramatic shift from direct company involvement to third-party purchase of houses owned by transferring employees. The third-party method is outlined in Exhibit 16. Numerous firms specializing in this type of service have emerged in recent years. A good source of information about such firms is *Mobility,* the bimonthly magazine of the Employee Relocation Council (ERC) in Washington, D.C.

In situations where a third party is not involved, it is customary for the employer to cover closing costs, brokers' fees, carrying charges, and any loss compared with an agreed-upon evaluation.

New residence search expenses. House hunting is a serious and sometimes traumatic experience for an employee. A married employee must be sensitive to the needs and tastes of the spouse and children. Company allowances need to specify the frequency and duration of visitations, provisions for trips by the family, and the types of expenses that are reimbursable (see Exhibit 16).

Temporary living expenses. This category often has two aspects. First, the employee frequently begins work at the new location before permanently vacating the old residence and, if married, before the family moves. In these cases, some arrangements must be made to pay for the employee's meals and lodging. The timing of transfers can be a

Exhibit 16. Elements of a recruiting-oriented relocation policy.

Category	Transferee	New Hire
House hunting	Seven days plus two additional days, if needed	Seven days plus two additional days, if needed
Transportation to new location	Paid	Paid
Lease cancellation	Three months	Three months
Sale of old residence	Third party makes offer based on two appraisals. Employee may accept immediately or elect to market home for up to 60 days. Dual mortgage payments relieved during this time. An advance of 95 percent of estimated equity is made available. If third party offer is rejected, employee may take a personal loan. Closing costs will be paid. If third party offer is rejected and new home is purchased, mortgage payments relieved for up to three months.	Third party offer based on two appraisals, less 6 percent. Home listed for 90 days. If sold, employee pays all closing costs and is responsible for mortgage payments to time of sale. If unsold, third party takes administrative control of title and continues the sale process. Closing costs paid at time of sale and mortgage payments absorbed by third party beginning with the inventory period (91st day). An advance of 85 percent of estimated equity is made available.
Temporary living	60 days	45 days
Auto rental	Up to 45 days, if needed	Up to 45 days, if needed
Visit family	Every two weeks	Every two weeks
Moving family	One trip	One trip
Temporary living (family)	Two weeks	Two weeks
Moving household goods	Yes, plus storage for three months	Yes, plus storage for three months
Movement of household pets	$200	$200
Assistance in purchasing new residence—loan	Personal loan if third party offer is rejected (interest paid for 3 months).	None
Assistance in purchasing new residence—closing costs	Normal closing costs paid	None
Mortgage interest differential	Difference between the new interest rate (if higher) and the old rate times mortgage balance of old home at time of sale times three (paid quarterly for three years)	Difference between the new interest rate (if higher) and the old rate times mortgage balance of old home at time of sale times three (paid quarterly for three years)
Miscellaneous expense allowance	Five percent of gross annual income	Five percent of gross annual income
Tax status	Company will gross up expenses which are taxable income and will pay these taxes for employees.	Company will gross up expenses which are taxable income and will pay these taxes for new hire.

Source: Howard G. MacMillan, Jr., "Your Relocation Policy as a Recruiting Tool," *Mobility,* November–December 1980.

critical factor in controlling these costs. A man who is transferred in February may not want to move his family until the end of the school year in June. This means that the company may have to pay his living expenses for five months. Obviously, operating requirements have a higher priority, but major shifts of personnel might be timed to avoid extended allowances whenever possible. A little foresight can save the company considerable expense.

The second aspect is the need to cover living expenses for the entire family for some period of time. For instance, a woman might want to move in September in order to enroll her children in school, but the house she is buying might not be ready for occupancy until November. Again, some sensitivity on the part of management, plus specific allowances with some flexibility, are needed to accommodate these kinds of problems.

House-purchase allowances and loans. Prior to the late 1970s, the principal form of employer assistance in this category of relocation costs was an equity loan if needed. These loans, which are still generally granted when requested, provide the transferred employee with funds to purchase the new house while waiting to receive proceeds from the sale of the old residence. The loan is usually limited to 80–90 percent of established equity in the house being sold, and either it is non-interest bearing or the interest is at a very low rate.

The sharp escalation in mortgage interest rates starting in 1979 caused most employers to adopt mortgage interest differential (MID) programs. MID allowances became a practical necessity when a transferred employee had to surrender a 6 percent mortgage and accept a 17 percent rate in the new community. The MID described in Exhibit 16 is the prototypal design, except for the method of payment. Most firms either make a lump-sum payment at time of transfer or pay in installments over a specified period of time (about 18 months in many companies).

Some leading edge companies use both the old and new mortgages in calculating the MID. In one formula for doing this, first the average of the two mortgages is multiplied by the difference between the two mortgage rates. The resulting number is then multiplied by some weighting factor determined by the company, typically a number between two and four, to calculate the total MID. The following example illustrates how this is done.

$$\frac{\$50,000 \text{ (old mortgage)} + \$80,000 \text{ (new mortgage)}}{2} = \$65,000$$

$$16\% \text{ (new rate)} - 8\% \text{ (old rate)} = 8\%$$

$$\begin{array}{r} \$65,000 \\ \times\ .08 \\ \hline \$\ 5,200 \\ \times\ 3 \text{ (weighting factor)} \\ \hline \$15,600 \text{ (MID)} \end{array}$$

Another area of coverage that has emerged as a standard in recent years is purchase closing costs. The most common benefit today is to reimburse all normal and reasonable nonnegotiable buyer closing costs.

In addition to the various specified allowances, many firms provide a general allowance to cover miscellaneous expenses resulting from relocation. As indicated in Exhibit 16, this can be expressed as a percentage of pay.

Spouse employment assistance. It is now estimated that in most corporations the percentage of management employees with working or career-oriented spouses is between 25 and 50 percent. This reflection of changing work and family values has further challenged relocation policies and created some additional considerations. At a minimum, most employers provide job market counseling, referrals, and résumé circulation. Companies that will employ spouses generally try to locate the person within the firm; companies with antinepotism policies sometimes make exceptions for spouses of transferred employees.

Some employers now cover job search expenses, including outplacement and employment agency fees. One company is reported to be providing a working-spouse allowance of one and a half months of former pay to help replace lost income while the spouse is looking for a new job. Although these are presently exceptional allowances, sometimes handled on an ad hoc basis, the continuing increase in dual-career marriages will undoubtedly cause employers to formally adopt policies to cover the need.

Practical assistance. Another company service that can create much goodwill when transferring employees and their families is practical assistance in relocating. At a minimum, it can include providing maps and brochures about the new area, and referral to real estate brokers and banks. Beyond that, the service is typically a function of how much time the personnel staff and the new boss are able to devote to the needs of the relocated employee. A motor tour of selected residential areas, visits to the homes of peers, and discussions with recently transferred employees can be extremely valuable aids to a smooth transition. Since management time is often not available for this type of assistance and counsel, some companies utilize outside agencies.

TAX TREATMENT

Under current federal tax law, all payments to or on behalf of a relocated employee are reportable as income. The IRS allows a moving expense deduction for persons making a job-related move of 35 miles or more, subject to the following limits:

1. Expenses of traveling (including meals and lodgings) from the old to the new residence.
2. Expenses of moving household goods and personal effects.
3. Expenses of traveling from the former residence to the new place of work for the principal purpose of searching for a new residence, and costs of meals and lodgings (up to 30 days) while waiting to move into permanent quarters (maximum $1,500).
4. Qualified expenses incident to a sale, purchase, or lease of a residence.
   (The sum of 3 and 4 cannot exceed $3,000.)

For most employees these deductions do not come close to matching the amount that must be reported as income for tax purposes. To compensate for this, most companies have adopted tax-assistance policies. Typically, this is handled as a gross-up of income using either a standard percentage (for example, 25 percent) or a graduated scale based on salary level and the amount of nondeductible reimbursement.

EMPLOYER CONTROL

Generous relocation allowances can facilitate transfers and create employee goodwill. But unless they are governed by specific and clearly written policies, misunderstandings and runaway costs can occur. Moving companies should receive explicit instructions about allowances and limitations on packing, storage, insurance, and convenience services. Employees should receive a complete policy guide so that false expectations do not lead to dissatisfaction at a later date. The policy should not be silent on any point that experience indicates may arise. If it is the company's intention not to pay for maid service when the employee vacates the old residence, it is a good idea to state that fact.

Exhibit 17 is a checklist that a national moving company has distributed to its clients as an aid to establishing a moving policy. Another source of guidance on policies is the previously mentioned Employee Relocation Council (ERC), a nonprofit organization that facilitates the exchange of information among company personnel responsible for administering the employee relocation and housing function.

Product and Service Discounts

Companies dealing in consumer goods and services have an excellent opportunity to provide their employees with nontaxable savings on the purchase of company products. The recruitment literature of airline firms and department stores gives testimony to the ascribed value of this type of benefit to employees. Certainly firms producing and selling cosmetics, toiletries, food products, and small appliances will have a workforce with great interest in obtaining the products they help bring to the market. Being able to buy these products at factory cost or at the wholesale price is an important saving to the employee. For the employer, the purchase of his products by employees is a sign of pride in the company and, on a strictly commercial note, a form of promotion to the public. Liberal discount privileges can also help control pilferage.

The sale of noncompany products to employees at a small discount is a service offered today by relatively few employers, although in plants at remote locations it could serve the same convenience purpose as a military post exchange. However, the company store seems to be out of phase with the modern philosophy of employee benefits. As employees spend less and less time at the work site, they no longer want to be dependent on the employer for commodities that are available with greater choice and at comparable prices in area shopping centers. It is hard to imagine that any employer would regret

Exhibit 17. Checklist for establishing an employee relocation policy.

A company issues one, sometimes two, policy statements.

One is a statement of overall, internal policy, usually for the guidance of management only. The other encompasses internal policy and is distributed to employees when they move.

The checklist below can be used as a guide to establish either policy.

BASIC QUESTIONS

_____ Who is authorized to approve relocation expenses?

_____ Under what conditions will the company pay for or reimburse an employee for relocation expenses?

_____ How is the mover selected and paid for his services?

_____ Who may approve unusual expenses?

PROGRAM ADMINISTRATION

_____ Assignment of responsibility for the program.

_____ Appointment of a Moving Administrator at one or more locations.

_____ Description of Moving Administrator's responsibilities.

RULES LIMITING EXPENDITURE

_____ Company will pay all moving and relocation expenses.

_____ Expenses will not exceed $_____.

_____ Employer will pay the actual cost of packing and moving _____ pounds of household goods.

_____ _____ percent of the employee's annual base salary will govern the maximum relocation expense.

_____ Job classification will determine the applicable moving and relocation allowance.

HOMESALE EXPENSES

_____ Third party buyout.

_____ Mortgage differentials.

_____ Guarantee against loss on homesale or penalty on unexpired lease.

_____ Full or partial reimbursement of homesale expenses.

_____ Tax gross-up for any reimbursable expenses.

MOVING ALLOWANCE AND LIMITATIONS

Routine Services Provided by the Mover

_____ Packing and crating services.

_____ Transportation, as authorized.

_____ Temporary storage limits (30 days, 60 days, etc.), and final delivery to the home.

_____ Extra pickup or delivery services.

_____ Permanent storage.

_____ Servicing of appliances, before and after moving.

_____ Insurance or transit protection provided by carrier.

_____ Insurance provided by employer.

(*continued on next page*)

Exhibit 17.   Continued

Convenience Services that May or May Not Be Allowed

_____ Janitor or maid services.
_____ Rug and drapery cleaning.
_____ Shipment and/or storage of frozen food.
_____ Shipment of pets, cars, boats, and other items (like lumber, bricks, etc.) not ordinarily considered to be household goods.
_____ Shipment of merchandise having no personal or intrinsic value and that is clearly not worth the expense of moving.

INCIDENTAL RELOCATION EXPENSES

Travel and Temporary Living Allowances

_____ Mode and class of transportation for employee and family.

_____ Basis for reimbursing the employee for living expenses during the course of moving.
_____ Exploratory trip to the new community by the employee and spouse.

Unusual Expenses

_____ Child care.
_____ Trips by employee to visit family before household good are moved to the new location.
_____ Purchase of items for new home—drapes, carpeting, miscellaneous fixtures, etc.
_____ Express shipments of personal or professional items needed immediately upon arrival in the new community.
_____ Removal and installation of appliances, TV antennas, special electrical or plumbing connections, cabinet work, etc.

Source: The Bekins Company.

discontinuing the sale of noncompany products to his employees, and unless there is an obvious convenience to the employees in having the service, its discontinuation can probably be accomplished with little upset.

Credit Union

A service that exists in about two out of every three firms today is an employee credit union. A credit union is an organization in which a group of people agree to save their money together and to make loans to each other at low interest. The members elect their own officers and set policies in accordance with standards set by the Bureau of Federal Credit Unions in Washington, D.C., or by a state league of credit unions. Although people who belong to the same fraternal order, church, or labor union may form a credit union, more than two-thirds of all credit unions serve employee groups. Some of the reasons for the popularity of this institution with employers are:

- Garnishments, loan requests, and pay advances drop sharply when a credit union is installed in a company.
- Employee worries about financial problems can be relieved.
- Management does not have to get involved with an employee's financial affairs.
- Serving as volunteer directors in the credit union gives employees firsthand experience and insight into business operations.

The company cannot regulate an employee credit union, but there are many ways in which it can encourage and support the employee group: through providing space, equipment, and materials at no charge or at a reduced rate; through urging those managers with expertise in investments, auditing, credit, and accounting to serve on credit union committees; through publicity in the house magazine and through bulletins, newsletters, and payroll envelope stuffers; and, perhaps most important, through payroll deduction for credit union savings and loan purposes.

Subsidized Food Service

An indication that a fully subsidized cafeteria is definitely an employee benefit was contained in a decision of a major insurance company some years ago. This company decided to discontinue the practice of providing free meals to employees and announced that the cafeteria would charge "reasonable" prices. To offset the additional expense, salary adjustments of up to $400 a year, depending on length of service, were put into effect.

Today, most employers subsidize their food operations, but very few provide free meals. The subsidy usually consists of provision by the employer of space, equipment, utilities, and (sometimes) labor. The employee than pays only for the actual cost of the food and obtains low-cost meals at a considerable saving compared with costs at outside restaurants with a profit objective. Many firms prefer to have outside caterers operate their food-service operations because of the special expertise required. This need not have any direct bearing on the company's subsidy objective.

The principal purpose for having a company cafeteria is to serve lunch, or one basic meal for shift workers. However, in many firms the cafeteria is used for the coffee break, and in some firms for breakfast. The latter service is considered to be a deterrent to tardiness. A candy manufacturer that offers a bonus to employees for getting to work on time opens its cafeteria for breakfast in advance of the basic plant starting time to help employees achieve their bonuses.

Companies that operate employee cafeterias generally believe the service permits a shorter lunch period, typically 30 or 45 minutes, than would be required if employees had to leave the plant or office. The service therefore benefits the employer by saving time and the employee by saving money. Also, by restricting the length of the meal period the company can more easily pass the "convenience of employer" test that the IRS uses to determine if the company subsidy should be included in employees' taxable income.

Commutation Assistance

In 1973 the 3M Company was faced with the need to construct a new $2.5 million parking garage to accommodate the automobiles resulting from growing employment at its St. Paul, Minnesota, headquarters. Instead, management decided to offer 12-seat vans to groups of employees for their daily commute. In return, the riders would pay 3M monthly fares to cover the costs of acquiring and operating the vans.

The Commute-A-Van program was an instant success at 3M, and subsequently, the van pooling concept has been adopted by some 600 organizations throughout the United States, including Prudential Insurance, SmithKline, Corning Glass, Chrysler, Texas Instruments, and the Tennessee Valley Authority. Some of the advantages cited by employers are cost savings in constructing and maintaining parking spaces, improved attendance and punctuality, and enhanced morale. In most cases, the program pays for itself or costs the company very little.

Employees who participate in company van pooling perceive it as a valuable benefit that produces tangible savings in commutation costs plus reduced wear and tear on personal automobiles. Passengers enjoy the convenience of avoiding daily driving, and the driver usually rides free and has use of the van on weekends and evenings.

Since van pooling supports federal and state efforts to conserve energy, reduce vehicular pollution, and relieve traffic congestion, it is strongly supported and promoted by both levels of government. The Energy Tax Act of 1978 specified investment tax credit opportunities for employers providing vans or buses, and most states now offer assistance to companies in setting up ride-sharing programs.

Other ways in which companies assist employees in commuting to and from work are by:

1. Providing an information clearinghouse for car pool inquiries and arrangements.
2. Arranging special routes and schedules with local bus companies to accommodate large numbers of employees.
3. Subsidizing parking in public lots and garages when company parking space is unavailable.

Group Social and Recreation Programs

Major social events for all company employees are no longer in vogue, at least in large companies. The annual picnic or Christmas party for an organization of a thousand or more employees has very little appeal to today's employee, who is also a home owner, PTA member, civic worker, Boy Scout adviser, and evening student. Not only are the employees unfamiliar with all but a few immediate co-workers, but they cherish limited spare time and reserve it for prime interests.

These facts suggest that a wide choice of activities that collectively appeal to the many diverse hobbies and interests of employees is the preferred approach to company social and recreation programs. As firms have moved in this direction, there has been a shift from employer control of the activity to a facilitative approach. The National Employee Services and Recreation Association (NESRA) reports that employees exercise significant control in most programs today, and there are few, if any, instances in which employees are given no voice. Rather than running a picnic or dinner dance, the company provides a subsidy to any group that demonstrates enough interest in an activity and then supports it through internal publicity.

Employees are involved in the management of the program and can gain satisfaction, and even good experience, from this kind of participation. They benefit by being able to join with coworkers from all levels and areas of the company in something of common interest. In some situations, such as group travel plans and bowling leagues, there can be substantial savings for the employee, since group rates are lower than individual costs. Again, in small or remote communities, company-sponsored programs may fill a local need for leisure-time activities.

For the employer, a balanced program of social, cultural, educational, and athletic activities, from which most employees can select at least one function in which to participate, is a positive factor in maintaining good morale.

Health Services

To ex-military personnel, the company health center may seem like the post dispensary. The impression may exist that any visitation is an encounter in which the employee tries to establish that he or she is too sick to work, and the company doctor or nurse is like Horatius at the bridge, blocking the route to the exit. In reality, modern occupational health programs are concerned with detecting malingerers, but more importantly, they are designed to maintain, conserve, and improve employee health.

At one time, employers avoided setting up medical programs, other than for preplacement physical examinations, in the belief that they might be in conflict with private practitioners. The risks of occupational accidents and illnesses, the growth of occupational medicine as a specialized field, and the relative shortage of general practitioners have all led to a major reversal of that position.

Companies that are able to employ one or more full-time physicians for employee health purposes can offer periodic medical examinations, health education, and immunization programs to all employees. A company doctor can evaluate the work environment in order to detect and assess health hazards, mental as well as physical. Without usurping the role of the family physician, the company M.D. can counsel with employees about health conditions that may adversely affect their job performance, and recommend a program or source of treatment. Employers that cannot justify the retention of a staff physician can utilize nurses and other paramedical personnel to run a health program with the aid and advice of outside doctors.

A recent development in company health services programs has been a greater emphasis on wellness intervention and health promotion. Rather than just passively reacting to signs of illness, some firms have taken a more aggressive stance with regard to preventive medicine. One such program is *Good for Life*®, which is offered free of charge to employees of American Hospital Supply Corporation on a voluntary and confidential basis. According to Karl Bays, chairman and chief executive officer of this company:

> American has introduced *Good for Life*® to safeguard our most important resource: our employees. It's designed to increase our knowledge of how health is affected by everyday actions we take, or don't take. It's also designed to acquaint us with how we can live more healthy lives.[4]

The basis for individual involvement in this program is a personal health profile that is developed by a health professional from responses to a questionnaire and a health assessment. The health professional reviews the profile with the employee, who then may choose one or more of the following seven life-style programs: hypertension, nutrition, weight control, smoking cessation, stress, exercise or fitness, and employee assistance.

This is an exceptionally comprehensive program that may be beyond the reach of most employers at this time. However, it is possible to implement at least some of the component elements, and many firms have. The cost–benefit effectiveness of avoiding coronary bypass surgery or a lifetime of medical treatment for a significant number of employees should be sufficient incentive for more employers to follow this lead.

Employee Assistance Programs (EAPs)

Closely related to health promotion or wellness intervention are employee assistance programs (EAPs). When these counseling programs began to gain acceptance in the early 1940s, they were identified

---

[4] American Hospital Supply brochure on *Good for Life*®, 1981.

closely with alcoholism treatment. That was the basis of the pioneer programs at New England Telephone Company, DuPont, and Eastman Kodak. In 1945 Caterpillar Tractor Company introduced what has become known as the "broadbrush" type of EAP, and this is the direction that most companies have since taken.

Today a typical EAP is designed to help employees deal with practically any type of physical, mental, emotional, or personal problem that might be interfering with job performance. In addition to alcoholism and other health-related problems, the EAP usually offers counseling related to marital, family, financial, legal, and career difficulties. Because of the diversity of problem areas covered, a broadbrush EAP cannot provide intensive in-depth counseling, but an employee (or family member) can obtain knowledgeable assessment, short-term counseling, referral, and follow-up service.

Most EAPs are in-house programs administered by a director and one or more counselors. In many instances, the EAP is part of, or closely allied with, an employee health department. An alternative approach is to utilize an outside organization, such as Priority Systems of Summit, New Jersey, which in late 1980 was offering EAP service to more than 20,000 employees (and their families) of 12 client corporations. In this type of arrangement, the employer usually pays a per capita fee based on the employee population. There are no charges to the employee for using the service.

In both approaches, much emphasis is placed on preserving confidentiality, and this is essential for program success. Employees will utilize EAPs only if they feel secure that by revealing problems they are not putting their jobs in jeopardy. However, an employer may direct employees to seek help from an EAP whenever it appears that personal problems are adversely affecting job performance.

Companies that provide EAPs as an employee benefit believe that the costs are easily justified. McDonnell Douglas calculated that it saved $4 million over ten years with its EAP, and other firms also report lowered costs for medical and disability insurance, fewer accidents, and reduced absenteeism.

Service Awards

Probably no act of employer beneficence has received more ridicule than the presentation of the symbolic gold watch in recognition of long company service. Cynical barbs, such as "That must add up to $2.28 per year," are all too familiar. Still, a service recognition program continues as a standard benefit in a substantial majority of companies. And the Economic Recovery Tax Act of 1981 provided a potential boost for these programs by raising the limits on employer deductions for award items. Specifically, the cost of any item up to $400 is now deductible, and, if the average cost of all awards does not exceed that amount, an individual item costing up to $1,600 can be deducted.

Employees normally begin to receive recognition awards after five years of service. Beyond that, practice varies according to the age of the company, turnover experience, emphasis on seniority, and employee interest. A fairly common profile is to provide awards of progressively greater value at five-year intervals. The more traditional approach has been to limit gifts to jewelry items and to specify an item for each milestone. Some programs provide greater flexibility by including a variety of jewelry and household articles, travel vouchers, theater tickets, time-off allowances, and cash, with provisions for employee choice.

Surveys of employer views on award programs, conducted by manufacturers and wholesalers of the symbolic recognition items, tend to make the programs sound like panaceas. The satisfied customers cite "drop-in-the-bucket cost," "recognition from coworkers," "stronger company identification," "tie-in with family," and "a visible thank you from the employer" as reasons for giving service awards. The minority position is that senior employees may view the program as a form of tokenism and younger employees may perceive it to be crass paternalism.

Although the costs for service awards are relatively small, they have the potential for receiving either very high or very low ratings on the employee satisfier–dissatisfier scale. This suggests that program sponsors need to pay close attention to the appropriateness, quality, attractiveness, and utility of awards, and be alert to shifts in styles and preferences.

CHAPTER 8

Leading Edge Benefits

A leading edge benefit is defined here as one that is not yet standard but appears to have the potential for achieving that status by the end of this decade. There are no guarantees that the predictive part of this definition will be fulfilled, but clearly each of the benefits discussed in this chapter has already generated considerable interest among employees. Not every company can be expected to adopt all these benefits, so the challenge becomes one of picking the most appropriate ones for a particular organization. Fortunately, as flexible (cafeteria) benefits programs become more prevalent, employers will not have to shoulder that burden alone—employees will be making many of those decisions for themselves.

The most important leading edge benefits at the beginning of the 1980s are:

Dental benefits.
Vision care.
Prescription drug plans.
Dependent life insurance.
Adoption benefits.
Child care assistance.
Group legal services.

Financial counseling.

Flextime.

Flexible (cafeteria) benefits programs.

Dental Benefits

Among large organizations, a dental assistance plan is already a standard benefit, and rapid growth continues among small and medium-size companies. In 1965 only about 2 million people were covered by group dental plans. Today that figure is estimated to be 60 million, and by 1985 it is expected to reach 95 million. The principal reasons for this growth have been:

- Identification of dental assistance by the big unions in the early 1970s as the "next benefits frontier" beyond major medical insurance and supplementary unemployment benefits.
- Rapid success of these unions in gaining dental care benefits through negotiations, and the leadership of such firms as IBM and DuPont in adopting plans.
- Heightened public concern over dental disease.
- Technical advances that have made dental treatment progressively less painful.

SOURCES OF COVERAGE

The principal sources for obtaining a group dental plan are private insurance carriers, dental service corporations, and Blue Cross/Blue Shield organizations.

The insurance companies have gained a predominant position as providers of group dental benefits. This is undoubtedly due to their well-established role in covering other medical expense benefits. Most employers utilizing an insurance company for dental benefits tend to use the same carrier that handles their major medical coverage. In some companies, the two coverages are integrated, but in a majority of firms, the plans operate separately.

Dental service corporations, coordinated nationally through Delta Dental Plans Association, are sponsored by state dental societies. Participating dentists agree to render service under specified terms and conditions and to receive direct payments from the plan. The plans cover charges from nonparticipating dentists, but the benefits tend to be smaller. The "Blues" offer dental benefits in all states, in some cases in conjunction with a Delta plan.

In selecting an underwriter for a group dental plan, an employer should develop a list of critical questions to be answered by candidates. A good starting point would be the following basic set prepared by a benefits planning executive:[1]

1. Do you currently have enough profile information to enable your claims personnel to process claims adequately on a reasonable and customary basis?
2. If you were selected as an underwriter for our dental plan, how long would you be willing to guarantee rates?
3. What percentage of our employees would have to enroll to constitute an acceptable group?
4. How many offices do you have to process dental claims? Where are they located?
5. Will you permit us to design a specific plan with our exclusions and limitations, or must we accept those recommended by you?

COVERED SERVICES

Although dental care is a form of health care, the benefits structure in dental plans tends to be quite different from the traditional group medical plan design. The latter is oriented toward *treatment* and covers expenses incurred as a result of illnesses and injuries. For the most part, dental care is elective and of a nonemergency nature. However, neglect can lead to serious dental and medical problems with large long-term costs. Because of this, most dental plans stress *hygiene* by covering all or most of the costs for diagnostic and preventive services. Conversely, since orthodontic care is generally conceded to be a lower level health priority, many plans exclude this category entirely or provide very limited coverage.

The usual classification of services and levels of coverage in a model group dental plan today are:

Diagnostic services—routine oral examinations and X rays. These are usually covered fully without deductibles or coinsurance payments but subject to frequency limits.

---

[1] Richard A. Harvey, "Designing a Corporate Dental Plan," *Compensation Review* (3rd Quarter 1975).

Preventive services—cleaning and scaling, fluoride treatments, and space maintainers are normally covered on the same basis as diagnostic services.

Basic restorative services—fillings, inlays, crowns, removal of dental decay, and so on. Subject to specific limits on payment for the use of precious metals, these services are typically covered on a reasonable and customary charge basis. Quite often, a small deductible (for example, $25 per person) is applied. (These same conditions usually apply to oral surgery, endodontics, and periodontics.)

Oral surgery—generally excluding surgery required as the result of an accident. That would be covered under a major medical plan.

Endodontics—procedures used for prevention and treatment of diseases of the dental pulp, such as root canal work.

Periodontics—treatment of gums and other supporting structures of the teeth.

Prosthodontics—construction, replacement, and repair of dentures and bridgework. Many plans utilize a schedule or cover a smaller portion (for example, 50 percent) of reasonable and customary charges for these major and costly procedures.

Orthodontics—correction of malocclusion and abnormal tooth position. This coverage (when provided) is frequently restricted to dependent children, and the benefit level is similar to that for prosthodontics. It is also common to apply a lifetime maximum (for example, $1,000) per person.

OTHER PLAN DESIGN CONSIDERATIONS

The dental plans negotiated by the major unions in the early and mid-1970s did not require employee contributions, and that pattern has continued to prevail as denta' benefits expand throughout industry. In addition to wanting to be competitive with plans credited to union initiative, most employers have been influenced to sponsor noncontributory plans by the antiselection argument. These companies believe that when employees have to contribute to a dental plan, those who have neglected to care for their teeth join and quickly make maximum use of the plan. Conversely, those employees with good teeth tend to stay out of the plan because of the contribution requirement. This so-called antiselection phenomenon distorts the risk-spreading foundation of a group plan and puts upward pressure on costs.

Since employers typically do not require employee contributions, several other cost-control techniques are used in dental plans:

Deductibles are usually quite small (for example, $25 or $50) and not applicable to diagnostic and preventive services.

Coinsurance is achieved in most plans by payment of a specified percentage of reasonable and customary costs for various services. For example:

$$
\left.\begin{array}{l}
\text{Restorative services} \\
\text{Oral surgery} \\
\text{Endodontics}
\end{array}\right\} 80\%
$$

$$
\left.\begin{array}{l}
\text{Periodontics} \\
\text{Prosthodontics} \\
\text{Orthodontics}
\end{array}\right\} 50\%
$$

Annual maximums limit the plan's total annual liability on behalf of any one participant.

Lifetime maximums often are imposed on payments for particular services, such as orthodontics and periodontics.

Predetermination of benefits is a common requirement whenever dental fee quotations exceed a certain amount (for example, $100 or $150). The dentist and the patient are advised in advance of treatment what portion of the projected fee will be covered by the plan. This may result in a decision to proceed with a less costly alternative.

Waiting periods of six months or a year are utilized by some firms to guard against transient workers taking early and full advantage of dental benefits and then leaving. This may be a prudent safeguard in some industries, but it obviously detracts from the value of the benefit in recruiting efforts. It is not a common practice.

Vision Care

Vision care was secured as an employee benefit by the United Auto Workers (UAW) in their 1976 contracts with the major auto companies. This was heralded as another pattern-setting achievement for the UAW, but so far, the growth of vision care as a group benefit has been restricted mainly to the auto industry, some peripheral manufacturing companies, trucking, and parts of the public sector. Only 10 percent of major companies had such plans in 1981, according to the

Hay/Huggins Noncash Compensation Comparison.[2] Reasons for this relatively slow growth include the higher priority given to dental benefits, the constraints of the 1979–1980 federal pay guidelines, and the greater emphasis given to direct pay adjustments by both unions and employers in the late 1970s. However, with approximately half of the U.S. population over age 3 using corrective lenses, interest in this benefit is bound to accelerate.

Vision care plans are almost universally noncontributory, and typically they cover eye examinations, corrective lenses, and frames. But, because many choices available to employees involve fashion and cosmetic considerations, several forms of cost controls are built into most plans. As shown in Table 9, design features used to limit costs include scheduled cash allowances, coinsurance percentages, frequency limits, deductibles, and maximum benefits. The standards for "medically required" contact lenses are usually related to post-cataract surgery and/or the restoration of 20/70 visual acuity. Extra costs for tinted lenses, photosensitive lenses, and oversized frames are normally excluded from group plan coverage.

Prescription Drug Plans

A substantial majority of employers cover prescription drug expenses under their group hospital and major medical plans. When administered during hospital confinement, the full cost of medicines is absorbed by the basic plan; otherwise, payment is subject to the deductible and coinsurance provisions of the major medical plan.

The alternative concept of prepaid prescription drug plans gained national attention in 1967 when the UAW negotiated this benefit with the major auto and farm implement companies. The strong attraction of these plans for employees is the absence of the relatively high (for example, $100) deductible used in major medical plans. A prototype prescription plan will cover the full cost of an individual prescription (and insulin purchases) after the employee or dependent pays the first $1–3. In many cases, there are no limits on the frequency or number of prescriptions covered. In some plans, however, benefits vary depending on whether the order is filled by a participat-

[2] The Hay Group, Philadelphia, Pennsylvania.

Table 9. Typical plan features in vision care plans, 1982.

Coverage	Plan A *Office Employees*	Plan B *Office and Nonoffice Employees*	Plan C *Nonoffice Employees*	Plan D *Office and Nonoffice Employees*
Eye examination	*Biennial* $35 maximum allowance	*Annual* 100% of reasonable and customary charges ($5 deductible)	*Annual* 80% of reasonable and customary charges	*Annual* $25 maximum allowance
Lenses Single	*Annual (2 Lenses)* $9 each	*Annual (2 lenses)* 100% of reasonable and customary charges	*Biennial (4 lenses)* 80% of reasonable and customary charges	*Annual (2 lenses)* $15 each
Bifocal	$16 each	Same as above	Same as above	$25 each
Trifocal	$21 each	Same as above	Same as above	$35 each
Contact lenses Medically required	*Annual* $150 each	*Biennial* $200 total	*Biennial* 80% of reasonable and customary charges	*Annual* $100 total
Not medically required	Not covered	$100 total	Not covered	Not covered
Frames	*Biennial* $25	*Biennial* 100% of reasonable and customary charges ($5 deductible on lenses and frames)	*Biennial* 80% of reasonable and customary charges	*Annual* $15

ing or nonparticipating pharmacy. Such arrangements are common in plans offered by Blue Cross/Blue Shield associations. Participating pharmacies contractually agree to accept specified payments from the association, and the subscriber pays only the small deductible amount. Claims for purchases from nonparticipating pharmacies must be submitted to Blue Cross/Blue Shield for reimbursement.

Payment is then normally 75 percent of the charge in excess of the deductible. Similar features are included in plans underwritten by insurance companies and specialized service organizations, such as Pharmaceutical Card System, Inc., a national firm headquartered in Phoenix, Arizona.

Employers who have adopted prescription drug plans tend to believe that they are at least as cost-effective as having prescription costs covered under a major medical plan. They mention the leverage that the plans exert on pharmacists' charges plus the desirability of encouraging outpatient drug therapy as an alternative to more costly hospital confinement and extended absences. There is also a sense that employees view prepaid prescriptions as a particularly useful benefit. Their needs may range from antibiotics for treating an infection to daily doses of insulin, but inevitably most employees will utilize plan benefits and appreciate the fact that they are saving money.

Dependent Life Insurance

When the workforce was dominated by the married male breadwinner with a wife at home caring for their children, the need for dependent life insurance was quite apparent. While the husband was covered by employee group term life insurance, the nonworking wife was not, and, despite importunate efforts by the insurance industry, in many instances she had no personal life insurance coverage either.

The idea of dependent life insurance responded to the need for protection against burial expenses if a noninsured spouse should die suddenly during the survivor's active working years. It was generally presumed that the surviving spouse (husband) would not be able to save for such a contingency, and the associated expenses would create a hardship for him. On the basis of these premises, a relatively small number of firms offer modest levels of coverage, usually on an employee-pay-all or contributory basis.

A typical dependent life insurance plan covers a spouse for $2,000 and dependent children on an age-based scale reaching a maximum of $1,000 at about age 5. Some plans specify the spouse's death benefit at 50 percent of the employee's group term life coverage, with a maximum that rarely exceeds $5,000. A number of states restrict the amount of this benefit, and the Internal Revenue Code has noted that a benefit of more than $2,000 on a spouse or child may cease to be "incidental" when determining the tax treatment to the employee of employer contributions.

With half of all married women now working, and probably covered by group term life insurance plans, it would seem that interest in dependent life insurance should be declining. However, the incidence of this benefit increased markedly during the 1970s, according to the previously cited Conference Board studies:[3]

	Percentage of companies offering dependent life insurance	
Category	*1973*	*1980*
Office employees	15	25
Nonoffice employees	11	21

Although this may not be a benefit for everyone, it continues to answer a need for a significant number of employees. As long as employees pay at least half of the cost, employers should be willing to offer it as an elective benefit.

Adoption Benefits

Adoption benefits are an excellent example of employer initiative in meeting unique needs of employees. In 1972 IBM introduced an Adoption Assistance Program that according to Harold P. Kneen, Jr., director of employee benefits, filled a perceived void:

> We were already assisting in the medical expenses associated with childbirth when an employee's family is enlarged in that way, yet provided no assistance to those families where the family was enlarged through adoption. Use of the program is by under one percent of the population, but it does provide meaningful assistance and a degree of equity.[4]

Currently, the IBM plan reimburses employees for 80 percent of legal, court, and agency charges and pregnancy expenses for the natural mother, with an overall maximum of $1,000 per adoption. Similar

[3] *Profile of Employee Benefits* (1974 and 1981).

[4] *Rethinking Employee Benefits Assumptions* (New York: The Conference Board, 1978).

plans have been installed by Xerox, S. C. Johnson, Pitney Bowes, Hallmark, and many pharmaceuticals companies. Most plans pay benefits upon final adoption out of general assets, and since many allowances are taxable income to the employee, taxes are withheld.

In addition to covering adoptions of newborns and other young children, many plans reimburse employees for costs associated with adopting a spouse's natural children from a previous marriage.

This is a relatively low-cost benefit that is not apt to be utilized by very many employees or used frequently by those who do. Certainly, subject to maintaining control on maximum allowances for each adoption, it should be an easily affordable benefit in most firms. Considering the tremendous employee goodwill that most plan sponsors have reported, the best answer to the question "Why have an adoption benefits plan?" seems to be "Why not?"

Child Care Assistance

"By 1990 you'll see the child care benefit as often as you see group medical insurance today."[5] This is a daring prediction, perhaps intended to be self-fulfilling since it comes from a child care industry executive. Nonetheless, employers need to be aware of the growing need within their workforces for this assistance. For many years, the stereotype of the working woman had been a cycle of work until marriage, leave the workforce to raise a family, and return to work when the children are self-sufficient. Now nearly half of all mothers of children under age 6 are working. With their husbands also working— and parents living far away or working too—these women have a critical need for child care assistance, in terms of both adequate and convenient facilities and financial aid. The problem is not strictly a woman's problem either, as the award-winning movie *Kramer vs Kramer* demonstrated so effectively.[6]

[5] Richard J. Grassgreen, executive vice president, Kinder-Care Learning Centers, Inc., Montgomery, Alabama. Cited in *Business Week* (December 21, 1981).

[6] A report, "Families at Work: Strengths and Strains," conducted for General Mills in 1980–1981 by Louis Harris and Associates, provides useful insights into various views on how benefits might help employees balance family and work responsibilities.

As of 1981, according to the U.S. Department of Health and Human Services, only 160 companies, unions, and government agencies provided child care assistance. One such program is operated by Corning Glass Works at Corning, New York. Aided by a start-up grant from the company-sponsored foundation, a child care center is operated for preschool children in a church across the street from the main plant. Employees with children in the center pay about two-thirds of the operating costs—a bargain compared with fees of commercial day-care facilities.

Obviously, employees benefit from company-provided or -subsidized child care assistance, and a 1981 federal tax code revision made the benefits nontaxable. Although there is not yet much data to support the contention, sponsors of child care centers claim that such centers help to reduce absenteeism and turnover, particularly in organizations with a high percentage of female workers. Even if this were not the case, employers should consider the view of Amory Houghton, Jr., chairman of the board of Corning Glass Works: "It's the right thing to do. It's one of those little pockets of excellence which corporations are judged by."[7]

Group Legal Services

The American Bar Association has pointed out that 70 percent of Americans lack adequate legal representation. That portion of the population consists mainly of the middle-income working class, since it is generally conceded that the wealthy can afford specialized legal services and the unemployed have access to Legal Aid Societies. This suggests that employees should have a strong interest in employer-subsidized group legal plans; yet to date, this benefit has been adopted by barely 1 percent of major employers.[8]

The failure of group legal services to catch on as a fast-track new benefit in the late 1970s was surprising for two reasons. First, the Tax Reform Act of 1976 provided a tax incentive. Both employer contributions to a group plan and benefits received by employees through a plan were exempt from federal income tax. These exemptions were scheduled to expire at the end of 1981, but the Economic Recovery

[7] *Business Week* (December 21, 1981).
[8] *Hay/Huggins Bulletin,* September 1981.

Tax Act in that year extended the provisions through 1984. Second, the UAW negotiated a legal services plan with Chrysler covering 140,000 active and retired workers that many benefits authorities expected to be a pattern setter. But because of a long delay in issuance of IRS regulations, restrictive state regulations, lack of strong support from the legal profession, apparent apathy from the insurance industry, and the reasons previously stated in relation to vision care benefits, group legal services have grown very slowly as an employee benefit. Still, as consumer awareness and litigious attitudes become more evident, expansion of this benefit seems inevitable.

Under present tax law, a group legal plan qualifies for favorable tax treatment whether it is funded by an insurance company, by a legal service group, or through a self-funded trust. There are two basic models for group legal services. A *closed panel* plan is based on a group of lawyers or law firms contracting with an employer to provide specified legal services to employees for prepaid fees. An *open panel* plan allows an employee to choose any attorney for covered services. The employee pays the attorney's fees and then submits a claim for reimbursement under the plan. Benefits under either model may be limited by scheduled maximum hours or costs for specific services, deductibles, and/or coinsurance ratios.

Most group legal plans provide a limited amount of telephone consultations and office time of an exploratory nature to determine the extent, if any, of legal problems. Such contacts frequently involve prospective review of contracts, leases, sales agreements, and other documents and may serve to prevent future time-consuming complications. Some of the legal services covered under a typical group plan are:

Simple wills and trusts.
Real estate transactions.
Landlord–tenant disputes.
Divorce.
Adoption.
Bankruptcy proceedings.
Defense in traffic cases that could result in loss or suspension of licenses.
Legal defense in criminal and civil actions.

Normally excluded from plan coverage are:

Actions involving the employer.

Class actions.

Actions relating to an outside business or profession.

Routine tax matters.

A 1977 Supreme Court decision (*Bates* v. *State Bar of Arizona*) opened the door for lawyers to advertise their services. Employee awareness of the need for legal representation undoubtedly will be stimulated as firms such as Jacoby & Meyers engage in direct promotion to the public in certain states, including New York, New Jersey, and California. Interest in group plans is bound to follow. Assuming that this benefit continues to receive favorable tax treatment, it could easily become a standard benefit by 1990.

Financial Counseling

With increased flexibility in the design of benefits plans comes greater complexity. Twenty years ago, the employer made virtually all decisions and the employee had very little choice of options. Today an average employee has to weigh the advantages and disadvantages of starting an individual retirement account, participating in an employee savings plan or contributory profit sharing plan, investing in the various accounts available in capital accumulation plans, and electing deferred or current distribution from such plans. Participants in cafeteria benefits programs have even more choices to make.

Decisions in these matters tend to be interrelated, with a variety of personal financial considerations. Many companies have traditionally offered financial counseling as a perquisite for executives, and a session on financial planning is a standard component of most preretirement programs. But until recently, very little attention was given to the needs of all employees.

During the late 1970s, a few companies, notably Gulf & Western, Braniff, Transamerica Corp., and the Electric Boat Division of General Dynamics Corp., began offering personal financial planning programs to employees on a group basis. One packaged course used by several of these firms is marketed by Manufacturers Hanover Trust Company (New York City), which also offers the program to its own employees under their tuition-refund plan. It is a six-lesson home study course that covers: investments; employment benefits; building a financial foundation; taxes, gifts, and jointly held property; trusts and wills; and plans and prospects. Each participant receives a computerized financial analysis statement based on responses to a confidential questionnaire and is assigned to a program administrator who can be contacted, by phone or letter, to answer questions or to resolve problems. As of early 1982, the group rate for this program was $95 per enrollee.

In a column on group financial counseling in *Newsweek* (March 12, 1979), Jane Bryant Quinn challenged employers with the comment: "Every company president who gets help with his own finances should think about the troops in the trenches and let this benefit trickle down to them."

Considering the universal applicability, high visibility, and relatively low cost of this benefit, it seems to be assured of significant growth—resulting from grass-roots efforts if not from trickle-down largess.

Flextime

As mentioned in Chapter 1, flextime (also called flexitime, gliding work time, or flexible work hours) is a no-cost consideration for employers that can produce meaningful benefits for employees. The key element in installing flextime is the shift in control over work time away from management to employees. While management retains the final word and establishes the time structure, rank-and-file workers gain some of the freedom once reserved for managers and professionals. Exhibit 18 depicts a typical flextime arrangement.

Although only 16 percent of the labor force was reported as being on flextime in 1981,[9] it is likely that this percentage is unrealistically low because of difficulties in classifying programs and differences in terminology. Also, there is little doubt that the concept is spreading rapidly, as such major employers as Control Data, Prudential, Metropolitan Life Insurance Company, Scott Paper, Gulf Oil, Hewlett-Packard, and the Social Security Administration have adopted programs within the past ten years.

For employees, flextime permits rearrangement of work hours to

[9] John Perham, "The New Corporate Goodies," *Dun's Review* (July 1981).

Exhibit 18. Typical flextime model.

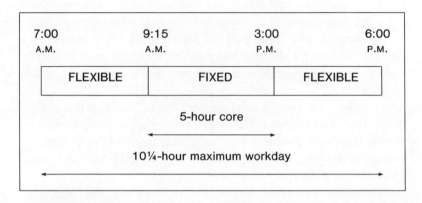

7:00 A.M.	9:15 A.M.	3:00 P.M.	6:00 P.M.
FLEXIBLE	FIXED	FLEXIBLE	

5-hour core

10¼-hour maximum workday

1. Under the schedule outlined above, an employee may start work any time between 7:00 and 9:15 A.M. and stop work between 3:00 and 6:00 P.M. These hours are called the flexible work hours. The minimum that an employee may work is 5 hours in any one day, and those 5 hours are the "core day" (the fixed hours) of 9:15 A.M. to 3:00 P.M.
2. The flexible work hour preferences of employees will be subject to work requirements of the department and to the approval of the immediate supervisor.
3. Although starting and quitting times are flexible, employees work a 40-hour, five-day (at least 5 hours a day) week.
4. The lunch period (45 minutes) is not flexible.
5. Hours worked in excess of 40 in a week may not be "banked" for a following week.

meet family requirements, schedule personal appointments, and handle emergency situations without necessarily losing pay. Employers maintain that tardiness is reduced when employees are no longer required to meet a rigid starting time. Absenteeism declines because employees do not call in "sick" to avoid reprimands for losing time because of personal reasons. Some companies believe that productivity increases under flextime, but the reasons for this are not yet clear. Theories are evolving that it is probably due to a combination of employees selecting work hours that coincide with their most alert and efficient periods (for example, "morning people" versus "evening people"); the assurance of full staffing during core time; and a "Hawthorne effect" (that is, positive reactions to a sign of employer interest in the individual worker).

Firms subject to the Walsh-Healey Act, which requires that certain employees be paid at a time-and-one-half rate for all hours worked in excess of 8 in a 24-hour period, are somewhat limited in using flextime. However, the requirement does not apply to exempt (or to all nonexempt employees) in these firms, and proposals are currently being formulated to amend the act to permit greater flexibility in weekly work schedules without penalty or premium pay requirements.

Flexible Benefits Programs

The concept of a benefits program in which employees are given freedom to select the types and levels of coverage that best fit their individual needs is not new. A detailed description of how such a program might be designed was the subject of a 1970 article entitled "The Employee Benefit Smorgasbord: Its Potential and Limitations."[10] The first edition of this book, published in 1972, referred to the "recent development of the 'cafeteria' or 'buffet' program in which the employee has a 'meal ticket.' " (With these kinds of metaphors, it is a wonder that most employees did not conclude that the programs were just a form of food service!)

When TRW and Educational Testing Service (ETS) launched flexible benefits programs in 1974, many observers predicted that other large companies would rush to get on the bandwagon. However, the tax laws at that time imposed some limitations, and employers were concerned about antiselection, administrative complexities, and the consequences of employees making "wrong" decisions. During the past few years, each of these impediments to growth has been removed or minimized. It now appears that a major movement toward flexible benefits is under way.

REMOVING OBSTACLES

Initially, cafeteria benefits programs were inhibited by the tax doctrine of constructive receipt. That doctrine had held that if an employee could choose between a taxable benefit (for example, cash) and a nontaxable benefit and chose the nontaxable benefit, he or she could be taxed as if the taxable benefit had been selected. The Reve-

---

[10] L. M. Baytos, *Compensation Review* (1st Quarter 1970).

nue Act of 1978 and the Miscellaneous Revenue Act of 1980 eliminated this tax application for flexible benefits programs.

Antiselection (or adverse selection) is a risk/insurance management
concept based on the assumption that people select coverages that
they are most likely to use. Because employees who know they have
serious illnesses are apt to select high levels of group life insurance
coverage and those whose children have lots of cavities in their teeth
will surely opt for dependent dental care coverage, plan costs can be
adversely impacted under a cafeteria plan. A totally altruistic employer might take the view that this is what benefits are for, but a
more pragmatic approach is to place some limitations or restrictions
on employee choices. Some of the ways in which employers have tried
to control the effects of antiselection in flexible benefits programs are
to:

○ Combine coverages such as dental and vision.
○ Require a medical examination whenever an employee (or dependent) elects to increase group life insurance coverage.
○ Use age-related insurance rate tables rather than uniform rates to
  allocate costs.
○ Provide core-level coverage through employer contributions;
  offer supplementary coverage on an employee-pay-all basis.

The administrative complexity of flexible benefits programs cannot
be minimized. When American Can Company tested its program in
1978 on 700 employees of their consumer towel and tissue division, it
was necessary to develop a complex data processing system capable of
handling 10,000 different benefits plans. However, automated employee information systems are now common in large companies.
Small firms can utilize time-sharing options on computers and obtain
packaged software systems to meet their needs.

Also essential to the development and operation of a cafeteria benefits plan are the detailed planning and review that must be handled
by specialists in law, taxes, insurance, finance, and employee communications. Fortunately, a number of consulting firms, especially
Hewitt Associates, Lincolnshire, Illinois, have gained expertise in all
aspects of these programs and can save clients the agony of starting
from scratch. Another potential resource for information is The Employers Council on Flexible Compensation in Washington, D.C.,
which is a membership-by-invitation organization.

The "wrong choice" argument against flexible benefits programs should not be too difficult to deal with from a legal standpoint. The key is making sure that employees receive accurate and adequate information and have sufficient time to make informed decisions. It is advisable to have employees sign a statement acknowledging these points and the fact that the election of benefits for the designated period is irrevocable. What many employers fear though is the bad press that results from such situations as when the long-service employee becomes disabled and receives a minimum weekly income replacement benefit from the company. The reason for the small payment could be that the employee chose more life insurance or vacation time under a flexible program, but the employee and coworkers might still blame the company. Such reactions probably cannot be avoided entirely, but certainly they can be minimized by effective communications that stress individual responsibility.

TYPES OF PLANS

There are three basic models for flexible benefits programs:

Core type (carve-out method).
Participant option (opt-up/opt-down).
Additional allowance type (add-on).

American Can Company's program is an example of a core-type plan. As illustrated in Exhibit 19, a core was carved out of the pre-flexible program and flexible credits were created for each employee by reducing certain coverages. For example, credits were generated by introducing a Social Security offset in the calculation of pension benefits, raising the medical plan deductibles, lowering the standard amount of group life insurance, eliminating dental insurance, and lowering the long-term disability benefit. With the exception of the pension plan, employees had the option of using their flexible credits to recreate their pre-flexible coverage. However, they had many other options, and in the original pilot phase, only 14 percent of the participants elected to preserve the status quo.

TRW Systems Group, based in Redondo Beach, California, has a participant option type of program with many levels of choice in the categories of life insurance and hospital and medical insurance. There is also a provision for dependent life insurance. A participant may elect an "average" level of coverage without contribution. If "liberal" coverage is chosen, the employee contributes through payroll deduc-

Exhibit 19.   Concept for flexible benefits program.

The concept

The idea behind flexible benefits is very simple: it reflects our belief that each individual should have the ability to choose the benefits that are most meaningful to him or her. Under flexible benefits, you'll have a basic foundation—or core—of coverage and an allowance to use in putting together your own benefit program around that core.

The Development of Flexible Benefits

Think of our pre-flexible benefit program (the program we had before flexible benefits) as a circle divided into five parts—medical benefits, life insurance benefits, vacation, disability, and retirement and capital accumulation benefits. Over the past few decades, we worked hard to build a benefit program that stands among the best available in industry today. The trouble is, no one program—however rich—can ever meet everyone's needs equally well. People are too different for that.

Now, picture an inner circle of benefits which we'll call the core. This core area represents fundamental protection that can't be changed under the flexible benefits system. It's a basic foundation of security for all employees—security no one can opt out of.

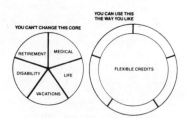

How Flexible Credits are Figured

The difference between the core and your pre-flexible benefits is transformed by insurance and actuarial calculations into flexible credits which are allocated to you in dollars. You can then use those dollars for benefit options. With them, you can build your own benefit program around the core. The amount of flexible credits you are allotted will vary from year to year. That's because they depend on your particular age, pay, family status, and years of service with the company. You'll be given your flexible credit allowance on the form you use to make your benefit option decisions. This same principle holds even if you joined us without having ever been covered by the pre-flexible program. Your flexible credit allowance will be figured the same way.

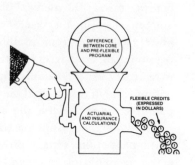

Source: American Can Company.

tion. If "conservative" coverage is opted, the employee may receive cash, which of course is taxable in the year received.

The Educational Testing Service program typifies the additional allowance alternative. Flexible credits are calculated each year on the basis of an employee's salary and years of service. The employee may elect additional benefits in a variety of areas, including life insurance, dental care, annual physical examination, additional vacation, educational subsidies, mutual fund investments, and cash. These add-ons may be obtained through use of the flexible credits, salary deduction, or both.

EMPLOYER INTEREST

In addition to finding that the earlier obstacles are no longer insurmountable, employers have discovered many positive features in flexible benefits programs. One company has said it is interested in setting up a program because of a desire to change employee perceptions from "What have you done for me lately?" to "How can I best spend the money you make available to me?"

Other advantages and objectives cited by firms with, or planning for, programs are:

○ Better able to meet benefits needs of employees.
○ Participants become more aware of benefits costs and values by exercising options.
○ A way to break the lockstep relationship between negotiated benefits and benefits for nonunion employees.
○ Permit addition of coverages, especially special-purpose benefits, with minimal cost.
○ Reintroduce employee contributions for benefits on a selective basis.
○ Responsive to two-career marriages where both spouses were paying for coverages that were not fully usable; now provision of benefits can be coordinated.
○ A distinctive recruitment attraction.

FUTURE OF FLEXIBLE BENEFITS

In the study "Families at Work: Strengths and Strains,"[11] a sample of working men and women was asked: "Would it help you and your

[11] Louis Harris and Associates, 1980–1981.

family a great deal, somewhat, hardly at all, or not at all to have the freedom to pick and choose the employment benefits that are best for your family's needs?" Of the 1,503 respondents, 50 percent said "a great deal" and another 24 percent replied "somewhat." In the same study, a group of human resources officers was asked how much each thought freedom to pick and choose benefits would help employees and their families. Among 104 who responded to the questionnaire, 33 percent said "a great deal" and 44 percent indicated "somewhat"; 70 percent of this latter group said that their organization was most likely to adopt such a program within the next five years (that is, by 1985–1986).

Not all companies can be expected to install programs as complex and ambitious as those now in place at TRW, ETS, and American Can Company. Some may achieve the goal of increased flexibility by simply building additional options into existing plans. An outstanding example of this was the approach taken by Honeywell in 1982. The Minneapolis-based company designed an IRA-type retirement savings plan to accept tax-deductible employee contributions of up to $2,000 a year. At the same time, it also designated 4 percent of each employee's pay as "pay conversion contributions" to the plan. In accordance with Section 401(k) of the Internal Revenue Code, this effectively reduced employees' taxable income by that percentage. However, employees could elect to take back all or any part of the conversion dollars as pay (subject to taxes). The savings plan offers three choices of investment funds.

Another approach is the "Bene-Trade" option designed by the Marriott Corporation. This program allows employees to trade a portion of their unused sick leave and/or vacation to help pay their contributions to medical, dental, and disability plans.

Whichever direction employers decide to take, it appears that monolithic benefits programs will become a dinosaur in the 1980s. Employees are nearing the point of demanding flexibility, and perceptive employers now recognize that a program offering choices within stated limits is a sensible and cost-effective response. Given those realities, substantial changes in the design of employee benefits plans and programs seems imminent.

CHAPTER 9

Costs: The Other Side
of the Coin

The success of a company's employee benefits program is largely dependent on satisfying employees' needs and meeting the employer's goals. In measuring program performance, the primary emphasis is on benefits provided through the various plans. But inevitably attention turns to the other side of the coin—namely, costs. Top management must have information on the costs of benefits for use in planning, budgeting, and reporting to employees and stockholders, and for evaluation of any proposal to adopt or liberalize a particular benefit. Supervisors and personnel representatives need data on the costs of benefits for carrying out their employee communications responsibilities. Under ERISA, employees must be given summary annual reports, with cost information on all covered pension and welfare plans in which they participate. Unions have been given rights to obtain information on employer costs for benefits through the Labor Management Relations Act.

In recent years, the soaring costs of health care have caused employers to focus special attention on this component of group benefits. In particular, companies with noncontributory plans have been searching for new ways to contain costs. Initiatives aimed at improving health and preventing illness, such as fitness programs and periodic examinations, have been favorably received by employees. But some other efforts, such as the insertion in the United Mine Workers health care plan in 1977 of a 40 percent employee payment requirement, up to a family maximum of $500 per year, have triggered strikes and other negative reactions.

Obviously, dealing with costs is an integral part of managing employee benefits. It is essential to know what they are, how they interrelate with direct compensation, how to express them meaningfully, and how to control them effectively. A caveat for benefits managers though is to be careful not to undermine employee satisfaction with benefits by overemphasizing cost control. Cost-effectiveness is a desirable objective; cost-obsessiveness can be counterproductive.

Relationship to Direct Compensation

Some management people take the view that employees should not be concerned about the company's costs for benefits. They say, "After all, isn't it the value to the individual that counts? What difference does it make to employees if our firm can set up a pension plan for less money than some other outfit?"

What matters to employees is that they now consider benefits as part of their total compensation, and indeed employers have cultivated this view. One major company even describes its program as "Your Benefit Pay." However, unlike the costs for wages and salaries, which are displayed on each paycheck stub, the costs of benefits are not always decipherable on an individual basis, and if management appears to be evading the issue of benefits costs, the credibility of the total compensation program is certain to suffer.

Some of the ways in which employers provide employees with individual accounting of benefits expenditures are:

Paycheck stubs that provide details on the amount and cost of paid time off on a current and year-to-date basis.

Personalized benefits reports that compare employee and employer costs. For example:

A. This year's estimated total cost for the employee benefits the company makes available for you and your family is [$15,000].

B. Your contribution to the cost of these benefits, including your share of Social Security, was [$2,500].

C. The company's costs for your benefits was [$12,500].

Periodic statements of amounts contributed by the company to individual account plans (for example, savings plans, profit sharing, money purchase plans).

Payroll inserts and other reminders of mandatory employer payments for Social Security, unemployment compensation insurance (UCI), and (where applicable) temporary disability benefits (TDB), which are based on individual rates.

In addition to automatically providing benefits plan participants with summary annual reports containing cost information, employers are required by ERISA to make available on request the full reports filed with the federal government. These complete reports reveal considerable detail about such items as expenditures, investment earnings, dividends, retroactive rate refunds, and reserves. Although it is not easy for an employee to translate this kind of information into paycheck language, there is at least assurance that company money is being spent in the employee's behalf.

In relating the costs of benefits to direct compensation, whether for employee communications or expense analysis purposes, it is important to distinguish between inside-payroll and outside-payroll items. The former are those benefits described in Chapter 5 and classified as "the hidden payroll." Paid vacations, holidays, sick leave, personal days, and rest periods share a dual identity; they are benefits that are included in pay. For communications purposes, it is critical to recognize this duality, since it would be inaccurate to tell employees that the total amount of company payments for benefits was in addition to salary. To illustrate this point:

Chris Wallace is a systems engineer for Progress Unlimited Corporation earning $36,000 a year. The company spends $12,000 on benefits for Chris, of which $4,000 is for inside-payroll items. The ratio of benefits expenditures to salary is 1 to 3, or 33⅓ percent ($12,000 to $36,000). However, since $4,000 is already included in the salary, the cost of total compensation is $44,000. This can be arrived at in either of two ways:

1. Pay for time worked ($32,000) + pay for time not worked ($4,000) + cost of outside payroll benefits ($8,000) = $44,000.
2. Salary ($36,000) + cost of outside-payroll benefits ($8,000) = $44,000.

Outside-payroll benefits of course include all the statutory and private programs and plans into which the employer makes payments on behalf of employees and dependents. Clearly, these are adders to direct pay and should be included in total compensation.

In analyzing benefits costs, it is useful to recognize the effect on benefits of any increase in base pay. Additional benefits costs resulting from base-pay increases are called roll-up costs. Costs of inside-payroll benefits roll up automatically with pay adjustments, but it should be noted that employees receiving identical pay increases can be affected quite differently. For example, assume that a company providing ten holidays and one to five weeks' vacation per year according to seniority grants a general wage increase of 50 cents an hour. For a relatively new employee, the roll-up cost for these benefits would be $60 a year (10 holidays + 5 vacation days × 8 hours × 50 cents). For a long-service employee, the cost would be $140 a year (10 holidays + 25 vacation days × 8 hours × 50 cents). The two employees might not perceive this cost differential, but an employer should analyze and evaluate the full impact of a general pay increase on the costs of benefits before committing to any change in compensation. The roll-up costs might suggest a need to look at alternatives.

Outside-payroll costs that are tied to pay include payroll taxes for FICA, UCI, and TDB; lump-sum separation allowances; profit sharing and savings plan contributions; pension benefit accruals; and many group life insurance plans. Generally unrelated to wages and salaries are the costs of health insurance, educational assistance, suggestion plan awards, free or discounted products, and most employee services.

Comparing Benefits Costs

Anyone who has ever been involved in a wage or salary survey appreciates the importance of job comparability. To paraphrase Gertrude Stein, "A product manager is not necessarily a product manager, is not necessarily a product manager, . . ." Identical titles are no guarantee of comparability. It is essential for participants in a survey to compare job content carefully. Traditionally, surveys of benefits costs have been more difficult to administer and comprehend because of different concepts of what should be included and how costs should be expressed. For example, Company X classifies overtime and shift premium pay as a benefit and analyzes its increase in benefits from one year to the next, as shown in Table 10. On the basis of this infor-

Table 10. Increase in base pay and benefits over one-year period.

Company Costs	1981	1982
Base Pay	$1,000,000	$1,150,000
Benefits		
Overtime and premium pay	50,000	180,000
Legally required	100,000	115,000
Employer programs	200,000	230,000
Total	$ 350,000	$ 525,000

mation and the classification of overtime and premium pay as a form of benefit, Company X would claim that its cost of benefits had risen 50 percent in one year—three and a third times the rate of increase in base pay. The ratio of benefits costs to base pay would have increased from 35 to 46 percent.

Since overtime and premium pay are considerations for time worked, most employers do not consider them benefits. They recognize these payments as costs to the company for scheduling added work, and they group them with wages and salaries. Therefore, a more typical analysis of Company X's benefits costs is given in Table 11. Using the more acceptable measurements, benefits costs rose 15 percent, compared with a 27 percent increase in payroll costs. The ratio of benefits costs to payroll costs actually decreased from 29 to 26 percent.

Another contributor to inflated quotations of benefits costs is the kitchen-sink approach to compiling information. Such items as parking lots, space for a credit union, shoe-polishing machines in executive washrooms, reading-rack booklets, umbrellas for rainy days, and company newspapers all may be helpful to some employees, but they

Table 11. Adjusted increase in payroll costs and benefits over one-year period.

Company Costs	1981	1982
Base pay	$1,000,000	$1,150,000
Overtime and premium pay	50,000	180,000
Gross Payroll Costs	$1,050,000	$1,330,000
Benefits		
Legally required	100,000	115,000
Employer programs	200,000	230,000
Total	$ 300,000	$ 345,000

seem marginal for inclusion in any summary of cost of benefits. Most surveys of benefits exclude such items. If employees thought that their company was taking credit for them as benefits costs, they would be very doubtful of survey comparisons with other companies.

To ensure use of a common language, and a high degree of standardization and continuity, many industry groups and area associations have adopted the survey format used by the Chamber of Commerce of the United States (CCUS). Unquestionably, the CCUS studies, which began in 1947, are the most widely used and frequently quoted source of information on benefits costs for private industry. Originally published biennially, the reports have been issued on an annual basis since 1977. Data from approximately 1,000 reporting companies are arranged according to industry group, geographic region, and company size. The categorization of included benefits was shown in Chapter 1. An important point to note for companies using the CCUS results for comparative purposes is that the data are, in general, limited to employees who are *not* exempt from the overtime provisions of the Fair Labor Standards Act. However, for banks and financial institutions, all nonsupervisory employees and working supervisors are included, regardless of their method of wage payment.

Ways of Expressing Costs

There are six commonly used ways of expressing the cost of benefits: total annual cost, percentage of payroll, average cost per employee per year, average cents per hour, actual cost for each employee, and employer–employee cost ratio.

TOTAL ANNUAL COST

Total annual cost is the basic summary figure from which other forms of expression are derived. The information for an annual report of benefits costs is available from standard payroll and accounting records.

Exhibit 20 is an example of a statement prepared by an accounting department according to personnel department specifications. Most of the benefits are available to all classifications of employees, but if separate reports are needed for hourly and salaried employees, relocation expenses might be eliminated from the former's analysis and

Exhibit 20. Example of statement of total compensation and benefits costs for 1,500 employees for one calendar year.

Benefit	Company Costs	Totals
Social insurance payments		
Social Security taxes	$1,500,000	
Unemployment insurance	380,000	
Workers' compensation	370,000	$ 2,250,000
Private health and security plans		
Group insurance premiums	$1,250,000	
Disability plan	175,000	
Retirement plan	1,750,000	
Savings plan	375,000	3,550,000
Pay for time not worked		
Vacations	$1,250,000	
Holidays	875,000	
Sick pay	300,000	
Personal absence	250,000	
Severance pay	125,000	
Rest periods and wash-up time	625,000	3,425,000
Extra payments		
Suggestion awards	$ 50,000	
Educational assistance	25,000	
Relocation expenses	160,000	
Service awards	15,000	250,000
Employee services		
Cafeteria subsidy	$ 150,000	
Products discounts	45,000	
Recreation programs	50,000	
Medical services	55,000	300,000
Total cost of benefits		$ 9,775,000
Total payroll (exclusive of pay for time not worked and salary expenses included in cafeteria subsidy and medical expenses)		21,400,000
Total compensation		$31,175,000

(*continued on next page*)

Exhibit 20.   Continued.

Reconciliation to salary and wage payments	
Pay for time not worked	$ 3,425,000
Cafeteria subsidy (salary expense)	125,000
Medical services (salary expense)	50,000
Total payroll (exclusive of above)	21,400,000
Total payroll	$25,000,000*

* Includes overtime and shift premiums totaling $1.5 million.

wash-up time deleted from the latter's. Also, if the company wants to analyze benefits for outside sales representatives, it should exclude rest periods, wash-up time, cafeteria subsidy, and recreation programs. In this case, allowances peculiar to sales personnel—sales bonuses, company cars, or expense accounts—should be added.

The total annual cost is an important figure to the benefits manager, who is accountable for performance against the current year's budget and for the following year's plan. Top management also wants benefits expenses expressed in this way so that the data will conform to other types of business expenses for financial analysis and planning purposes. Although they are not concerned with all the details, boards of directors and stockholders want to know the total cost of benefits, for they too recognize that there is more to employee compensation than wages and salaries.

Total annual cost is probably the most impressive statistic for broad publicity purposes during and after union negotiations and for general recruiting literature. For example: "Employees of XYZ company now receive more than $10 million in benefits on top of outstanding wages and salaries," or "Contract settlement reached; wage and benefit increases to cost company $3 million over next two years," or "Our company spent $25 million last year for employee benefits and services."

PERCENTAGE OF PAYROLL

Percentage of payroll is normally calculated by dividing the total cost of benefits by total payroll. Using the data in Exhibit 20, the applicable percentage would be 39.1 percent:

$$\frac{\$\ 9,775,000}{\$25,000,000} = 39.1\%$$

This is the standard basis for developing a percentage figure, but several other methods are used. Some companies use only straight-time pay for time worked as the denominator. This, in effect, eliminates pay for time not worked plus overtime and shift premiums from the gross payroll amount. In Exhibit 20, this would mean deducting $3,425,000 and $1,500,000 from the $25 million total payroll. As a result, the benefits–cost ratio would be higher:

$$\frac{\$\ 9,775,000}{\$20,075,000} = 48.7\%$$

Another approach, indicated previously, is to count overtime and shift premiums as benefits costs. Using the same data as above, this would produce an even higher percentage:

$$\frac{\$11,275,000}{\$20,075,000} = 56.2\%$$

Some calculations include overtime but not shift differentials as part of payroll, and there are other minor variations of each of the methods cited here.

As long as the same basis of measurement is used, percentage of payroll is an excellent way to make comparisons with other companies, since it overcomes variations in size. On the other hand, it is important to realize that a high benefits–cost ratio can result from low wages as well as from high benefits. This relationship is particularly important when comparing domestic and overseas operations. Using the standard calculation method described above, benefits costs in South America and some European countries are 50–100 percent of payroll when compared with a typical 35–40 percent in the United States. These higher percentages are caused in part by higher legally required payments in other countries, but they are attributable also to much lower wage levels outside the United States.

AVERAGE COST PER EMPLOYEE PER YEAR

Average cost per employee per year is an impressive figure to use in employee communications. It is personalized, easily related to the

W-2 statement, and usually large enough not to be ignored. The standard method for obtaining this figure is to divide the total cost of benefits by the average number of employees on the payroll during the year. Again using the data in Exhibit 20:

$$\frac{\$9,775,000}{1,500 \text{ employees}} = \$6,517$$

The average number of employees can be determined by averaging monthly employment reports or by using payroll hours to construct the number of full-time equivalent employees. This can be done by adding time actually worked and time paid for but not worked by all employees to obtain a figure for gross payroll hours for the year, then dividing that figure by the number of payroll hours worked by a typical full-time employee. For example,

$$\frac{3,300,000 \text{ hours}}{2,200 \text{ hours}} = \$1,500 \text{ (full-time equivalent employees)}$$

The latter method, although more complicated, should be used in organizations that have wide variations in hours worked by employees, a large number of part-time or seasonal employees, or a significant amount of overtime work.

Employers should realize that an average cost of the total package may mean very little to employees who are not eligible for or do not participate in the major plans. If there are long waiting periods for participation and if large numbers of employees are excluded from certain plans, the average cost could be a very misleading figure. In such cases, it would be preferable to compute actual costs for participants on a plan basis.

AVERAGE CENTS PER HOUR

Average cents per hour is usually derived by dividing the total cost of benefits by total payroll hours, or, using the information above,

$$\frac{\$9,775,000}{3,300,000 \text{ hours}} = 296¢ \text{ or } \$2.96 \text{ per hour}$$

Another common method of calculating cents per hour is to use only production hours as the denominator. This means excluding hours paid for but not worked, such as vacation time, holidays, and sick leave, and might involve the following deductions:

Benefits	Hours per year
Vacations	120
Holidays	80
Sick leave	40
Paid personal absence	20

$$\begin{array}{r} \overline{260 \text{ hours}} \\ \times \ 1,500 \text{ employees} \\ \hline 390,000 \text{ person-hours} \end{array}$$

The total productive, or work, hours would be 2,910,000 (3,300,000 − 390,000). Then the measure of cents per productive hour would be

$$\frac{\$9,775,000}{2,910,000 \text{ hours}} = 336¢ \text{ or } \$3.36 \text{ per hour}$$

Using either method, this form of expression is especially effective in communications with employees who think of their pay in terms of hourly rates. An employee who is paid $8.00 per hour worked is apt to be quite favorably impressed when made aware that benefits amount to an additional $2.96 or $3.36 per hour. For those paid on a weekly, biweekly, or semimonthly basis, it is relatively easy to convert the hourly cost to comply with their particular mode and frequency of pay.

ACTUAL COST FOR EACH EMPLOYEE

The actual cost for each employee is perhaps the ideal form for expressing cost information. It is also the most difficult and expensive to develop. But, as mentioned above, statements using averages can be misleading and subject to criticism by employees. For example, younger employees will point out that they do not benefit from pension contributions; single employees will claim that they gain nothing from employer-provided dependent coverage payments; and employees who do not participate in thrift plans will be reminded that they receive no credits from company funds. Furthermore, an employee who has had perfect attendance will realize that others have been "rewarded" by payments for time off due to illness and personal reasons.

Information on some benefits costs—the cafeteria subsidy and recreation program expenses—usually have to be averaged, but most other items can be computed individually. With computers becoming increasingly versatile and efficient, this type of information is now being developed in conjunction with total employee information systems by many large firms. Smaller companies have opportunities to produce comparable reports by sharing outside computer services on a cooperative basis with other small organizations.

EMPLOYER–EMPLOYEE COST RATIO

The employer–employee cost ratio is most meaningful in organizations that have contributory benefits plans. Virtually all working people contribute to the cost of Social Security coverage. In some states, employees pay for a part of unemployment compensation and disability income benefits. It is still common for employees to share the costs of group insurance coverage with their employer, and most thrift plans are predicated on employee contributions.

Since employee contributions are normally handled through payroll deductions, employees are constantly made aware of their costs. If the company newspaper carries a report that stresses only the employer's costs, employees are bound to become resentful and to expect equal space. In most instances, the employer will be on the favorable side of the ratio, so there should be no reason to hold back information. Care should be taken to report net costs. For instance, dividends from insurance plans should be applied against premium costs. A large manufacturing company created a serious bargaining snag some years ago by attempting to hide its dividend credit, only to have the union attorney obtain a photostatic copy of the report the company had received from the insurance carrier.

Table 12. Employer and employee benefits costs.

Cost	Employer Payments	Employee Payroll Deductions
Total annual cost	$9,775,000	$2,650,000
Percentage of payroll	39.1%	10.6%
Average cost per employee	$ 6,517	$ 1,767
Average cost per hour	$ 2.96	$ 0.80

A comparison of employer and employee benefits costs can be expressed in any of the forms described in Table 12. The actual cost ratio for each employee would, of course, have to be calculated on an individual basis.

Collective Bargaining Implications

Unions tend to be skeptical of cost data presented by employers and often claim that management attempts to overstate benefits expenses as a means of forcing down cash increases in bargaining. At the same time, employers have accused unions of giving inflated cost figures to the press when announcing contract settlements. The inference is that unions try to use exaggerated amounts as leverage in subsequent negotiations with other employees.

Another problem that unionized companies encounter is the ambivalence of unions in shifting between bargaining on benefits *values* and benefits *costs*. Whichever way the focus is turned, union negotiators are often suspicious of management motives. A management proposal to improve hospital and surgical benefits may be rejected because there is no "assurance" that this plan will require additional company costs over a two- or three-year period. Nevertheless, unions may not be satisfied that the company will have to spend a large sum of money to fund a benefit if members cannot collect immediately. A 1970 analysis by Rudolph Oswald and J. Douglas Smyth of the AFL–CIO research department stated:

> Total employer costs for fringe benefits cannot be equated with total income of the employee because a number of benefits, such as pensions, provide the worker with no immediate additional income. Other benefits, such as supplemental unemployment benefits (SUB), provide economic security against a circumstance which may never materialize.

Because of the uncertainty that unions seem to have about dealing with benefits as a cost or value item, management must be prepared to face a two-edged sword at the bargaining table. However, by computing cost information on the initial union demands, the company negotiators will be able to discuss both cost and value effects of subsequent proposals and counterproposals throughout the bargaining process.

Exhibit 21. Confidential cost analysis of union demands.

A = Bargaining unit, 50 employees; average rate $8.00/hour
B = Nonexempt staff, 25 employees; average salary $250/week
C = Exempt staff, 10 employees; average salary $25,000/year

Union Proposal	Added Cost Next Year
1. Add 10% general wage increase	
A—50 × 80¢ × 2,080 hours	$ 83,200
B—25 × $25 × 52 weeks	32,500
C—Not directly affected	—
2. Add two additional holidays	
A—50 × $8.80 × 16 hours	7,040
B—25 × $55 × 2 days	2,750
C—10 × $100 × 2 days	2,000
3. Eliminate 4% employee contribution for pension plan	
A—30 participants × 4% × $8.00 × 2,080 hours	19,968
B—10 participants × 4% × $250 × 52 weeks	5,200
C—7 participants × 4% × $26,000	7,280
4. Provide fourth vacation week after 15 years	
A—20 employees × $9.90 × 40 hours	7,920
B—5 employees × $330	1,650
C—6 employees × $750	4,500
5. Eliminate offset in jury duty pay	
A—Estimate 5 employees × $50	250
B—Estimate 3 employees × $50	150
C—Estimate 2 employees × $50	100
6. Roll-up costs (wage-related benefits = 25% of pay)	
A—50 × 80¢ × .25 × 2,080 hours	20,800
B—25 × $25 × .25 × 52 weeks	8,125
TOTAL	$203,433

Exhibit 21 illustrates how a small company might organize an analysis of the cost of a union's demands for wage and benefits improvement. While it does not project secondary-effect cost increases, such as overtime or the impact on salary increases for the exempt staff, it is the type of analysis that unionized companies should tailor to their own needs in order to bargain intelligently on benefits.

Internal Comparisons

When making comparisons with other companies, firms are not likely to reveal actual costs of benefits or to discuss these costs in relation to sales or earnings. However, large employers with many divisions or profit centers may want to compare actual costs between and among such units as a means of evaluating performance, as well as for checking consistency of coverage.

The same type of comparison would be useful as a first step toward integrating employee benefits after an acquisition or merger. Although it might not be possible to have identical programs, it would help maintain good morale if employees could be shown that the companies had equivalent ratios for benefits costs.

Cost-Control Issues

In a speech given to a group of pharmaceuticals industry production and engineering executives in 1960, Homer M. Elwell of the Upjohn Company introduced the terms "benefat" and "benefruit." Elwell created these words to characterize two polarized views about the costs of employee benefits. The benefat was described as a person who tends to become alarmed about rising costs, the apparent failure of benefits expenditures to spur productivity, and a trend toward more and more benefits for less and less work. The benefruit, according to Elwell, sees benefits as part of the fruits of labor and feels that since they are earned rights they should be returned for the laborer's contribution to industrial progress without undue regard for cost.

During the past 20 years, it appears that each of these conflicting viewpoints has had its share of influence on employee benefits. Surely the benefruit view has contributed to the increases in the costs of benefits depicted in Exhibit 1. But there are definite signs that the benefat influence has been limiting the rise in employer costs. Notable among these efforts are:

1. Maintenance of the contributory principle.
2. Use of deductibles, offsets, coordination of benefits, and co-insurance features.
3. Application of age-related benefits exclusions and reductions.

4. Self-funding.
5. Greater assertiveness in dealing with outside resources.

EMPLOYEE CONTRIBUTIONS

Not too many years ago, it appeared that contributory benefits plans were becoming outmoded. Many companies had originally installed pension, health, and life insurance plans on a shared-cost basis, but gradually employee contributions were phased out. The prevailing viewpoint held that since the costs were generally tax deductible for the employer, but not for the employee, it was more sensible and equitable to make the plans noncontributory. This position was championed by labor unions, many of whom had considered contributory plans merely as a foot-in-the-door compromise to secure new benefits.

The dramatic changes in workforce demographics, the development of special-purpose benefits, and the introduction of cafeteria benefits programs all influenced the renewed acceptability of contributory plans in the late 1970s. Generally, employees have been willing to spend aftertax dollars for additional life insurance, group auto insurance, or a thrift plan when the choice has been completely voluntary and the benefits seemed to be a good buy. The contributory principle has been further extended in flexible benefits programs, where the employee chooses among alternative coverages and the passed-over benefits become part of the price paid for the alternatives selected.

DEDUCTIBLES, OFFSETS, COORDINATION, AND COINSURANCE

Since most employees now own homes and/or cars, the concept of a deductible amount in an insurance policy is well known. As price-conscious consumers, today's employees clearly understand the inverse relationship between the amount of the deductible and the premium cost for insurance coverage. However, employers, perhaps intimidated by the 1977 coal miners' strikes, have been rather timid in raising the $100 deductible that has been traditional in major medical plans since the 1950s. Still, The Conference Board recently reported that 13 percent of surveyed companies had deductibles in excess of $100 in 1980 compared with 6 percent in 1973.[1] The approach

[1] Mitchell Meyer, *Profile of Employee Benefits: 1981 Edition.*

taken by American Can Company in raising deductible amounts to create flexible credits to be used in tailoring coverages to individual needs could be a breakthrough in overcoming employer reluctance to change deductibles.

The idea of offsets and coordination of benefits has always seemed logical and reasonable to employers. After all, why should anyone ever receive more than 100 percent of lost income or expense replacement? The response of some employees has been, "When we have to pay for a benefit, we expect full value, not a discounted amount!" Even if a benefit is noncontributory, employees may resent being told that it is part of their compensation, then having a scheduled payment reduced because it is covered under a spouse's plan. Nonetheless, these plan features continue to be effective cost containers. They may become less repugnant to employees when more benefits tradeoffs are allowed by their employers.

Coinsurance is expected to increase employee involvement in cost containment. The predetermination of benefits provisions in many dental plans is a good example of this concept. If an employee is responsible for 20–50 percent of a dentist's charges, chances are good that some questions will be raised and, in some cases, less expensive treatment elected. It is especially helpful from a cost-control standpoint to include copayment features in coverages where costs can fluctuate a great deal and utilization is somewhat elective. This is the case in certain aspects of dental care, vision care, and group legal plans. On the other hand, companies have recognized that when an employee is seriously ill, treatment is hardly elective; therefore, most major medical plans today stop the copayment requirement after an employee has paid $1,000 or $1,100 out of pocket.

AGE FACTORS

Both ERISA and ADEA contain provisions that permit employers to legally discriminate on the basis of age in determining eligibility and entitlement to benefits plans. Many employers have adopted these provisions, primarily for cost-control reasons.

Under ERISA, it is not necessary to enroll an employee in a pension plan prior to age 25, or to consider years of service prior to age 22 for purposes of vesting in most instances. Also, it is legal to exclude from participation in a defined-benefit pension plan an employee hired within five years of the plan's normal retirement age (typically 65).

ADEA permits suspension of pension benefits for employees who continue working past age 65, and reductions are allowed in group life insurance and disability benefits because of the higher premium costs for these older workers.

Not all employers take full advantage of every exclusion and reduction sanctioned by ERISA and ADEA, but surveys indicate that the provisions are widely reflected in plan design.

SELF-FUNDING

The advantages of self-funding health insurance plans were listed in Chapter 4. Self-funding, or self-insurance, has become increasingly attractive to larger companies with sufficient cash to handle targeted levels of claims in hospital–medical–surgical, disability, and workers' compensation plans. Although it is arguable whether or not the costs of claims become higher without the full services of an insurance carrier, the higher earnings potential for funds that would otherwise be earmarked for premium payments has become irresistible for many companies. For firms using the self-funded approach, the high level of investment earnings on liberated reserves has continued to be an effective hedge against increases in benefits costs in the early 1980s.

CONTROLLING OUTSIDE RESOURCES

In the 1940s and 1950s, when the management of employee benefits was in its infancy, company executives were often at the mercy of outside "experts." Insurance and financial industry specialists and consultants developed and installed benefits plans for groups, with very little input from clients. Certainly the experts deserve a large measure of credit for innovations and technical refinements. However, without clear specifications or informed challenges from customers, some suppliers did not always provide the best fit. Surely self-interest was a factor too. An insurance company representative is unlikely to propose self-funding a health insurance plan, and a bank trustee is not apt to recommend an insured group annuity pension plan.

In recent years, as the level of benefits expertise within companies has risen, employers have become increasingly assertive in dealing with outside resources and in so doing have gained more respect. Examples of this include the trend toward self-funding; more shifts in carriers, plan trustees, and investment managers; active participation in local coalitions for containing health care costs; and greater specificity in requests for proposals and performance standards. It is difficult to be entirely objective, or precise, about this changing relationship, but it seems to be approaching a healthy equilibrium. Employers are not always right, but they should know what they want and what their cost limitations are. An effective supplier can always adapt to those conditions.

CHAPTER 10

Communicating with Employees

The true measure of the success of a benefits program is the degree of credibility, awareness, understanding, and appreciation that it gains from employees. Effective communication is the key to attaining these objectives. All the preceding chapters have included references to some aspect of benefits communication. In order to provide an overview, this final chapter deals with some of the general concepts.

Credibility has to come first. Employees must believe that benefits plans are sound and secure, and that they will do what the company claims they will do. M. Scott Myers, a noted consultant in organizational psychology, has described a typical employee reaction to company benefits communications as "the big print giveth, and the little print taketh away." Once employees are told by a hospital administrator that physician calls, X rays, anesthesia, and certain forms of therapy are not fully covered under the group insurance plan, they discover the reason for the fine print in the policy and lose faith in the company for burying that information.

If the company tells employees that benefits are part of their pay, those employees expect to receive some accounting of benefits costs. If they do not receive this information, an impression of flimflam develops. Employees know that the company has tax and purchasing advantages in providing benefits, and they expect to share in those advantages.

Exhibit 22. Communications model for employee benefits.

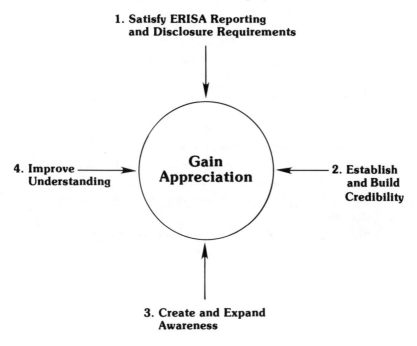

**1. Satisfy ERISA Reporting
and Disclosure Requirements**

**4. Improve
Understanding**

**Gain
Appreciation**

**2. Establish
and Build
Credibility**

**3. Create and Expand
Awareness**

To gain full value from their benefits, employees must understand the eligibility rules and workings of the various plans. Procedures for submitting health care claims should be as simple and clear as possible to expedite reimbursement. Options in pension, profit sharing, and savings plans should be carefully explained to help the employee make the best choices. Suggestion award plans, tuition-aid plans, and employee services should be publicized regularly to ensure employee awareness and to encourage participation and utilization.

Employee appreciation for benefits is the ultimate objective. An employer cannot expect employees to give standing ovations for benefits. But if they are honestly appreciated, benefits will fulfill their purposes of helping to attract, satisfy, motivate, and retain competent and committed workers. Unfortunately, many companies try to gain employee appreciation for benefits through dramatic and flamboyant promotional techniques without paying enough attention to the need for establishing credibility, creating awareness, and ensuring understanding (see Exhibit 22). If the investment in benefits communication is to have any chance of success, each of those objectives must be consciously addressed.

ERISA—A Foundation

The ERISA requirements for reporting and disclosing information about benefits plans (see Exhibit 23) have helped in opening the books and removing a fundamental cause for employee distrust—namely, secrecy. Although benefits specialists continue to complain about "the paper chase" created by ERISA, the requirements for forthright and understandable communication seem to have been more of a help than a hindrance to employers when examined objectively.

Certainly the summary plan description (SPD) is an essential document for plan participants (including beneficiaries receiving benefits). In addition to describing the main features of a benefits plan ("written in a manner calculated to be understood by the average plan participant"), an SPD is required to include an "ERISA rights" statement. This statement must advise participants of their rights to additional information and to appeal claims that may be denied or ignored. They must also be informed that any questions about the statement or their rights can be referred to the nearest area office of the U.S. Department of Labor, Labor-Management Services Administration.

Benefits plan summary booklets did not originate with ERISA, but it is evident that the 1974 law has led to wider distribution, more prompt revisions, and an overall improvement in the comprehensibility of these documents. Some companies even go beyond the requirement of automatically giving SPDs to plan participants. They issue copies to all employees on the presumption that eventually everyone will be eligible to participate in the plans.

The requirement for issuing a summary of material modifications (SMM) within 210 days after the end of a plan year seems reasonable. In most instances, when an employer makes any significant changes in a plan, the information is communicated to employees on or before the effective date. In many cases, the SMM requirement can be satisfied by these current written announcements of changes.

The annual report (Form 5500) is intended primarily for filing with

Exhibit 23. Summary of key ERISA requirements for reporting and disclosing information to pension and welfare participants, for plans with 100 or more participants. Some exemptions and exceptions apply to plans with fewer than 100 employees.

| Item | Due | Participants to be given | | To Government |
		Automatically	On written Request	
1. Summary plan description	120 days after plan establishment; new participants—90 days after becoming eligible	Yes	Yes	Yes (DOL)
2. Summary of material modifications	210 days after end of plan year	Yes	Yes	Yes (DOL)
3. Annual report (Form 5500)	7 months after end of plan year	No	Yes	Yes (IRS)
4. Summary annual report	9 months after end of plan year	Yes	No	No
5. Benefits statement for terminating vested participants (pension plans only)	7 months after end of plan year	Yes	No	No

(continued on next page)

Exhibit 23.   Continued.

6. State- ment of accrued/ vested benefits (pension plans only)	30 days after written re- quest; no more than once in 12- month period	No	Yes	No

the IRS, but a participant is entitled to receive a copy upon written request, and the employer must make a copy conveniently available for inspection by employees. Most employers report that a minimal number of employees ever exercise either of these rights. That is easy to understand, because employees seem to be almost apathetic about the summary annual reports (SARs) they receive automatically.

As indicated in Exhibit 23, an SAR is supposed to be given to each participant in a plan no later than nine months after the end of the plan year. However, the due date can be extended by as much as two and a half months with IRS permission. One firm that obtained a two-month extension without informing employees reports that no one in the company inquired about the overdue reports. A few years ago, another company decided to test the readership of an SAR by inserting an extraneous sentence that invited participants to: "Bring this booklet to Personnel within one week and receive a cash bonus." No one came forward to claim the bonus!

The obvious lack of interest in SARs has inspired numerous proposals to eliminate the automatic distribution requirement for these documents. Employers claim that the costs of producing and distributing SARs are out of line with their utility. Since employees seem to be more interested in individual benefits accounting and are apparently content that the government monitors the 5500 reports, the SAR may soon be extinct.

The benefits statement for terminated vested employees is directly related to Schedule SSA, which is part of the annual report filed with the IRS. Both are required within seven months after the end of a pension plan year. However, many employees satisfy the requirement to disclose this information to participants by including it in a letter immediately following the actual termination date. This ordinarily provides the individual with useful information at a much earlier date.

Companies that issue personalized annual benefits statements to employees can easily include a section describing the employee's accrued pension plan benefits and the percentage of those benefits that are vested. In that way, they would satisfy the ERISA requirement without having to respond to individual requests. Actually, when employers do not furnish this information automatically, relatively few plan participants submit the necessary written requests for information. Since it is in the employer's interest to communicate the information, a proactive approach seems preferable.

Building Credibility

All too often, an employee will become disenchanted with company benefits because of incorrect or misleading information given prior to employment. Because recruiters frequently operate in a sell mode, they may tend to oversell the value of benefits or minimize waiting periods and vesting requirements. To illustrate:

Leslie Samuels, in recruiting for a production supervisor position, tells ' candidate Tim Horne that Consolidated Rust Inc. (CRI) has a profit sharing plan that pays a 15 percent annual bonus. Assuming that this plan would add $4,500 to a $30,000 starting salary, Tim accepts CRI's employment offer. He joins the company on February 1 and attends an orientation meeting at which benefits are discussed. At this session he learns the following facts about the profit-sharing plan:

1. Participation begins on the January 1 or July 1 after completion of one year of employment.
2. While the plan can pay a maximum of 15 percent—and did achieve that percentage in the most recent year—the average contribution for the past five years has been 8 percent.
3. Vesting is on a class-year basis, and each year's contribution takes four years to become fully vested.

One of the outcomes of incidents like this is a bitter feeling on the part of the newly hired person toward both the benefits plan and the recruiter. Defensive responses, such as "Why didn't you ask for more information?" or "All the details were in the literature we gave you," do not help alleviate the dissatisfaction.

Although this illustration may seem exaggerated, there is little doubt that much of the reason benefits plans lack credibility with employees stems from early disappointments of this type. To deal with the problem employers should:

1. Authorize only certain people to communicate information about benefits during recruitment. For example, outside recruiters and/or supervisors could be prohibited from discussing benefits with prospective or new employees.

2. Conduct training sessions for recruiters periodically and when benefits are being added or materially modified.

3. Provide recruiters with a brief and authoritative summary of employee benefits for selective distribution to prospects and applicants (and make sure that outdated material is destroyed).

4. Arrange for an early audit of how well a new employee understands the benefits plan, as a form of quality assurance that recruiters are giving accurate information.

Other ways in which employers can build employee trust and confidence in their benefits plans are discussed below.

Provide for two-way communication. For many years, communications specialists have urged company management to recognize that employee communication is a two-way process. A steady barrage of literature and talks about benefits from the employer, with no opportunity for employees to express their views, can have a deafening effect on them. Unfortunately, the usual response to any expert advice about giving some attention to vox populi is a question-and-answer column in the employee newspaper or a few minutes for that purpose at the end of a group oral presentation. Measures like these usually have very little effect.

Before planning and developing any type of benefits program, an employer should arrange to listen to the questions, complaints, and suggestions that arise constantly about all benefits plans. This can be done through individual interviews, special surveys, informal visitations throughout the company, small-group discussions, hot-line telephones, or whatever technique might be appropriate to a particular firm.

By listening to employees, retirees, and family members, management will obtain countless suggestions for improving the benefits program. Some patterns will form, and action may be taken on the basis of a partial consensus. But conflicting and impractical ideas will inevitably be generated. New employees will want longer vacations sooner, and long-service employees will want longer vacations than new employees. Younger workers will want better maternity benefits and tuition-aid plans. Older workers will want improved pension benefits and scholarships for their children.

After digesting all the questions and criticisms about the benefits program, management may decide to make some modifications in plans, but major changes take time to implement, and cost factors must be weighed. In many instances, it will be clear that what is needed is not change but explanation. Announcing an improvement in a benefits plan may be a more enjoyable assignment for management, but the clarification of terms in existing coverages may be just as important. Clearly, the latter is the more difficult task.

Involve employees as communicators. The model for this approach is Texas Instruments Incorporated (TI), which for many years has involved rank-and-file workers in benefits communication. By identifying and training department representatives, TI provides a readily available, on-the-spot resource for answering employee questions. At the same time, the company demonstrates a willingness to take non-supervisory employees into its confidence and uses the group as a sounding board for benefits planning purposes.

Promote a "use but don't abuse" philosophy. This is a phrase that insurance companies have used in explaining coordination of benefits (COB) provisions in group health coverages. The intended message is that employees should utilize their benefits, but in order to control costs (and permit future plan improvements), they should cooperate in the nonduplication of payments from two or more plans. As indicated in Chapter 9, employees are not thrilled with these arrangements that can reduce payments from a secondary plan.

An antidote for the negative attitudes that can arise from COB reductions and from Social Security offsets in pension plans is proactive communication of other programs. Such benefits as educational assistance, a suggestion plan, product and service discounts, an employee assistance program, group social and recreation activities, matching gifts, commutation assistance, child care, and financial counseling are utilized largely through employee initiative. Unless they are promoted aggressively, employees may overlook them. A company can build a good measure of credibility for the benefits program by periodically publicizing the availability of these benefits and encouraging their use.

Creating Awareness

The body was discovered behind a file cabinet, but a day passed before anyone could identify it. Someone in the Accounting Department recalled that a new employee hadn't been seen lately. At last, a janitor acknowledged that the deceased had asked directions from the Accounting Department to the washroom. The coroner's report confirmed that the janitor, although the last to see the new employee alive, was innocent of murder, for the cause of death was listed as "acute informational bombardment with digestive dysfunction."

In just two days on the job, the employee had been confronted with so much information so fast that his ability to assimilate it had been severely impaired. Thus, he had expired in a vain struggle to separate in his mind the vesting provisions of the company pension plan, from the firm's corporate objectives, from the way to the washroom. The murderer: the company's orientation program.[1]

This fictitious account of communications overkill may remind many employees of the first-day introductions to their companies. In attempting to help employees understand the benefits program, over-exuberant orientation leaders discuss in detail every benefit in the handbook. Some benefits are of immediate concern to everyone, but it is unlikely that an 18-year-old worker will have much interest in the joint and survivor annuity option in the pension plan. When employees are forced to endure a blizzard of information, much of which is not immediately relevant, their awareness of benefits becomes obfuscated.

THE BENEFITS ORIENTATION "LOCAL"

Rather than operating benefits orientations as an express train, with an extraordinary amount of information delivered in a few hours, more thoughtful employers have switched to a "local" schedule. A model schedule would consist of an initial briefing, followed by in-depth coverage of major plans at later times, closer to eligibility dates. For example, a new employee would follow this type of schedule:

Date of hire: Receives plan booklets and attends a brief (for example, one to one and a half hours) company orientation, in which highlights of the benefits plan are covered in a 12-minute sound-slide pre-

[1] "Murder on the Orientation Express," in Towers, Perrin, Forster & Crosby publication *Communications and Management* (January–February 1977).

sentation. Emphasis is on health insurance, holidays, recreational programs, the product discount plan, subsidized food service, commutation assistance, and other benefits that are immediately available. Eligibility dates for other coverages are mentioned, and a timetable of future sessions is distributed.

After 30 days: Scheduled for an individual conference with a personnel department representative. Encouraged to ask questions about any of the benefit plans. Reminded of date for next session.

On or before 90 days: Scheduled to attend a group session in which the life insurance and disability plans are described in detail. At 90 days, becomes eligible for supplementary life insurance and long-term disability coverage on a contributory basis. Plan options and costs are discussed, and enrollment cards distributed.

Between 11 and 12 months: Scheduled to attend a group orientation to the savings plan, which has a one-year waiting period. Features discussed include employee contributions, company matching, investment choices, vesting, and withdrawal rules. Enrollment cards are distributed.

When eligible: Scheduled for a retirement plan orientation session. This plan is noncontributory and enrolls participants on January 1 or July 1 (whichever date occurs first) after employee has completed one year of service and has reached age 25. All plan features are discussed.

EVENTS-CENTERED COMMUNICATION

Central to the concept of a benefits orientation "local" is the notion that employee awareness will be heightened when information is provided close to the time when benefits become available. Two corollaries that relate to employee awareness of benefits in terms of certain events are:

1. Employees should be reminded of benefits roll-ups when they receive pay increases. Since most benefits are pay related, it is not unusual for the roll-up to be 25–30 percent of salary. Supervisors can be given particulars to communicate to their employees in tandem with information about pay increases.

2. Employees' needs for benefits information are most acute when such events as illness, disability, retirement, and termination occur. Also beneficiaries need prompt, accurate, and complete information about relevant company benefits when an employee or retiree dies. At

Exhibit 24. Alternative paragraphs for retirement plan section of a termination letter.

RETIREMENT PLAN

(Select one of the following paragraphs.)

Code 1. Our records indicate that you were not a plan member and therefore you have no vested pension rights.

Code 2. Our records indicate that you were a member, but were employed for less than 10 years and made no contributions to the plan. Therefore you have no vested pension rights or refund entitlements.

Code 3. Our records indicate that you were a member but were employed for less than 10 years and therefore you have no vested pension rights. You are entitled to the return of your contributions of $_____ and interest. The amount will be forwarded to you by the plan trustee within 60 days.

Code 4. Our records indicate that you are vested in the retirement plan, with entitlement to a pension of $_____ beginning on the first of the month coincident with or following your 65th birthday. You may instead elect to receive an actuarially reduced pension at the beginning of any month coincident with or following the attainment of your 55th birthday. If this is your desire, please notify our benefits department.

---

these times, it is often difficult to remember details, or even which plans apply. For example, when an employee nears retirement or is leaving the company for other reasons, a variety of benefits are applicable. Trying to determine which ones apply can be overwhelming for the departing person.

To assist employees and beneficiaries in coping with these occurrences, some companies have developed standardized letter formats with variable paragraphs that both summarize and individualize plan information. For example, the format for a letter to terminating employees can include references to group insurance, the retirement plan, a savings or profit sharing plan, vacation pay, separation pay, and unemployment compensation. By using word processing equipment, choices can be made from alternative paragraphs and variable information inserted to produce a personalized letter. Exhibit 24 shows the retirement plan section of a termination letter format used by one company. A benefits assistant determines which of the four paragraphs applies and inserts specific information where appropriate. Similar sections for other plans are completed, and the material is sent to a word processing center, where an individually addressed letter is prepared.

PERSONALIZED BENEFITS REPORTS

Every January employees receive W-2 and 1099 forms summarizing their pay and miscellaneous income for the preceding year. This distribution creates awareness of how much direct compensation they received in that year, but it also reminds them of their tax obligations.

In an ever-increasing number of firms, employees now receive an annual report showing benefits entitlements and values on an individual basis. These reports probably have contributed more toward raising employee awareness of benefits than any other type of employer communications effort. And unlike the above-mentioned government forms, the benefits reports describe a portion of total compensation that is predominantly tax free or tax deferred.

Exhibit 25 is an example of a typical personalized benefits statement that is computer printed. All information is current and, in the case of retirement benefits, profit sharing, suggestion awards, and educational assistance, cumulative accruals and payments are shown. This particular company developed its own benefits statement program as part of an overall employee information system. However, many benefits consultants and computer software firms now offer packages that can be installed by companies that do not have sufficient internal know-how (or time) to do it themselves.

The issue of how to distribute personalized benefits statements has generated some controversy. It appears that most companies prefer to mail these reports to employees' homes, where information can be openly shared with family members. Certainly, this seems to be the best way to expand awareness, and in many instances, spouses, children, and parents living in the household are named beneficiaries in the various plans.

Some employees, however, raise strong objections to the release of information that they consider to be private and confidential. Rather than alienating that element in their workforces, a significant number of companies now distribute the reports to employees at the office or plant. Although this method saves on mailing costs, it does not have as good a readership potential as the first alternative.

Exhibit 25. Typical personalized computer-printed benefits statement.

Medical Expense Benefits (for non work-related illness or injury)
Basic Benefits

HOSPITAL EXPENSES - 100% OF SEMI-PRIVATE ROOM & BOARD, PLUS SERVICES AND SUPPLIES, UP TO 120 DAYS PER PERIOD OF DISABILITY FOR YOU AND EACH COVERED DEPENDENT.

IN-HOSPITAL PHYSICIAN VISIT EXPENSES - UP TO $15 DAILY FOR THE FIRST 3 DAYS AND $7 DAILY FOR THE NEXT 117 DAYS.

SURGICAL EXPENSES - SURGICAL FEES UP TO $1600 AS SPECIFIED IN THE PLAN, PLUS ADDITIONAL COSTS FOR SECOND OPINION.

DIAGNOSTIC EXPENSES - UP TO $150 A YEAR FOR REASONABLE DIAGNOSTIC X-RAYS AND LABORATORY TESTS REQUIRED BY ILLNESS OR ACCIDENT, PLUS ADDITIONAL COSTS FOR SECOND OPINION.

ACCIDENT EXPENSES - UP TO $50 FOR PHYSICIANS' TREATMENT AND X-RAYS REQUIRED WITHIN 90 DAYS OF AN ACCIDENT.

MATERNITY EXPENSES - TREATED SAME AS ANY OTHER CONDITION FOR EMPLOYEES AND SPOUSES.

Major Medical Benefits
IN ADDITION TO YOUR BASIC BENEFITS, 80% OF MOST MEDICAL EXPENSES IN EXCESS OF AMOUNTS ABOVE AFTER YOU PAY A $100-PER-PERSON, (OR $250-PER-FAMILY) ANNUAL DEDUCTIBLE. AN INDIVIDUAL'S UNREIMBURSED COVERED EXPENSES BEYOND $1100 IN ANY ONE CALENDAR YEAR ARE PAID IN FULL. $500,000 LIFETIME MAXIMUM.

Dental Assistance Plan
100% OF USUAL CHARGES FOR PREVENTIVE CARE. PARTIAL PAYMENT FOR OTHER SPECIFIED DENTAL SERVICES. ANNUAL $750 MAXIMUM PER PERSON. 50% OF CHILDREN'S ORTHODONTICS UP TO $1,000.
Dependents Covered   TWO OR MORE

Benefits For Your Survivors — If You Die While an Employee

Lump-sum Benefits

IF YOUR DEATH IS FROM ANY CAUSE:
$ 48,000 GROUP LIFE INSURANCE
$ 15,411 PROFIT SHARING ACCOUNT (LESS ANY 1982 PAYOUT)

$ 255 SOCIAL SECURITY DEATH BENEFIT

$ 63,666 TOTAL

IF YOUR DEATH IS THE RESULT OF AN ACCIDENT, YOUR BENEFICIARY WOULD ALSO RECEIVE:
$ 12,500 FROM OUR GROUP LIFE INSURANCE PLAN AND
$ 144,000 FROM OUR BUSINESS TRAVEL ACCIDENT
           INSURANCE PLAN IN CASE OF ACCIDENT
           WHILE YOU ARE TRAVELING ON COMPANY
           BUSINESS.

Plus Estimated Family Monthly Payments

$ 957 A MONTH IS THE MAXIMUM SOC. SEC. BENEFIT
           FOR A FAMILY WITH THREE OR MORE ELIGIBLE
           DEPENDENTS.

ANY WORKER'S COMPENSATION PAYMENTS WOULD BE IN ADDITION TO THE SURVIVOR BENEFITS DESCRIBED ABOVE.

Unless a very large percentage of employees oppose the home mailing method, it would seem preferable to follow that course while allowing individuals to designate office distribution on an exception basis.

REGULAR REMINDERS OF BENEFITS VALUES

Every paycheck stub reminds employees of *their* costs for benefits. Deductions for Social Security, insurance coverage, a savings plan, purchases of company products, and unemployment insurance (in some states) can be irritants whenever they decimate gross earnings weekly, semimonthly, or biweekly. To counter this potential for creating negative feelings about benefits, an employer needs to accentuate the positive aspects—namely, values—on a regular basis. The personalized benefits statement is fine, but it's produced only once a year. Some other vehicles that can be used selectively for this purpose are:

Company newspapers or magazines.
Contests.
Paycheck and claim check enclosures.
Posters.
Loop filmstrips.
Letters and memorandums.
Wallet cards.
Calendars.
Soundsheets (audio recordings).
Recorded messages that can be dialed on the telephone.
Closed-circuit TV.
Employee meetings.
Displays (in lobbies, cafeterias, lounges, and other meeting places).
Newsletters.

Improving Understanding

CONVERSION PRIVILEGE

The Group policy provides that if the insurance under the Group policy terminates because of termination for any reason whatsoever of the employment of an Employee the Employee, if he has been insured under the Group policy for at least three months, shall, subject to the conditions hereinafter stated, be entitled to have issued to him without evidence of insurability, a policy of insurance (hereinafter referred to as the "converted policy") by making written application therefor and paying the first quarterly premium, or at the option of the Employee a semiannual or annual premium, to the carrier within thirty-one days after such termination of insurance.

Thanks to ERISA, and many state insurance commissions, it is unlikely that a sentence such as this excerpt from a group insurance policy, circa 1970, would appear in an employee benefits booklet in the 1980s. ERISA prescribes that material should be written to be understood by the average plan participant, and the states have begun to impose readability standards on insurance company policies. Employer consciousness about the importance of clarity in written benefits communication has been raised, and several quantitative systems have been used to assess readability.

THE FOG INDEX

There are several ways to evaluate readability. One of the easiest to understand and apply is Robert Gunning's "fog index."[2] This approach considers the number of words per sentence and the percentage of hard (polysyllabic) words in the passage, to obtain a score that can then be related roughly to school grade level. The steps are as follows:

1. *Determine the average sentence length.* Count the number of words in successive sentences. Count the number of sentences to obtain average sentence length. Do not count articles (a, an, or the) as words.

2. *Find the number of hard words per 100.* Simply count the number of words that have three or more syllables. Do not count words that are capitalized or are combinations of short, easier words (bookkeeper) or are verbs made into three syllables by adding -ed or -es. Divide the number of hard words by the total number of words in the section to obtain the rate.

3. *Calculate the fog index.* Add Factors 1 and 2, and multiply by 0.4.

4. *Determine the reading level.* The table here shows the approximate reading levels that correspond to various fog index numbers.

---

[2] *The Technique of Clear Writing* (New York: McGraw-Hill, 1952).

Fog Index	Reading Level (by Grade)	Fog Index	Reading Level (by Grade)
17+	College graduate	11	H.S. junior
16	College senior	10	H.S. sophomore
15	College junior	9	H.S. freshman
14	College sophomore	8	Eighth grade
13	College freshman	7	Seventh grade
12	H.S. senior	6	Sixth grade

As an example, let's apply this formula to the "Conversion Privilege" quotation at the beginning of this section.

$$
\begin{aligned}
\text{Average sentence length} &= 92 \\
\text{Number of hard words}/100 \text{ words} &= \underline{30} \\
&\quad\ 122 \\
&\times\ \underline{0.4} \\
\text{Fog index} &= 48.8
\end{aligned}
$$

According to the table, this passage demands more than two and a half times the reading skill of the average college graduate! Of course, the fog index is merely a diagnostic tool that, in this case, confirms the unintelligibility of the writing. But what company would want its benefits plans to be that hard to read?

Some benefits professionals have argued that the technical complexity of group insurance and pension plans makes it impossible to achieve a low fog index in plan descriptions. The following before-and-after examples[3] tend to deflate those arguments, however.

Example A: Benefits at Retirement

Maximum lifetime benefits for each covered person will be the difference between $50,000 and total benefits paid before retirement under the Company's Group Accident and Health Plan adopted August 1, 1962, as amended, but in no event will maximum benefits exceed $20,000 after retirement date.

$$
\begin{aligned}
\text{Average sentence length} &= 43 \\
\text{Number of hard words}/100 \text{ words} &= \underline{19} \\
&\quad\ 62 \\
&\times\ \underline{0.4} \\
\text{Fog index} &= 24.8
\end{aligned}
$$

[3] Sandra Fleming, "Getting Your Money's Worth from ERISA," *Personnel* (May–June 1975).

Rewrite

To figure your maximum benefit, subtract the amount you received before retirement from $50,000. This amount, limited to $20,000, is what you can expect.

$$
\begin{array}{rr}
\text{Average sentence length} = & 11 \\
\text{Number of hard words/100 words} = & 13 \\
\hline
& 24 \\
\times & 0.4 \\
\hline
\text{Fog index} = & 9.6
\end{array}
$$

Example B: Life Insurance Payments

If the insured employee dies from any cause, his life insurance under the group plan at date of death, determined in accordance with the Schedule of Insurance, will be paid to his beneficiary, as shown on the records of the policyholder, after receipt of due proof of death.

$$
\begin{array}{rr}
\text{Average sentence length} = & 43 \\
\text{Number of hard words/100 words} = & 14 \\
\hline
& 57 \\
\times & 0.4 \\
\hline
\text{Fog index} = & 22.8
\end{array}
$$

Rewrite

When you die, your life insurance will be paid to your beneficiary.

$$
\begin{array}{rr}
\text{Average sentence length} = & 12 \\
\text{Number of hard words/100 words} = & 17 \\
\hline
& 29 \\
\times & 0.4 \\
\hline
\text{Fog index} = & 11.6
\end{array}
$$

In addition to helping to achieve a low fog index, the following reminders[4] should be useful to any benefits communicator who strives to improve the comprehensibility of written material:

1. Keep your sentences short.
2. Use short words.
3. Avoid extra and unneeded words.
4. Use examples.
5. Use active, not passive verbs.
6. Use "you" and "we."

[4] Based on principles developed by the Gunning-Mueller Clear Writing Institute, Santa Barbara, California.

7. Avoid definitions.
8. Write the way you talk.
9. Tie in with your reader's experience.
10. Write to express, not to impress.

NONWRITTEN COMMUNICATION

ERISA rules concentrate on the availability, timing, content, and readability of written benefits material. There are no specific requirements regarding oral, audio, or visual communication. Yet communications specialists point out that the average adult spends far more time watching television, listening to the radio and recorded music, and viewing movies and plays in theaters than reading. Clearly, this suggests moving beyond written communication.

As discussed earlier in this chapter, two-way oral communication is essential for management to become informed about employee attitudes. It is equally important for the purpose of ensuring employee understanding of benefits. The following actual occurrence emphasizes that point.

A company with a profit sharing plan held a series of group meetings with employees to explain the performance of the plan's several investment funds. In each presentation, charts were shown comparing the performance of the common stock investment fund with the Standard & Poor index of 500 common stocks. The profit sharing fund's growth compared quite favorably. But in one session, a skeptical employee spoke up: "Those comparisons might be O.K. when you include just a bunch of standard and poor stocks; how do they compare with the *good* stocks?"

Fortunately, the moderator recovered from his initial shock quickly enough to assure the questioner (who was absolutely serious) that the Standard & Poor 500 index included many "good" issues and that there was no attempt to rig the comparisons. The significant point though is that there was an opportunity to correct a misunderstanding. If the company had not held the group meetings and had relied solely on written reports, one person's suspicion might have led to a nasty rumor. Both understanding and credibility would have suffered.

Another company, VSI Corporation in California, found that many employees did not understand the computerized statement of their savings plan benefits. Remembering the old Chinese proverb, "One picture is worth more than ten thousand words," they switched to a cartoon format to make the information more easily understood. A subsequent survey revealed that employees preferred the new format by a margin of 25 to 1.

Some traditionalists are offended by the use of cartoons and similarly styled artwork in communicating benefits information to adults. Realistically though, if employees are able to retain as much information from a cartoon about benefits as they do from a Peanuts or Doonesbury comic strip or a Muppets TV show, the technique is valid.

Sound-slide and videotape presentations have become relatively inexpensive to produce and can help enhance oral communications sessions. However, this is an area where the benefits department is well advised to seek assistance from in-house training and communications staff, professionals, or outside services.

Programs for Retirees

In keeping with the concept of events-centered communications, most large companies conduct preretirement planning programs for employees after they reach the early retirement age. Subjects usually covered in group sessions include company benefits plans, Social Security, health care, financial planning, legal matters, housing considerations, use of leisure time, temporary employment, and second careers. Although some employees view these programs as a gentle push into early retirement, the majority find them to be a helpful benefit and appreciate the employer's efforts. Very often spouses are invited to attend the meetings, and this creates positive feelings. Some companies supplement the oral presentation by giving the participants reading material and/or subsidizing membership in Action for Independent Maturity (AIM), the preretirement division of the American Association of Retired Persons.

The event of retirement itself is normally marked by parties, gifts, and various expressions of well-wishing from company executives. But once active employment ends, many retirees become cut off from their former employers. Benefits and personnel executives should remember that these people, particularly those who had long service with the company, want to be remembered and expect more than a monthly pension check and a supplement to Medicare coverage. Also, feedback from retirees on benefits plans is useful for planning and review purposes.

Without great expense or effort, some considerations can be extended to retirees that will help maintain communication between this group and the company. Perhaps the simplest action is to continue sending these people all employee publications. If there are employee discounts on company products or services, they can be extended to retirees as well. Also, retirees could be eligible to receive referral bonus awards if these incentives are offered to active employees.

Some firms have formed retiree clubs and associations, which are self-governed. With some assistance and subsidies from the company, these organizations conduct social and recreational events for their members. Annual reunion dinners at a company location are another popular activity that a club can coordinate that helps retirees keep in touch.

Showing an interest in retirees in these ways keeps communications channels open and permits two-way exchanges concerning applicable coverages. It is an admirable expression of a company's sense of moral and social responsibility. It's also good employee relations, because active employees will have fewer reasons to fear retirement.

Caveat Communicator

"Let the communicator beware" is an important caution for every employer who discusses benefits with employees. The employer must guard against four major pitfalls: misinformation, conflicting information, incomplete information, and overemphasis.

Misinformation can occur most easily when benefits plans and policies are not described to employees in a clearly written form. Without a clear written reference, oral communications about pension formulas, vacation allowances, holiday pay, or hospital insurance can lead to distorted and garbled interpretations. Unintentionally, supervisors and staff specialists may misinform employees about entitlements and eligibilities, or employees may form incorrect beliefs.

This failure in communication can result in embarrassing retractions or, if the company feels it must eat its words, in inconsistent administration. The best remedy is a well-written booklet about benefits that provides a definitive reference for all plans.

Conflicting information may occur when a company distributes explanatory booklets to supplement the official text of a plan. Such terms as "credited service," "continuous employment," "annual earnings," or "eligible dependents" need to be defined carefully and cross-checked with all written references in which they appear. Firms with union contracts must be sure that contract language is consistent with the language in their basic literature on benefits plans.

A sound safeguard against conflicting information is the inclusion of a "reservation of rights" statement in any booklet or bulletin that describes, explains, or interprets the basic text. Such a statement might read, "In the event any questions of interpretation arise, the complete and official text distributed to all employees will take precedence and govern."

Incomplete information is perhaps the most difficult pitfall to avoid. It is particularly critical in the area of counseling employees about their benefits. As long as employers provide employees with complete texts and policy statements on benefits, they are fulfilling the primary obligation to communicate. If employers undertake the responsibility of advising employees about their options under certain plans, they are bound to point out the risks and consequences as well as the advantages of each choice.

This doctrine was affirmed in a U.S. circuit court of appeals ruling against Anheuser-Busch, Inc.[5] In this case, the executor of the estate of a deceased employee recovered more than the full amount of pension benefits to which the employee would have normally been entitled, on the grounds that Anheuser-Busch, through its pension consultants, was negligent in providing clear advice. The employee had written to the company asking for guidance on selecting the method of receiving his pension benefit. The company referred the inquiry to its consultants, who advised the employee to postpone taking a lump-sum payment because he would collect a larger sum if he waited. They neglected to point out that if he died before the postponed date, his family would lose a sizable amount. When the employee died before collecting, the executor filed a suit against the company for

[5] *Gediman v. Anheuser-Busch, Inc.,* 299 F. 2d 537 (2d Cir. 1962).

$78,356. In his decision in favor of the executor, the presiding judge commented:

> By his letter the pensioner placed himself in the hands of the employer. The employer was not required to accept him. It could have suggested he consult his own advisers. Having undertaken to advise, the employer was bound to advise clearly. [The employee] should have been plainly warned that the risks incident to death . . . would continue until whatever date he picked for distribution. Although we are sure everyone was acting in the best of faith, that needed statement was not forthcoming. Though the error was by the employer's advisers, the employer adopted it and . . . is responsible.

As plans are designed and modified to offer more selectivity, and as the cafeteria plan approach becomes more widespread, employees will be confronted with many more decisions to make about their benefits. It appears that employers will have to either assume a hands-off posture in giving advice or devote much more staff time and effort to presenting the pros and cons of the various choices. Companies that believe in counseling as a natural extension of providing the benefits coverage may find it worthwhile to purchase employee-benefits liability insurance.

Insurance may be obtained to defend and pay for judgments against employers on claims resulting from error or omission in the administration and communication of information about benefits plans. Coverage can be applied to four areas: giving counsel to employees, interpreting plans, handling records, and effecting enrollment.

Overemphasis on benefits communication is far less common in industry than failing to communicate often and positively enough. But the tone of some of the messages could be tempered to avoid boastful claims and to permit employees to form their own conclusions about the value of benefits. Blatant publicity stressing the company's generosity to employees invites resentful reactions. Employees now tend to perceive benefits as part of their compensation, as something they earn because of their productivity and loyalty to the company.

Straightforward presentations about plan features and options will earn much more appreciation and respect from most employees than a hard-sell approach. The latter style is somewhat like the boy who cried "Wolf!" too often or the Player Queen in Hamlet who "doth protest too much." Unfortunately, some literature on employee benefits gives the appearance of having been written to impress rather than to inform. There is no reason why the communications cannot be unique and distinctive. But self-serving flag waving is a poor substitute for meaningful reminders and suggestions to help employees gain optimum advantage from the total benefits program.

GLOSSARY

accidental death and dismemberment insurance (AD&D)
Insurance providing benefits in the event of loss of life, limbs, or eyesight as the result of an accident.

accrual of benefits (pension plans)
For defined-benefit plans—the process of accumulating pension credits for years of credited service, expressed as an annual benefit to begin payment at normal retirement age.
For defined-contribution plans—the process of accumulating funds in the individual employee's pension account.

actuarial assumptions
Assumptions made by actuaries in estimating pension costs—for example, investment yield, mortality rate, employee turnover.

ADEA (Age Discrimination in Employment Act of 1967)
Federal legislation that made employees between ages 40 and 65 a protected class. The 1978 amendments to this act raised the minimum age limit for mandatory retirement from 65 to 70 for most nonfederal employees and removed completely any mandatory retirement age for most federal employees. This has had a significant impact on pension and welfare plans.

administrative services only (ASO)
Claims services arrangement provided by insurance carriers to employers with self-insured health and disability benefits plans.

administrator
The person or organization (frequently the sponsor) specifically designated by the terms of the instrument under which a pension or welfare plan operates.

adverse selection (antiselection)
The tendency of individuals in poor health (high risk) to select the maximum amount of insurance protection, while those in good health do not elect, or defer, coverage.

annuity
Periodic payments made for a specific term or for life.

annuity certain (also referred to as term or period certain)
 A form of annuity under which payments are guaranteed for a specified period (for example, five years or ten years).

basic medical benefits
 Name applied to insurance that reimburses hospital and doctor charges (usually at 100 percent) up to stipulated limits. Additional coverage can be provided by major medical insurance.

beneficiary
 The person, other than the plan member, designated to receive the benefit resulting from the death of an employee, such as the proceeds of a life or accident insurance policy or benefits from a pension plan.

business travel accident insurance
 Limited to indemnity for an accident while traveling on company business. Usually covers all accidents occurring while away from home and not merely those directly connected with travel.

cafeteria benefits
 Cafeteria, or flexible benefits, plans permit covered employees to select benefits they want from a package of employer-provided choices, some of which may involve employee contributions.

career average (pension benefits formula)
 A formula that bases benefits on the actual credited compensation of an employee over the total period of service or participation.

class-year plan
 A provision in a savings, profit sharing, or pension plan in which each year's contributions from the employer vest separately after a specified amount of time elapses. The length of time may vary from one plan to another, but under ERISA, the employee's right to the employer's contributions for any plan year must be 100 percent vested within five years.

coinsurance
 An insurance plan provision specifying that the plan will pay a certain percentage (for example, 80 percent) of eligible expenses and the covered person will be responsible for the remaining portion (for example, 20 percent).

compulsory retirement
 The date or age at which an employee must retire. Under ADEA, this may not be prior to age 70, except for certain high-level executives and tenured university faculty, who may be required to retire at age 65.

contributory plan

A plan under which part (or all) of the cost is paid by the participants (employees) and any remainder by the employer.

conversion privilege

The right of an individual covered by a group insurance contract to purchase individual insurance of a stated type and amount, when all or part of the group insurance is canceled, without meeting any medical requirements, provided application is made within a stipulated period (normally 31 days).

defined-benefit pension plan

A pension plan that specifies the benefits or the methods of determining the benefits but not the level or rate of contribution. Contributions are determined actuarially on the basis of the benefits expected to become payable.

defined-contribution pension plan

An individual account pension plan, in which the contributions are specified by a formula. The benefits are whatever the amount accumulated in the participant's account will buy.

early retirement age (pension plans)

The age when an employee is first permitted to retire and to elect either immediate or deferred receipt of income. If payments begin immediately, they are generally paid in a reduced amount. Company consent to the election may or may not be required.

effective date

The date on which a benefit plan or insurance policy goes into effect and from which time coverage is provided. Normally represents the dividing point between past and future service in a pension plan.

employee benefits

A collection of nonwage protections of income, income supplements, and services for employees provided in whole or in part by employer payments.

ERISA (Employee Retirement Income Security Act of 1974)

Landmark federal legislation that established communications and fiduciary standards for private pension and welfare plans and set eligibility, vesting, funding, and plan termination rules for private pension plans.

ERTA (Economic Recovery Tax Act of 1981)

A federal law that liberalized tax treatment of employee benefits plans.

ESOP (employee stock ownership plan)

A plan in which a company borrows money from a financial institution, using its stock as security or collateral for the loan. Over a prescribed period, the company repays the loan. Principal and loan interest repayments are tax deductible. With each loan repayment, the lending institution releases a certain amount of stock being held as security. The stock is then placed into an employee stock ownership trust (ESOT) for distribution at no cost to all employees. The employees receive the stock upon retirement or separation from the company.

experience rating

A system of taking into account the premiums, losses that are paid, reserves, and expenses of an insured group in calculating a refund of part of the premium paid. This procedure is also called the financial accounting for a benefits plan.

final or final average pay (pension benefits formula)

A formula that bases benefits on the credited earnings of an employee at or during a selected number of years immediately preceding retirement.

flat benefit (pension benefits formula)

A formula that bases benefits on a fixed amount rather than a percentage of earnings (for example, $20 per month for each year of credited service).

fringe benefits

A term first used about 1943 by the War Labor Board to describe such benefits as vacations, holidays, and pensions that were thought to be "on the fringe of wages." Now considered obsolete and inappropriate by most compensation and benefits professionals.

funding

Setting aside monies in a trust account, or in the possession of an insurance company or another third party, in advance of the date when benefits are payable.

future service (pension plans)

That portion of a participant's retirement benefit that relates to the period of creditable service after the effective date of the plan or after a change.

group term life insurance

Annual renewable term life (and disability) insurance covering a class (or classes) of employees in accordance with a stipulated schedule of benefits.

HMO (health maintenance organization)

Prepaid group medical service organization emphasizing preventive health care. Defined in the Health Maintenance Organization Act of 1973 as "an organized system for the delivery of comprehensive health maintenance and treatment services to voluntarily enrolled members for a prenegotiated, fixed periodic payment." Subject to meeting certain standards and conditions specified in the act and associated regulations, HMOs must be offered to participants in group health plans as an alternative choice for coverage.

indexing

An automatic adjustment of benefits in the course of payment to reflect changes in a consumer price, cost of living, or other index.

integration (of pension plans with Social Security)

The process of combining a private pension plan with Social Security in an overall scheme of retirement benefits for employees. Through integration, a company can cut pension plan costs by approximately the amount it pays in Social Security taxes.

IRA (individual retirement account)

This is a form of defined-contribution plan for individuals. A person may make tax-deductible contributions to his or her own retirement account and to a spouse's if the spouse is not employed. Contributions are currently limited to an annual maximum of $2,000 ($2,250 when spouse is included).

joint and survivor annuity

An annuity payable as long as the pensioner lives that is continued, either in whole or in part, after his or her death, payable to a named survivor or contingent annuitant, if living, until the latter's death. Also called contingent annuity.

Keogh plan

Also known as an H.R. 10 plan, this enables a self-employed individual to establish a qualified tax-deductible money-purchase plan, defined-benefit pension plan, or profit sharing plan. Contributions are currently subject to the same rules as contributions to corporate plans.

life-only annuity

An annuity payable as long as the annuitant lives, with all payments (except for return of any employee contributions) ceasing at death.

loading

The amount added to the pure premium for any type of insurance or pension program to cover expenses, profits, and/or possible deviation of experience.

major medical insurance

Protection for large surgical, hospital, or other medical expenses and services. Benefits are paid once a specified deductible is met and are then generally subject to coinsurance. Usually written in conjunction with a basic medical plan and referred to as a single-plan comprehensive medical program.

minimum premium plan

A group insurance financing arrangement in which the employer is responsible for paying all claims up to an agreed-upon aggregate level, with the carrier responsible for the excess. The insurer usually processes all claims and provides other administrative services.

money purchase plan

Involves predetermined contributions that may be expressed in absolute monetary terms or more frequently as a percentage of covered earnings. The benefits paid depend on the accumulated value of the contributions in an individual's account at the time the benefit becomes due.

noncontributory benefit plan

A plan in which the employer pays the entire cost of premiums and deposits in funds from which benefits are paid.

normal retirement age (pension plans)

The earliest age at which eligible participants are permitted to retire with full pension benefits. Since unreduced Social Security retirement benefits are available at 65, that is the most common normal retirement age.

offset pension formula

A formula by which some part (typically a maximum of 50 percent) of the employee's Social Security benefit is subtracted from a defined amount to determine the benefit from the pension plan.

past service

The period of employment with a company prior to the original effective date or change in an existing pension plan for which credited service is given.

pension

The amount of money paid at regular intervals to an employee who has retired from a company and is eligible under a retirement income plan to receive such payments.

pension trust fund

A fund consisting of money contributed by the employer, and in some cases the employee, to provide pension benefits. Contributions are paid to a trustee, who invests the money, collects the interest and earnings, and disburses the benefits under the terms of the plan and trust agreement.

portability
A pension plan feature that allows participants to change employers without changing the source from which benefits (for both past and future accruals) are to be paid.

profit sharing plan
Plan established and maintained by the employer to provide for participation in its profits by the employees or their beneficiaries. Under ERISA, deferred profit sharing plans are considered to be defined-contribution pension plans.

qualified plan (pension or profit sharing)
A pension plan that meets certain statutory requirements. It must not discriminate in favor of officers, shareholders, supervisory personnel, or highly compensated employees. It has certain tax advantages for both employer and employee. It may be either a defined-benefit or a defined-contribution plan.

retention
The portion of the premium retained by an insurer to cover risk and expense charges and profit or contribution to surplus.

savings (thrift) plan
A plan established and maintained by an employer to systematically provide for the accumulation of capital by the employees in accordance with stipulated rates of contributions from the employees that are supplemented by the employer on the basis of some formula.

severance pay
Normally a lump sum payable on termination of employment in accordance with a stipulated formula (usually limited to involuntary termination).

Social Security
The Social Security Act of 1935 established what has become the federal Old-Age, Survivors, Disability, and Health Insurance system. The beneficiaries are workers who participate in the Social Security program, their spouses, dependent parents, and dependent children. Benefits vary according to earnings of the worker, length of time in the program, age when benefits start, age and number of recipients other than the worker, and state of health of recipients other than the worker.

Social Security option

A pension plan option under which the employee may elect that monthly payments of an annuity before a specified age (62 or 65) be increased and that payments thereafter be decreased to produce as nearly as practicable a level total annual annuity including Social Security.

split funding

Utilization of two different funding instruments in administering the assets of a pension plan (for example, an insurance company and a bank).

step-rate pension formula

A method of integrating private pension plan benefits with Social Security retirement benefits. A higher benefit multiplier is applied to earnings above a specified earnings level or breakpoint (for example, 1 percent up to $20,000; 2 percent above $20,000).

stock purchase plan

A program under which employees buy shares in the company's stock, with the company contributing a specific amount for each unit of employee contribution. Also, stock may be offered at a fixed price (usually below market) and paid for in full by the employees. Benefits are distributed in stock of the employing company.

stop-loss provision (health and disability insurance)

A provision designed to limit aggregate losses in self-funded plans to a specific amount. Typically, if total claims exceed an agreed-upon level for the year, the carrier will pay the policyholder (employer or administrator) for claims in excess of this amount. Alternatively, the provision may be structured on a per-case basis with a large deductible applied before the carrier is responsible for any payment.

SUB (supplemental unemployment benefits) plan

Employer-funded plan that supplements state unemployment insurance payments to workers during temporary periods of layoff. SUB plans are largely concentrated in the automobile, steel, and related industries.

TEFRA (Tax Equity and Fiscal Responsibility Act of 1982)

A federal revenue-raising measure with far-reaching implications for qualified pension plans, profit sharing plans, and group health care benefits.

total compensation

The complete pay package for employees, including all forms of money, benefits, services, and in-kind payments.

unemployment insurance

State-administered programs that provide financial protection for workers during periods of joblessness. These plans are wholly financed by employers, except in Alabama, Alaska, and New Jersey, where there are provisions for relatively small employee contributions.

variable annuity plan

Accruals and payments are expressed in terms of units of benefit rather than a fixed amount of money. Units are reevaluated periodically in relation to changes in cost of living, the investment portfolio, or some other index.

vesting

A pension plan provision that a participant will, after meeting certain requirements, retain a right to the benefits he or she has accrued, or some portion of them, even if employment under the plan terminates before retirement. Employee contributions are always fully vested. ERISA specifies standards for vesting of employer contributions.

welfare plan

A plan that provides medical, surgical, or hospital care or benefits in the case of sickness, accident, disability, death, or unemployment. Under ERISA, it may also include such other benefits as funded vacation or scholarship plans.

workers' compensation

Each state has its own workers' compensation law. The laws all have the goal of providing cash payment or medical care to cover health services for workers injured on the job and rehabilitation services to restore workers to their fullest economic capacity. All benefits are totally employer financed.

SELECTED REFERENCES

1. BOOKS AND SPECIAL REPORTS

Allen, Donna. *Fringe Benefits: Wages or Social Obligation?* Ithaca, N.Y.: Cornell University Press, 1964.

American Council of Life Insurance/ Health Insurance Institute. *A List of Worthwhile Life and Health Insurance Books.* Washington, D.C.: 1980.

Bankers Trust Company. *A Review and Comparison of Employee Savings Plans.* New York: 1979.

Barton, Paul E. *Worklife Transitions: The Adult Learning Connection.* New York: McGraw-Hill, 1982.

Brown, J. Douglas. *An American Philosophy of Social Security.* Princeton, N.J.: Princeton University Press, 1972.

Chamber of Commerce of the United States. *Employee Benefits Historical Data 1951-1979.* Washington, D.C.: 1981.

Committee for Economic Development. *Reforming Retirement Policies.* New York: 1981.

Diekman, Bernard A., and Metzger, Bert L. *Profit Sharing: The Industrial Adrenalin.* Evanston, Ill.: Profit Sharing Research Foundation, 1975.

Foulkes, Fred K., ed. *Employee Benefits Handbook.* Boston: Warren, Gorham & Lamont, 1982.

Foulkes, Fred K. *Personnel Policies in Large Nonunion Companies.* Englewood Cliffs, N.J.: Prentice-Hall, 1980.

Gorlin, Harriet. *Elements of Corporate Relocation Assistance Policies.* New York: The Conference Board, 1977.

Louis Harris and Associates, Inc. *Families at Work: Strengths and Strains.* Minneapolis: General Mills, 1981.

Lusterman, Seymour. *Health-Care Issues for Industry.* New York: The Conference Board, 1974.

Meyer, Mitchell. *Profile of Employee Benefits: 1981 Edition.* New York: The Conference Board, 1981.

Meyer, Mitchell. *Women and Employee Benefits.* New York: The Conference Board, 1978.

O'Meara, J. Roger. *Retirement: Reward or Rejection.* New York: The Conference Board, 1977.

President's Commission on Pension Policy. *Coming of Age: Toward a National Retirement Income Policy.* Washington, D.C.: Government Printing Office, 1981.

Rosenbloom, Jerry, and Hallman, G. Victor. *Employee Benefit Planning.* Englewood Cliffs, N.J.: Prentice-Hall, 1981.

Salisbury, Dallas L., ed. *America in Transition: Implications for Employee Benefits.* Washington, D.C.: Employee Benefits Research Institute, 1982.

Sehnert, Keith W., M.D., and Tillotson, John K., M.D. *How Business Can Promote Good Health for Employees and Their Families.* Washington, D.C.: National Chamber Foundation, 1978.

Spencer, Bruce. *Group Benefits in a Changing Society.* Chicago: Charles D. Spencer & Associates, 1976.

U.S. Department of Labor. *What You Should Know About the Pension and Welfare Law: A Guide to the Retirement Income Security Act of 1974.* Washington, D.C.: 1978.

Weeks, David A. *Rethinking Employee Benefits Assumptions.* New York: The Conference Board, 1978.

William M. Mercer Incorporated. *Employer Attitudes Toward Employee Benefits in the 1980's.* New York: 1979.

Yoder, Dale, and Heneman, Herbert G., Jr., eds. *Motivation and Commitment* (Volume II in *ASPA Handbook of Personnel and Industrial Relations*). Washington, D.C.: The Bureau of National Affairs, 1979.

2. PERIODICALS

Analysis of Workers' Compensation Laws (annual). Washington, D.C.: Chamber of Commerce of the United States.

Benefits News Analysis (monthly). New Haven, Conn.: Benefits News Analysis, Inc.

Business Insurance (biweekly). Chicago: Crain Communications.

Compensation Review (quarterly). New York: AMACOM.

Employee Benefit Plan Review (monthly). Chicago: Charles D. Spencer & Associates.

Employee Benefits (annual). Washington, D.C.: Chamber of Commerce of the United States.

Employee Benefits Journal (quarterly). Brookfield, Wisc.: International Foundation of Employee Benefit Plans.

Nutshell (monthly). Aspen, Colo.: The Country Press.

Pension World (monthly). New York: Communications Channels.

SPECIAL RESOURCES

1. SOURCES OF BENEFITS INFORMATION

Because of the dynamic nature of employee benefits, particularly in relation to government legislation and regulation, employers need access to a commercial loose-leaf information service. Firms providing these services include:

Bureau of National Affairs, Inc.
    1231 25th Street N.W.
    Washington, DC 20037
Charles D. Spencer & Associates, Inc.
    222 West Adams Street
    Chicago, IL 60606
Commerce Clearing House, Inc.
    4025 W. Peterson Avenue
    Chicago, IL 60646
International Benefits Research Associates, Inc.
    P.O. Box 241
    Old Greenwich, CT 06870
Prentice-Hall, Inc.
    Englewood Cliffs, NJ 07632

Also, the federal government and every state publish guides and handbooks related to specific statutory benefits. These are available for distribution to both employers and employees.

2. PROFESSIONAL ASSOCIATIONS AND RELATED ORGANIZATIONS

Action for Independent Maturity
(Division of American Association of Retired Persons)
    1909 K Street N.W.
    Washington, DC 20049
American Compensation Association
    P.O. Box 1176
    Scottsdale, AZ 85252
American Council of Life Insurance/ Health Insurance Institute
    1850 K Street N.W.
    Washington, DC 20006

American Management Associations
135 West 50th Street
New York, NY 10020

American Prepaid Legal Services Institute
1155 East 60th Street
Chicago, IL 60637

American Society for Personnel Administration
30 Park Drive
Berea, OH 44017

Association of Private Pension and Welfare Plans
1028 Connecticut Avenue N.W., Suite 909
Washington, DC 20036

Chamber of Commerce of the United States
1615 H Street N.W.
Washington, DC 20062

Clearinghouse on Business Coalitions for Health Action
1615 H Street N.W.
Washington, DC 20062

The Conference Board, Inc.
845 Third Avenue
New York, NY 10022

Council on Employee Benefits
1144 East Market Street
Akron, OH 44316

Credit Union National Association
5910 Mineral Point Road
P.O. Box 391
Madison, WI 53701

Employee Benefit Research Institute
1920 N Street N.W.
Washington, DC 20036

Employee Relocation Council
1627 K Street N.W.
Washington, DC 20006

The Employers Council on Flexible Compensation
1700 Pennsylvania Avenue N.W.
Washington, DC 20006

ERISA Industry Committee (ERIC)
1919 Pennsylvania Avenue N.W.
Washington, DC 20006

ESOP Association of America
  1725 DeSales Street N.W.
  Suite 400
  Washington, DC 20036
Health Insurance Institute
  (see American Council of Life Insurance)
International Association of Business Communicators
  870 Market Street, Suite 928
  San Francisco, CA 94102
International Foundation of Employee Benefit Plans
  18700 West Bluemound Road
  P.O. Box 69
  Brookfield, WI 53005
National Association of Employers on Health Maintenance Organizations
  Chamber of Commerce Building, Suite 1134
  15 South 15th Street
  Minneapolis, MN 55402
National Association of Suggestion Systems
  230 North Michigan Avenue
  Chicago, IL 60601
National Association of Van Pool Operators
  12208 West Kingsgate Drive
  Knoxville, TN 37922
National Employee Services and Recreation Association
  20 North Wacker Drive, Suite 2020
  Chicago, IL 60606
National Merit Scholarship Corporation
  One American Plaza
  Evanston, IL 60201
Profit Sharing Council of America, Inc.
  20 North Wacker Drive
  Chicago, IL 60606
Profit Sharing Research Foundation
  1718 Sherman Avenue
  Evanston, Illinois 60201
Society of Professional Benefit Administrators
  1800 M Street, N.W., Suite 1030 N
  Washington, DC 20036

INDEX

DATE DUE